DATE DUE

NOV 4 – 2002	
DEC 18 2003	

SHAKESPEAREAN LANGUAGE

SHAKESPEAREAN LANGUAGE

A Guide for Actors and Students

Leslie O'Dell

GREENWOOD PRESS
Westport, Connecticut • London

Library of Congress Cataloging-in-Publication Data

O'Dell, Leslie.
   Shakespearean language: a guide for actors and students / by Leslie O'Dell.
      p. cm.
   Includes bibliographical references and index.
   ISBN 0-313-31145-5 (alk. paper)
   1. Shakespeare, William, 1564–1616–Language. 2. Shakespeare, William,
   1564–1616–Versification. 3. English language–Early modern,
   1500–1700–Pronunciation. 4. English language–Early modern,
   1500–1700–Versification. I. Title.
   PR3072.O34 2002
   822.3'3–dc21   2001016059

British Library Cataloguing in Publication Data is available.

Library of Congress Catalog Card Number: 2001016059
ISBN: 0-313-31145-5

First published in 2002

Greenwood Press, 88 Post Road West, Westport, CT 06881
An imprint of Greenwood Publishing Group, Inc.
www.greenwood.com

Printed in the United States of America

The paper used in this book complies with the
Permanent Paper Standard issued by the National
Information Standards Organization (Z39.48–1984).

10 9 8 7 6 5 4 3 2 1

Contents

Preface

AN ACTOR'S GUIDE TO SHAKESPEARE'S LANGUAGE

This book divides quite neatly into two sections. In the first chapter, I make some general comments about how Shakespeare's language works for an actor in the modern theatre. The next part of the book explores Shakespeare's use of what I call the Iambic Code, the pattern of subtle variations on strict iambic pentameter with which Shakespeare suggests the emotional undercurrents at work in the scene. The focus then shifts to rhetoric, that classical art of using language to move one's audience, which was a central component of the Elizabethan school system and which can be found at work in the language of every one of Shakespeare's characters.

In developing my strategies for exploring the Iambic Code and rhetoric, I have taken insights gleaned from scholarly examinations of these topics and tested them in rehearsal halls, tutorials, and classrooms. My goal, throughout this process, has been to find a way of endowing a modern actor not only with the love of language that we associate with Shakespeare, for that comes quite easily as a natural byproduct of the regard with which society holds his plays, but also with the familiarity and sense of ownership with which his first actors would have rehearsed their assigned parts.

RECOMMENDED READING AND BIBLIOGRAPHY

Citations for the few works from which I quote directly are included in the Bibliography at the end of the book. Of far greater interest to most readers will be the list of titles in the Recommended Reading chapter. This represents only a small portion of the books that have been written about Shakespeare's language; it represents rather those writers whose ideas have most influenced my approach in the classroom and rehearsal hall.

CITATIONS

I often quote from one of Shakespeare's plays, and note the act, scene, and number of the first line in parentheses immediately following the quotation; I have used the line numbers found in *The Riverside Shakespeare*, edited by G. Blakemore Evans. I include the title of the play if that has not yet been indicated. For convenience, I have used a shortened version of many of the play titles, as follows:

12th Night	*Twelfth Night*
1HIV	*The first part of Henry IV*
2HIV	*The second part of Henry IV*
1HVI	*The first part of Henry VI*
2HVI	*The second part of Henry VI*
3HVI	*The third part of Henry VI*
A&C	*Antony and Cleopatra*
All's Well	*All's Well That Ends Well*
AYLI	*As You Like It*
Dream	*A Midsummer Night's Dream*
Errors	*The Comedy of Errors*
HV	*Henry V*
HVIII	*Henry VIII*
JC	*Julius Caesar*
John	*King John*
Lear	*King Lear*
LLL	*Love's Labour's Lost*
Measure	*Measure for Measure*
Merchant	*The Merchant of Venice*
Much Ado	*Much Ado about Nothing*
R&J	*Romeo and Juliet*
RII	*Richard the Second*
RIII	*Richard the Third*
Shrew	*The Taming of the Shrew*
T&C	*Troilus and Cressida*
Timon	*Timon of Athens*
Titus	*Titus Andronicus*

Two Gents	*The Two Gentlemen of Verona*
Wives	*The Merry Wives of Windsor*
WT	*The Winter's Tale*

I have also used the character names as they appear in *The Riverside Shakespeare* so that, for example, the heroine of *Cymbeline* is Imogen, not Innogen, and the man who eventually becomes King Henry IV is known as Bolingbroke, not Bollingbrook or Bullingbrooke.

I have assumed a familiarity with Shakespeare's plays, and so have explained the context of the quotations only if that is significant to what I am discussing. It is very difficult to avoid interpretation in these discussions; I cannot help but envision the scene in performance, the product of innumerable decisions every one of which can only be right for that one performance (imaginary or remembered), and none of which should be viewed as any more or less correct or valid than the decisions you might make in your productions.

QUOTATIONS

Although I have made use of *The Riverside Shakespeare* for line numbers, I have reproduced the quotations from Shakespeare based upon the 1623 folio edition, with some modifications. I have modernized most spellings, for ease of reading aloud. I have also, on occasion, adjusted the punctuation when it might completely mislead the modern reader. When the First Folio is clearly incorrect, or when I wish to quote lines only found in a quarto edition, I have made use of whichever alternative text is best regarded by experts in early modern printing practices.

There are a few significant differences, therefore, between the quotations in this book and those found in most editions of Shakespeare's plays. Close comparison between modern practices and those of Shakespeare's contemporaries reveal the following patterns:

- The early texts use far more capitalized words, usually nouns which we consider general and which they make proper, with some adjectives, and fewer verbs also so modified.

- The early texts use commas to mark places for the actor to breathe. Modern editors regularly modify these in accordance with rules of grammar.

- The early texts use other punctuation marks quite differently than we do today. Modern editors regularly "normalize" these, privileging grammar and correct usage over an evocation of the flow of ideas in spoken communication.

- The early texts seldom made a clear differentiation between the plural and the possessive, another grammatical "error" corrected by modern editors. Unfortunately, this requires them to choose between one of the two following interpretations of Ophelia's famous line, as in *The Riverside Shakespeare* where it appears as: "The courtier's, soldier's, scholar's, eye, tongue, sword" [*Hamlet* 3.1.151], when the folio reads: "The

Courtiers, Soldiers, Scholars: Eye, tongue, sword," leaving it open whether the eye, tongue, and sword in question belong to one or all courtiers, soldiers, and scholars.

- The early texts create compound words, or present as two separate words some common compound words, such as "myself" or "tomorrow."
- The early texts sometimes break up the lines of poetry differently than is customary in modern texts. In extreme cases, they present as prose entire passages which are reproduced as poetry by modern editors. In *Romeo and Juliet*, the Nurse's long meander down memory lane, in which a toddling Juliet gets a bump on her forehead, appears as prose in all three early editions. Mercutio's famous evocation of Queen Mab appears as poetry only in the first (1603) quarto; the second (1604) quarto and the First Folio both present this as prose.

Because I have recreated the choices made by the first editors, the quotations in this book might strike the modern reader as unexpected or even incorrect.

CAPITALIZATIONS

The First Folio presents no coherent pattern of making proper nouns of various objects and concepts, tempting modern editors to conclude that the practice was influenced as much by the availability of upper and lower case letters in the typesetter's box as it was by anything in the original manuscript. By including the First Folio capitals in this book, I have made it possible for you to judge for yourself, and glean what information you wish from these markers.

In making a comparison between modern punctuation and that found in the early texts, I have observed that modern editors quite often add an exclamation mark to reflect the strong emotion clearly expressed in the situation, when the first editor loaded on the capital letters and used a humble period. Consider, for example, that most famous of lines, "A horse! a horse! my kingdom for a horse!" [*RIII* 5.4.7], which in the First Folio appears as, "A Horse, a Horse, my Kingdom for a Horse." The four capital letters in that line evoke, for me, the shouting of a desperate man, a tidy equivalent to the three exclamation marks in the modern version.

Another speech from this play reminds us of the effect of linking individual and specific words to universal concepts. Here is the Duchess of York, mother of the title character, describing his childhood:

> No by the holy Rood, thou know'st it well,
> Thou camest on earth, to make the earth my Hell.
> A grievous burthen was thy Birth to me,
> Tetchy and wayward was thy Infancy.
> Thy School-days frightful, desp'rate, wild, and furious,
> Thy prime of Manhood, daring, bold, and venturous:
> Thy Age confirmed, proud, subtle, sly, and bloody,
> More mild, but yet more harmful; Kind in hatred:

What comfortable hour canst thou name,
That ever graced me with thy company? [*RIII* 4.4.166]

The capitalization in this speech transforms her memories into another "seven ages of man" speech, marking for us the universality of the stages of Richard's life, from his birth and infancy, through school days, to manhood and finally maturity, marked by the word "Age." When Jacques has a go at the same idea, his version makes use of similar capitalizations, describing "the Infant, / Mewling, and puking in the Nurses arms: / Then, the whining School-boy with his Satchel / And shining morning face, creeping like snail / Unwillingly to school" [*AYLI* 2.7.142].

FIRST FOLIO ERRORS

Using the first texts can open up all sorts of fascinating possibilities for the modern actor that arise from a more direct encounter with the irregularities that modern editors customarily remove from the plays. Here, for example, is a wonderful hiccup that appears at the end of an exchange between the young Duke of York and his uncle Richard:

Richard: What, would you have my Weapon, little Lord?

York: I would that I might thank you, as, as, you call me.

Richard: How?

York: Little. [*RIII* 3.1.122]

Modern editors, in an effort to clean up what they have assumed is an error made by the compositor of this particular page, remove the delicate little stutter, so that York is given no opportunity to telegraph his glee at the approaching punch line. I am more inclined to admire Shakespeare for his intuition about juvenile joke-tellers, and honor the "as, as," in performance.

Not all errors are so attractive. Here is the mess that the compositor has made of Romeo's final speech:

> For fear of that, I still will stay with thee,
> And never from this Palace of dim night
> *Depart again: come lie thou in my arms,*
> *Here's to thy health, where ere thou tumblest in.*
> *O true Apothecary!*
> *Thy drugs are quick. Thus with a kiss I die.*
> Depart again; here, here will I remain,
> With Worms that are thy Chambermaids: O here
> Will I set up my everlasting rest:
> And shake the yoke of inauspicious stars
> From this world-wearied flesh: Eyes look your last:

> Arms take your last embrace: And lips, O you
> The doors of breath, seal with a righteous kiss
> A dateless bargain to engrossing death:
> Come bitter conduct, come unsavory guide,
> Thou desperate Pilot, now at once run on
> The dashing Rocks, thy Sea-sick weary Bark:
> Here's to my Love. O true Apothecary:
> Thy drugs are quicke. Thus with a kisse I die. [5.3.106]

The same mess appears in the 1604 quarto, clearly the copy from which this was being set. The italicized section is customarily deleted in modern editions. However, I can't help but wonder if the two endings represent two different versions of the speech. Maybe the actors quickly discovered that the shorter version was more effective, and the compositors erred in printing out the shorter as well as the longer version.

Much scholarly effort has been expended on comparing the different early texts, in those cases where we have more than one option, and there is something to be said for the theory that Shakespeare's original version was quite a bit longer than the one actually performed. In this, he would be like most playwrights of my acquaintance, whose manuscripts bear the mark of a helpful editing process instigated by the first performers. It's fascinating to find evidence of the original as well as the amended version, one after the other, thanks to an error in the printing process: almost as good as getting our hands on a copy of the manuscript with Burbage's notes in the margins.

THE SIGNIFICANCE OF THE SELF

We are so accustomed to the modern compound pronouns that we are blind to the very special insights available whenever a character speaks of her individual selfhood. When Polonius advised Laertes, "This above all; to thine own self be true" [*Hamlet* 1.3.78], we hear only the maxim, not the originality of the thought. At a time when the individual was judged to be less worthy of primary loyalty than one's god, and one's liege lord, such loyalty to self was almost heresy.

Returning to *Richard III*, we find an exchange that loses much of its rhetorical power if given a modern spin on selfhood. Lady Anne is spitting out her hatred for the murderer of her husband and father-in-law, a man who is at this moment trying to win her love:

Anne: Vouchsafe (defused infection of man)
         Of these known evils, but to give me leave
         By circumstance, to curse thy cursed *Self*.

Richard: Fairer than tongue can name thee, let me have
         Some patient leisure to excuse my *self*.

Anne: Fouler than heart can think thee,
         Thou canst make no excuse current,
         But to hang thy *self*.

Richard: By such despair, I should accuse my *self*.

Anne: And by despairing shalt thou stand excused,
         For doing worthy Vengeance on thy *self*,
         That didst unworthy slaughter upon others. [1.2.78]

By italicizing the separate word "self," we can see the antithesis between the individual and all of his enemies presented in Anne's last lines. We are also reminded of the immense significance of cursing one's own soul to eternal damnation, the sin of despair, that Anne is wishing upon Richard.

LONG SPELLINGS

Anyone who has looked at a reproduction of the First Folio can testify to the difficulty it presents the modern reader, when even a familiar passage looks like this:

> But *f*oft, what light through yonder window breaks?
> It is the East, and *Iuliet* is the Sunne,
> Ari*f*e faire Sun and kill the enuious Moone,
> Who is already *f*icke and pale with griefe,
> That thou her Maid art far more faire than *f*eh. [*R&J* 2.2.2]

Because I place such importance on sight-reading Shakespeare aloud, I have adopted modern spellings for all of the quotations in this book. However, in doing so I have sacrificed an important set of clues contained in the old manuscripts, where patterns of spelling seem to have had significance for the delivery of the lines by actors in the theatre.

If we look at Romeo's words as he spies Juliet up on her balcony, we notice that he refers to the sun twice, but that when the word appears at the end of the second line it is spelled "Sunne," though in the very next line "Sun" is the spelling. Are we to believe from this that the typesetter could spell a simple word correctly and incorrectly, side by side? Are we to imagine that the typesetter voluntarily took the time to place into the frame two additional tiny lead letters for no particular reason? Common sense suggests otherwise. Although it is difficult to base an entire interpretation of a passage upon what might be the Elizabethan equivalent of a typo, something in the pattern of longer and shorter spellings suggests a heightened significance in direct proportion to the length of the word on the page.

If we think back to the days of hand-copied manuscripts, for example the spiritual texts so lovingly copied by monks in the great medieval monastery libraries, we can see this connection in the setting up of the words on the page.

The eye is naturally drawn toward the most important words like "soul" or "grace" by the copyist, who elongates the pen strokes and embellishes with curves and curls. Meanwhile, purely functional words are squeezed in and starkly drawn, perhaps even reduced to a shorthand whereby "your" becomes "yr."

It is possible that the copyists and typesetters who worked on the plays made use of a similar system of subtle emphasis, taking advantage of the fluctuation in accepted spelling to write or typeset "Sunne" and then "Sun" followed by "Moone" to suggest the relative intensity of the three words. We cannot know if, in doing this, they reproduced what appeared in Shakespeare's original manuscript, but we can acknowledge that the copyists and typesetters would have been influenced by the manner in which such words were spoken by the actors of the day.

HE OR SHE

In my writing I customarily use the word "actor" to refer to men and women; any reader alert to the nuances of language will note that I scatter male and female pronouns in connection with this noun randomly throughout the text. If I'm discussing Cleopatra or Romeo I will be more likely to have imagined a woman playing the first and a man the second, though historically the reverse has been true: the "squeaking Cleopatra" of Shakespeare's own theatre stands in memory beside Sarah Bernhard and Charlotte Cushman, two among many actresses renown for their portraits of Shakespeare's male protagonists. When appropriate, as in the sentence before this, I will use the term "actress" to make a point about the sex of the performer under discussion.

ACKNOWLEDGMENTS

I could not have completed *Shakespearean Scholarship* without the support and encouragement of my academic and theatre colleagues. In particular, I owe an immense debt of gratitude to the Stratford Shakespearean Festival in Stratford, Ontario, where I have had the privilege of working with those very artists whose enthusiasms, insights, and hard work have inspired this book. Above all, it is the support of my family that has allowed me to undertake this project, and it is to my mother Doris Woods O'Dell that I dedicate this book.

⤳ 1 ⤳

Sound and Fury

Life's but a walking Shadow, a poor Player,
That struts and frets his hour upon the Stage,
And then is heard no more. It is a Tale
Told by an Idiot, full of sound and fury
Signifying nothing.

Macbeth [*Macbeth* 5.5.24]

Between these two poles sits an attitude toward the published organization of words that we call *The Collected Works of William Shakespeare*. On the one extreme, we have Macbeth's suggestion that the sound and fury of idiots, and perhaps also of actors strutting and fretting upon a stage, signifies nothing. On the other extreme, we have an example of sound and fury that provides a climactic evocation of the disintegration of rational awareness, mirroring dissonant nature in the storm scene of *King Lear*, where the sound and fury of Lear's words have great significance, great impact, and enduring power.

This book is poised equidistant from the two poles. With every ounce of my being, I want the famous and admired words of William Shakespeare to be the repository of great significance. More specifically, I want to believe that buried in the Iambic Code are instructions from the author to the actor entrusted with speaking them, the thesis of the first section of this book. I even wish I could ascribe without hesitation to an Elizabethan attitude toward the god-given power of language, which forms the foundation of the second part of this book.

However, I must acknowledge the legitimate scoffing of those scholars who will point out that few, if any, of my assumptions about Shakespeare's strategies as an actor's playwright can ever be proven. I must also agree, in advance, with those actors who will observe that, although an understanding of rhetoric illuminates much of what is otherwise puzzling in the plays, it can never be substituted for the magical thing that actors do irrespective of any conscious knowledge of a four-hundred-year-old system of ordering words into persuasive argument.

The benefit of being caught in the double pull of skepticism and enthusiasm is that my thinking about Shakespeare's language remains fluid, open-minded, nondictatorial. I would not recommend any strategy outlined in this book be pursued unless it proves itself useful to a specific actor, role, production, situation. I do not advocate a single theory or approach, and in fact I could never prove absolutely the validity or effectiveness of the ideas I present. All I can say is that they've worked for some actors and not for others, of the several hundred with whom I have had the pleasure of working in the twelve years since I began my professional career as an acting coach and text consultant.

CORRECT SHAKESPEARE

> Speak the Speech I pray you, as I pronounced it to you trippingly on the Tongue: But if you mouth it, as many of your Players do, I had as live the Town-Crier had spoke my Lines.
>
> Hamlet [*Hamlet* 3.2.1]

The single most important proviso that I must present is that everything in this book is intended to spark interesting explorations in rehearsal, as a result of the private preparation an actor might undertake before and between rehearsals while working on a role. Absolutely nothing in this book is intended to have any direct influence upon how the language of Shakespeare's plays is spoken in performance. I do not believe that there is any one correct way to "speak the speech, I pray. . . ." I do not even believe that we are meant to take Hamlet's instructions to the players as Shakespeare's instructions to his actors. Every actor must find a way into the heart of the role and the play, within the context of the time and place of that particular production. If the guideposts I offer prove useful, it will be as a means by which an intensely personal and production-specific journey is undertaken into the labyrinth that is the language of Shakespeare's plays.

Not everyone reading this book is an actor. With those of you who only ever read these plays silently to yourself, I must take issue with the limits you have placed upon your experience of these plays, and urge you to "speak the speech." The words were written to be spoken aloud, by actors, listened to by audience members eager to find out what happens next, to have an emotional reaction to events, and to form temporary relationships with fictional characters. Shakespeare knew actors, he knew what it was like to act, he knew what sort of word patterns available within the conventions of his culture might best serve the purposes of the company seeking artistic success in order to thrive economically, and although it is dangerous to accredit him with god-like genius, it is difficult not to be in awe of how often his combinations of sounds, rhythms, thoughts, ideas, and words, words, words provide an actor with just what is needed to achieve a striking, compelling, haunting, unforgettable moment in the living theatre.

Even the name of his duties suggest the nature of the craft: he wrought dramatic structures which would showcase the talents of his colleagues, and he wrote and published poetry. He was not a "play-write." Shakespeare was first and foremost an actor and shareholder in a theatre company. He wrote plays for that company, and seems to have taken little interest in publishing his plays as works of literature. We must be very careful not to ascribe to him literary concerns and self-conscious explorations of language. From the report of Ben Jonson, who said Shakespeare "never blotted out a line" (23), it seems he wrote quickly and intuitively, seldom rewriting and polishing for a manufactured theatrical effect. I cannot help but feel that it would do us all a great deal of good if we took him off the pedestal whereupon bardolatry has placed him, and consider him a member of that most irreverent and improvising of professions. My guess is that he almost never knew exactly what he was about, and that every play, like every rehearsal process, was a journey of discovery with success the product of chance as much as effort.

Although I am happy to claim Shakespeare as a fellow toiler in the crucible of theatrical creation, I am not willing to ascribe to him contemporary attitudes or approaches to the craft of the actor, and it is in making such assumptions that very many modern actors find themselves at a loss for how best to bring these plays alive.

A CHALLENGE TO MODERN ACTING THEORY

A trend has emerged in recent years that is very much in opposition with the suppositions at work in this book. This trend places all of an actor's focus on the intuitive, personal development of the inner life of the character. The source of this acting style is the North American version of Stanislavky's theories of acting, known most commonly as The Method. At best, Method actors bring a passionate commitment to the human truth of every play and character. At worst, they indulge themselves in acting-as-therapy, placing personal emotional agendas before the requirements of a play or production. Any tendency toward character development that is the result of the interaction of the psyche of the actor with the character, rather than the actor's sensitive and thoughtful engagement with the words of the play itself, results in acting decisions that are first made and then superimposed upon the words the actor must speak.

In writing this book, I advocate a reversal in this process. First speak the words, discovering the character landmarks through the words, and then begin making acting decisions and developing a characterization that encompasses the landmarks in your own unique way, with all of the intensity and depth that a Method approach engenders.

In a modern play, an actor can more easily experience the development of the character and the speaking of the words as a unified, fluid exploration. All of the landmarks available in the text are absorbed consciously or intuitively with ease and confidence. The playwright lets it be known that your character dropped out of school after grade eight. Your character uses words like "incandescent" and "paradox" correctly. Two important landmarks suggesting an apparent contradiction: no formal education yet a university-level vocabulary. Immediately, the actor's mind begins to roam possible contemporary cultural phenomena that would explain the apparent anomaly.

Acting in Shakespeare's plays requires a scholar's awareness of social history and the connotation of words to grasp the significance of the landmarks. We don't even know when a character is acting according to or against expectations. When the grade eight dropout uses advanced vocabulary, we are invited to imagine how such an anomaly could come about. When Ophelia is visited by Hamlet in her closet, we don't know if he's violating every cultural taboo or doing what all love-sick young men are expected to do when the love-interest refuses to see them any more.

Just as the specific words "incandescent" and "paradox" become important landmarks buried in the text, so too can we find in Shakespeare's plays important clues embedded in the linguistic patterns and specific words he has selected. That is what playwrights do. They select words, either intuitively or consciously, that convey important information both overtly and subtly. An actor of Shakespeare needs to learn how to spot the landmarks that are four hundred years old and part of a social and theatrical context that is lost to us today. The purpose of this book is to point out some of the most subtle landmarks, the ones buried right into the way the words have been shaped to be spoken aloud.

THE MODERN ACTOR AND THE SHAKESPEAREAN TEXT

There is something about the training and workplace experiences afforded to modern actors that gets in the way of an automatic correspondence between experience, talent, and disciplined hard work and excellence in the speaking of Shakespeare's language. Peter Hall, in *Making an Exhibition of Myself* (1993), describes casting Sarah Miles as Imogen, the heroine of Shakespeare's late romance, *Cymbeline*, because he "admired the daring honesty of her film performances."

Within days I knew I'd made a terrible mistake. Sarah learnt the meaning of Imogen's verse with aptitude, and she worked hard to breathe in the right places and to develop her voice. But she had great difficulty in delivering the words as spontaneous descriptions of her feelings. Too often she sounded false, not to say calculating, and her tempo was very slow. I realised that her strength as an actress was in conveying emotions below and beyond the words. On film you can see what she is thinking and this makes her a great asset to the camera. But Shakespeare expresses everything by what he *says*. His characters have an ability to describe and illustrate what they are feeling *as* they are feeling it. So his actors have to give the impression of creating the text while they experience the emotion. This is hard; and it has nothing to do with naturalistic acting, where feeling is always paramount, and what is actually said often masks or disguises it. (344)

Hall persevered, in the belief that a director, having cast an actor, shouldn't be so quick to terminate a contract. He notes, "I had known many actors break through the barrier she was up against. But as she worked harder and harder, the problem became worse and worse. The spring of the verse, the skill needed to speak trippingly on the tongue, eluded her" (345). Finally, he realized she simply could not acquire the necessary skill, and brought in an actress who "had no time to worry about the technique; she had the instinct, and simply practised the verse round the clock" (345).

As an alternative to merely hoping that one has been born with, or has miraculously acquired by osmosis the "instinct" of which Hall writes, the modern actor can undertake a journey of training and acclimatization that will facilitate the encounter with Shakespeare's poetry, so that all of the intuitive connection that might transmit one's talent, sensitivity, and skill directly into the language and through those connections into the events and relationships, can occur naturally, without the sort of deadening labor that Sarah Miles found only decreased her capacity to play the role.

AN ACTOR'S GUIDE TO SHAKESPEARE'S LANGUAGE

Modern actors playing roles in Shakespeare's plays enjoy the unenviable task of building a bridge between our audience and a theatrical play-text written four hundred years ago. The bridge they build must also cross over the intervening years' obsession with the playwright and the poetry, and they must do their building under the intense scrutiny of professional and amateur contributors to bardolatry. When they fail, they please those who profess Shakespeare to be greater than any individual production, as well as the skeptics who have known all along that the gap is too wide and the payoff scarcely worth the effort even if it were achievable.

There are many who assist in the task of building this bridge. We might liken these individuals to the contractors who prepare a foundation for the bridge, but who are not themselves the structural engineers who construct the bridge so that it successfully reaches from shore to shore. Directors are often able to sink concrete piles into the bed of the river, offering support to the bridge as it spans the divide. Some coaches and mentors become sufficiently knowledgeable that we have some responsibility in preparing supportive structures for the bridge's structure midway into the four-hundred-year gap. For example, much of the information I bring to rehearsals about the social history of Shakespeare's England might, if we continue our metaphor, be a sort of preparation of the far shore for the bridge's structure.

Acting teachers are the ones who lay an important foundation on the near bank. To continue our metaphor, this training is like the multilane highway that leads to the bridge, and brings to it all of the intuition, the technique, the commitment, and the rich and free-flowing energy that are the construction materials for the bridge itself. However, a terrible traffic jam seems to form at the base of the bridge, partly because of conflicting advice received from one's teachers, coaches, and directors, but more importantly because modern acting technique has been created to facilitate the flow of acting energy into contemporary texts and acting challenges. I would argue that any training that succeeds in preparing an actor to achieve artistic excellence in a modern play would also be of use in Shakespeare, but seldom in as direct a manner as is readily apparent in the application for which the training has been developed. What is missing is any sort of an easy access ramp from the near shore to the beginning of the bridge proper.

It is fairly easy to take the practices of modern acting and apply them to the special challenges of Shakespeare's language. These applications then become the steel girders for the bridge. If we were not fairly skilled at building such bridges, we would have long ago stopped producing Shakespeare in modern theatres. What is missing, however, is a comprehensive training method that is as suitable to playing Shakespeare as Method acting is to playing Tennessee Williams, in other words, the clear off-ramp on the far shore that is adapted to that particular theatrical geography.

Many actors, directors, and audience members are sufficiently satisfied with a production that connects our near shore with something we sense is in the plays, that we little care if the bridge is anything more than an intuitive, flimsy accident and that the production never allows us to experience more than the predominant features of the far shore, those visible from the shoreline. I would have to agree that the view is stunning, and well worth the effort of crossing the bridge, and I have no interest in joining those who sneer, as a result of their extensive theoretical knowledge of the far shore, because the bridge is so flimsy that it cannot truly be said to stand the cold winds of criticism, much less comparison with all of the bridges that have been constructed before, to say nothing of the imaginary bridge that the critic champions (but could never build).

I think that far more bridges make it over the gap, and that actors quite regularly find themselves arriving on the other side of the four-hundred-year gap, fully attuned to the theatrical potential to be found there. However, unless they are profoundly intuitive explorers, or remarkably lucky, what most of them lack is any sort of a road that would be the Shakespearean equivalent of the acting training they received in order to maneuver in contemporary theatre.

SUB-TEXT AND SHAKESPEARE

Sub-text is the term that modern actors use to describe all of the emotional material that is added to the words of the play, to mirror that aspect of human communication wherein the surface words convey one meaning but the tone of delivery conveys more, or perhaps even an alternative meaning. Often a playwright hints at the sub-text by suggesting an emotion-filled delivery; more often, the actors inject the otherwise mundane language with highly charged sub-text in keeping with the situation being enacted.

This trick of juxtaposing tone and content, the one suggesting profundity and the other capturing language at its most benign, is one at which modern actors excel and modern playwrights use with regularity, so that it has become habitual to break up speeches and dialogue with silences in which the sub-text can be enacted, or to color words or phrases with striking vocal indications of feeling such as the breaking of a vowel, a stuttered consonant, or a purposeful slurred or exaggerated enunciation.

These habits of delivery work so completely against the language of Shakespeare's plays that coaches and directors have been given to announcing, "There is no sub-text in Shakespeare." This is, not surprisingly, a misrepresentation. There is no room in the delivery of Shakespeare's language for these particular modern tricks, not because there is no sub-text, but because the sub-text is conveyed differently. There is no need for artificial impositions of tonal quality, because all of the subtle and overt shifts in color and shape are written directly into the lines. And there is no need for the manipulation of rhythms or delivery because those two have already been shaped by the master actor-writer.

If a modern actor superimposes her own habitual vocal indication onto the finely tuned indicators Shakespeare has already placed in his dramatic language, then two unfortunate effects result. First, the modern indicators, which might resonate as "true" for the actor, ring false when used to voice what is clearly not modern language. Secondly, the modern tricks, successful as they might be within today's conventions, drown out the indicators that worked in Shakespeare's theatre, making it impossible for the actor to tap into the sub-text that has been charted in the text.

I would reword the dictum, "There is no sub-text in Shakespeare," to read, "There is no need for the vocal indicating that suggests sub-text in Shakespeare, because powerful and appropriate sub-text indicators are already there, waiting to be sounded and felt."

SENSING THE SOUND OF SHAKESPEARE'S LANGUAGE

> If music and sweet poetry agree,
> As they must needs, the sister and the brother,
> Then must the love be great 'twixt thee and me,
> Because thou lovest the one, and I the other.
>
> [*The Passionate Pilgrim*, VIII, 1]

I believe that the action of making sounds with lips, tongue, teeth, and breath is a viscerally emotional action. Yes, language has an intellectual component, but that is only the most obvious psychological process at work when we speak. If I say, "The rest is silence," to you, and we both know that this is a metaphor for death, we are both willing to commit to the emotions that might be aroused by such an event. But the *sound* of that combination of vowels and consonants, echoed a few seconds later in, "And flights of Angels sing thee to thy rest" [*Hamlet* 5.2.358, 360], and more importantly the physical sensation of making those sounds, links the mind to the body and grounds the actor in the physiological root of all language.

Every child loves the discovery of those words that sound like what they mean. An actor who has developed, or rather rediscovered, the connection between sound sensations, speaking sensations, and emotional content finds onomatopoeia all around. Doesn't "hungry" capture the twist in the empty stomach just as "ping pong" recreates the ball hitting the paddle back and forth so quickly? Consider these striking images that come out of the mouth of Caliban, surely one of the less appealing of characters in *The Tempest*:

> Be not afeard, the Isle is full of noises,
> Sounds, and sweet airs, that give delight and hurt not:
> Sometimes a thousand twangling Instruments
> Will hum about mine ears; and sometime voices,
> That if I then had waked after long sleep,
> Will make me sleep again, and then in dreaming,
> The clouds methought would open, and show riches
> Ready to drop upon me, that when I waked
> I cried to sleep again. [3.2.135]

The sounds and patterns of stressed and unstressed syllables, matching so effectively the intellectual meaning and also the emotional associations of the words, are the reason why we call this "poetry." They are also the reason why saying the words without any preconceived intention of feeling anything in particular, or of conveying any particular emotion or attitude, will arouse an emotional connection between the speaker and the words spoken.

This connection won't be particularly useful in performance if it is not linked to more visible and audible acting choices, but it makes a good place to begin looking for actions and attitudes that can result in the integration of action and text into a vivid, exciting performance.

Fashions in Delivery of Shakespearean Verse

Earlier masters of Shakespearean verse speaking were praised for their ability to find the operatic scale of the passions and the language; in reaction to lesser talents who produced the sound and fury only, the pendulum has swung quite far in the direction of unforced, natural, delicately nuanced delivery. The arrival of the technology by which an actor could deliver the verse to a camera in close-up removed the need to use the voice to fill the space of a large theatre; when raging fury is called for, the camera can pull back and the human figure can shrink on the screen so that the scale of delivery still appears "natural."

Now, the pendulum has swung just about as far as it can go in the direction of an approach to the verse that is deeply felt and minimally articulated, what might be called "thought Shakespeare." We have learned the limits of mumbling, and many among us miss the sound and the fury. Concurrently, there has been a reconsideration of the tenets of Method acting, not limited to the incompatibility of hyperrealism with the prenaturalist classics and postmodern experimental theatre. The result has been a fearless return to the celebration of the musicality of the verse, quite separate from motivation and given circumstances, so that the sound in and of itself is held to signify something profound and theatrical.

Everything Old Is New Again

As the pendulum swings away from "thought Shakespeare," and all the related problems of "realistic" verse speaking, the observations of two or three generations ago suddenly transform from "dated and embarrassing" to "thought-provoking and insightful." Some of the funky retro scholars who are now worth a second look are George Bernard Shaw, Harley Granville-Barker, and Sir John Guilgud. My university library has a copy of David Hedges's *Speaking Shakespeare*, in which these past-masters are extensively quoted. Inside the front cover a disgruntled student has written, "This is pure B.S.!!" Ten years ago everyone would probably have agreed with that assessment of Hedges's backward-looking description of the old way of doing things. Today, a forward-looking assessor of the swing toward the power of Shakespeare's music as a vehicle for compelling human communication will appreciate many of Hedges's comments, provided a copy of the book can be found! It was published in 1967 by The American Press, and I doubt very much that it will ever be reissued.

One of the attributes of a good Shakespearean style of delivery, which remains unchanged and unchallengeable, is the necessity of knowing what it is that you are actually saying. For this, a modern actor must be prepared to undertake a considerable amount of effort, and expand upon simplistic definitions that spring from modern associations or are provided by footnotes.

KNOWING WHAT YOU ARE SAYING

What is meant by this phrase in Macbeth's well-known eulogy to sleep?

> Macbeth does murder Sleep, the innocent Sleep,
> Sleep that knits up the ravelled Sleeve of Care,
> The death of each days Life, sore Labours Bath,
> Balm of hurt Minds, great Natures second Course,
> Chief nourisher in Life's Feast. [2.2.33]

The modern reader, upon first encounter, would liken "course" to "feast" and assume that Macbeth is talking about the second serving in a banquet. But this doesn't serve us well, unless there were only two courses in a meal, neatly corresponding to waking and sleeping. And is the second course the chief nourisher of the feast?

The primary meaning of "course" given in the *Oxford English Dictionary* is, "The action of running, or moving onward." People and horses do this, as do sailing ships and heavenly bodies, following a particular path. The definition expands to suggest implications of a race or any swift and violent motion, and hence, "The rush together of two combatants in battle or tournament; charge, onset; a passage at arms, bout, encounter." This meaning links "Great nature's second course" with the images of balm and sore labour and Macbeth's status as Scotland's premier warrior.

Other meanings in this same category: a raid, riding to hounds, the flow of liquid, the circulation of money, and in general the capacity to move in this manner. The second general category of meaning is given as, "The path, line, or direction of running." We use this today when we speak of an obstacle course or a race course, for example. Blending these two meanings, which spring from the same observable activity of motion in a linear pattern, we can think of the type of motion or flow of events that would shape Macbeth's waking hours, in contrast to the second type of motion and pattern of movement offered by Nature which takes place while asleep.

There is a third category of meaning listed in the O.E.D. which suggests that this particular image was a common one. This category is identified as figurative rather than literal, in reference to time, events, or action. These definitions and examples expand our sense of what concepts might be at work in this metaphor: "The continuous process (of time), succession (of events); progress onward or through successive stages.... The space of time over which any process extends; length (in time), duration." "Life viewed as a race that is run; career." "The continuous connected purport or tenor of a narrative; drift." Macbeth might be drawing upon his awareness that one's experience of life's events is like the running of a race or the reading of a story. But Nature offers a second, parallel race, journey, or story, during the time of sleep.

The next meaning makes direct reference to nature in the sense of the ordinary or customary: "Habitual or ordinary manner of procedure; way, custom, practice. Course of nature: the ordinary procedure of nature; the natural order, esp. in regard to its constancy or regularity." This meaning strikes at the heart of the experience of insomnia: what is ordinary, habitual, customary, and natural, i.e., a regular night's sleep, is lost.

Other meanings leap off the page with potential significance, not as a direct explanation of what the image means, but as an associated image that can resonate at this moment of the play. One of the meanings of "course" is "Systematic or appointed order, order of succession," which is exactly what Macbeth is setting out to disrupt by murdering Duncan and seizing the throne from his two sons. The word was also used to mean "The prescribed series of prayers for the seven canonical hours," and Macbeth has just finished describing his inability to respond to the simple prayer "God bless us" with an appropriate "Amen."

This examination of a single word, which we thought we understood, reveals that the complexity of meaning available in such words resonates profoundly in connection with the themes of the play. When an actor absorbs both the complexity and the clarity of specific words, the energy that is thereby released into the acting of the moment elevates the delivery effortlessly from the mundane, conversational, ordinary to the heightened, significant, glorious.

UNDERSTANDING WHAT YOU ARE SAYING

The bottom line for an actor is that many of the constructions used by Shakespeare are simply not the way we put thoughts together today.

These sentences usually leap out at you almost immediately, because they make no sense in a very specific sort of way. The key functional words don't function. When you hit the word and think that it's a landmark for one type of transition or connection, you make all sorts of assumptions about what will follow, and instead something quite different takes place.

In most cases, once you've found your way to the end of the thought and retraced your steps to the puzzling functional word, you can place an intonation on that word so that, by sheer force of will, it means what you need it to mean for the sentence to make sense.

Here is Celia attempting to cheer up her cousin Rosalind:

If my Uncle thy banished father had banished thy Uncle, the Duke my Father, so thou hadst been still with me, I could have taught my love to take thy father for mine; so wouldst thou, if the truth of thy love to me were so righteously tempered, as mine is to thee. [*AYLI* 1.2.9]

The tricky, functional word in this speech is "so," which we are accustomed to see used to mean "so that" or "even so." Naturally, when we start saying a sentence that begins with "if," we know we're listing the conditions. When we reach the first "so," we assume that it follows immediately after those conditions, and therefore we're supposed to be saying, "If your father had banished my father so that you were still with me. . . ." But that can't be right! We need to push forward to the end of the sentence and then retrace our steps. We discover that the phrases have been rearranged, and the real meaning is something like, "If your father had banished my father, I could have taught my love to take your father as my own, provided that ("so") you were still with me."

There is little difficulty for the actor saying or hearing these lines once they are delivered with a vocal shaping to suit the meaning, because the emotional and intellectual heart of the lines does not rest upon the functional word. The temptation, and one to be avoided is to toss away the offending word, underplaying or rushing it, and filling those words that are clear and obviously significant ("father" and "love" and "banished") with lots of acting stuff. In actual fact, what the audience requires is a clear and strongly energized delivery of the functional word that is Shakespearean rather than modern in usage.

The hierarchy of a sentence is quite different from word order. By that I mean what actors do all the time when placing an intonation onto a piece of dialogue. Here is a simplistic example.

Ben: You've got your red dress on.

Is it significant that the other person is wearing a dress, or that it's the special dress identified by its color? If the former, then the word at the top of the sentence hierarchy is dress; if the latter, then red, the adjective, swells to match or even top the noun, dress. Following along, in a lower position, is the active verb, here the colloquial "got." Since this is not a vivid verb, it is not likely to rival the noun. It carries the preposition along with it, because the verb phrase is "have got on"; the "have" blends in with the pronoun as a result of the contraction. The two pronouns vie for last place. The first, which sets the direction of the aural connection, is stronger than the possessive pronoun, which is, after all, implied by the first, and can drop away a bit to serve as a springboard for the top-ranking adjective/noun combination. In all of this I simply describe what any actor would do with a simple line like that. When you get to a complex line like one of Shakespeare's, then the subtle pattern of intonation that sets the various words into a hierarchy of relative significance can become very complex.

When you are confronted with words that are unexpected, which will cause a glitch in the auditory experience of the audience, they need to move up slightly on the hierarchy, from the position they would normally occupy given their function, so that the audience receives some assistance from the actor in understanding the sense of the sentence.

Here is a simple example, again from *As You Like It*:

Orlando: Or Charles, or something weaker masters thee. [1.2.260]

Today, we would say "Either Charles, or something weaker masters you." The proper noun and the adjective "weaker" would compete for first place, depending on the context. Commonly, the first mentioned would be in first place, with the second mention dropping just slightly, unless the second was a surprise, sneaking up from behind and topping the first. The two functional words, "either" and "or" would rank somewhere down the ladder, as their function is so standardized as to require little intonation to do their job. "Or" might creep up in significance if whatever is mentioned second is unexpected, to create a strong set-up for the surprise.

But with Shakespeare's use of the double "or" to serve the same function, the first "or," being in itself unexpected for a modern audience, needs just a tiny little push in significance, to affect the bridging in the inner ear of the audience. This is easily accomplished if the energy of discovery is injected into the first sound of the sentence, so that the character's investment of significance into the entire realization gets hooked a little bit onto that first "or."

THE EVOLUTION OF SHAKESPEARE'S LANGUAGE

We do not know the exact order in which the plays were written, but even so we can trace broad general patterns in the evolution of Shakespeare's language, in particular with regard to his use of the strategies of rhetoric. This is of great significance to actors, because it is tempting to lump all of the plays into one category of Shakespearean language, when plays from different periods represent different experimentations and require different blends of modern and period approaches.

In the earliest plays, actors discover the tricks of language sitting very much on the surface, sometimes to the irritation of our modern sensibilities. In particular, history plays such as *Richard III* require a strong command of rhetorical strategies and the sublimation of personal emotion to the larger issues under debate. The early comedies such as *The Taming of the Shrew* require a love of language games as an expression of passion and sexuality, of mockery and trickery, and just for the fun of the game.

In contrast, the mature comedies and tragedies of the middle period, those plays that are most often performed and studied, although they make use of all of the same tricks of language, present a better balance of substance and form. A modern actor can be excused for thinking that no language arts are required, the words seem so natural an expression of feeling and personality. Of course that is just the surface, and the hard muscle of rhetoric is readily apparent, providing the shape and power to the tragic events and sparkle and exuberance to the comic. *Hamlet, Othello, As You Like It,* and *Measure for Measure* provide us with striking examples of Shakespeare's mastery of dramatic writing.

As Shakespeare began to wind down his full-time career as an actor and shaper of plays, he moved into some new territory in his experimentations with dramatic language. It was at this time that he pushed against the envelope of the Iambic Code, until the underlying heartbeat is almost lost under the variations and permutations. He also, on occasion, seems to be seeing just how complicated a syntactical tangle he can weave and still convey the essential argument. We can find examples of these extremes in *The Winter's Tale* and *The Tempest.* A modern actor might not even notice the complexity of the verse rhythms, in fact might welcome their prose-like naturalness, but the syntactical messes are monstrous stumbling blocks to even the simple communication of the meaning of the text. It is here, when they are most threatened, that the modern actor most needs a firm understanding of the language conventions with which Shakespeare is playing.

BACK TO BASICS

One of the most discouraging discoveries for those who wish to make use of the Iambic Code or understand the rhetorical strategies used by Shakespeare, is that they have only a vague understanding of the basic rules of pronunciation and grammar, even though they use the rules correctly and effectively all the time in ordinary conversation.

I include below a brief introduction to the basics and trust that the reader is not offended by the simplistic presentation. It is not so much a matter of learning these things, as of bringing these elements of language into our conscious awareness.

Introduction to Scansion

Perfectly intelligent, well-read, well-spoken individuals who have come through the public school system during the years when language studies were dominated by the goal of unlocking personal creativity have no conscious understanding of the way in which words are pronounced. They have acquired a large spoken vocabulary orally, and an even larger comprehensive vocabulary by encountering words they have never spoken aloud in written or verbal presentation, and which they understand by context or by conscious effort, asking what a word means or looking it up in a dictionary.

These individuals have no strategy for scanning a line of iambic pentameter. If asked to read the line aloud, they can. But if you ask them if "below" is accented on the first or second syllable, they won't know for sure, even if they say it aloud. They represent an extreme instance of a gap that most of us experience to a lesser degree: we use language much more effectively than we are able to explain or analyze intellectually. Those of you who have no trouble telling the difference between stressed and unstressed syllables can jump over this section. Those of you who struggle, please don't despair. Here are a few suggestions to help you understand consciously what you already do without thinking.

To "stress" a word means to give it added significance within the context of the sentence. As we acquire sophisticated language skills, usually before we even begin school, we know the subtle difference between "I'm going to get you a RED dress for your birthday," and "I'm going to get you a red DRESS." In the first instance, you have several dresses but not a red one. In the second, you have several red items of clothing, but not a dress.

But when we talk about the stress or accent in a word with more than one syllable, we are talking about a simple technique of shaping the sound of the word so that one syllable is more pronounced and therefore we understand which word is being spoken. And we have many, many words that are pronounced exactly the same but with two different stresses, and which therefore can mean two different things.

"I am going to convert the heathen."

"I'm a recent convert to Roman Catholicism."

The first example makes use of the word with the stress on the second syllable. It is the verb form, and if we were recording the stress we might write it as conVERT. The second example is the noun form of the word, and we put the stress on the first syllable, CONvert. Here are other examples that demonstrate this aspect of the spoken language:

I have heard conFLICTing reports from Belfast about the CONflict in Northern Ireland.

Each of the following sentences contains only one word of more than one syllable.

I think that the answer is five point two.

When did you discover the clue?

Why did you go before Sue?

If you find that you need to say the word aloud in order to be sure where the stressed syllable lies, then don't be at all worried about mastering scansion. You're going to want to say Shakespeare's words aloud at every opportunity. However, if you find that you're still guessing even after saying a word out loud, then you may need to have someone say the line for you, speaking slowly and slightly overemphasizing the stressed syllable in a multisyllable word. You will need to work a bit to transfer a conscious awareness from an intellectual source, such as a dictionary, to consciously hearing the stressed syllable when someone else says the word, to hearing it when you say it. Just keep remembering that it is not a situation of your not knowing which syllable to stress when you say the word, but rather that you aren't consciously aware as you pronounce the word correctly of just what it is that you're doing with the sounds of the word.

Introduction to Grammar

If your schooling did not include an explanation of the rules of grammar, including the parts of speech and how they function, you will find it difficult to follow any discussion of how Shakespeare's language works. Here is a brief refresher, in the form of an analysis of Caliban's description of the music of his island home, quoted earlier as an example of a near-perfect union of sound and sense.

Nouns and Verbs

You can spot a noun because nouns do things or have things done to them. You will discover that many of them are concrete, such as "noises," "sounds," "instruments," "ears," "voices," "riches," and "clouds," things that are encountered with the senses, to be savored and experienced with as much immediacy as possible. Sometimes they are places, an invitation to the imagination of the actor: what exactly is this "Isle" where we find ourselves? Other nouns reflect familiar experiences, often charged with emotion: "delight" and "sleep" are two such words used by Caliban. Each one of us will bring a personal take to such nouns: what for you would be the most delightful of experiences? What associations do you bring to the idea of "sleep"?

We must not forget that pronouns stand in for nouns, as the speaker and the listener are capable of doing things and having things done to them. The "you" of this particular speech is implied; its focus is upon Caliban, who alone has had this remarkable experience, or at least that is what he thinks, and therefore the speech is filled with "I" and "me" and "mine."

Verbs are the doing or being done to that are connected with the nouns. For Caliban, the noises of the island "give" and do not "hurt," they "hum" and "make" him sleep. Then, the clouds "open" and "show" riches, until finally Caliban becomes active, reporting that he "waked" and "cried," above all longing for the most evocative of verbs, "to dream."

The most common and variable verb is Hamlet's very own "to be." "I am, I was, I will be, I have been, I will have been, I might be, I might have been" . . . these represent the time-frame within which the action occurs: present, past, future, on-going, just a possibility. Caliban's story of the music demonstrates the subtlety with which Shakespeare can move us from the simple and straightforward present ("the Isle is full of noises") to the complexity of a past event that might or might not take place ("if I then had waked"), to a longed-for impossibility ("the clouds methought would open") and finally to a simple report of a prior event ("when I waked I cried"). Through all of these shifts, we follow the speaker with minimal difficulty, such is the marvellous flexibility of that verb "to be."

Adjectives and Adverbs

We always want details. It's not enough to say "instruments." We label the specific orchestration "twangling." The sleep is "long," and the airs are "sweet," but otherwise Caliban is noteworthy for his minimal description. Here, for example, is an equally powerful description of the environment in which another deformed outcast finds himself; note Richard's use of adjectives, which I have italicized:

> Now is the Winter of our Discontent,
> Made *glorious* Summer by this Son of York:
> And all the clouds that lowr'd upon our house
> In the *deep* bosom of the Ocean buried.
> Now are our brows bound with *Victorious* Wreathes,
> Our *bruisèd* arms hung up for Monuments;
> Our *stern* Alarums changed to *merry* Meetings;
> Our *dreadful* Marches, to *delightful* Measures.
> *Grim-visaged* War, hath smoothed his *wrinkled* Front:
> And now, in stead of mounting *Barbed* Steeds,
> To fright the Souls of *fearful* Adversaries,
> He capers nimbly in a Ladys Chamber,
> To the *lascivious* pleasing of a Lute. [*RIII* 1.1.1]

Adverbs tell us more about a verb, as when Richard describes Grim-visaged War as he capers "nimbly." These modifies contain additional, specific details about the nouns and verbs, all of which invites our imagination to share in the riches of the speaker's invention.

Conjunctions and Prepositions

The simple little words that join phrase to phrase and demonstrate the relative relationship of ideas are easily overlooked, and yet they are of inestimable value because they are, for the most part, the same today as they were in Shakespeare's time. They almost always answer a question, so that we might reword Caliban's speech as a sort of dialogue, with Shakespeare's words italicized:

The Isle is full . . . of what? *Of noises, sounds* . . . and what else? *and sweet airs* . . . what type are they? *That give delight* . . . and what else? *And hurt not* . . . All the time? *Sometimes a thousand twangling instruments will hum* . . . where? *About mine ears* . . . and then what? *And sometimes voices* . . . what kind of voices? *That if I then had waked* . . . when? *After long sleep, will make me sleep again* . . . and then what? *And then in dreaming, the clouds methought would open* . . . and then what? *And show riches ready to drop* . . . where? *Upon me* . . . and then what? *That when I waked I cried* . . . for what? *To dream again.*

Analysis of a Sentence

Let's have a look at a single prose sentence and identify the parts of speech and how they function. Here is Rosalind addressing the audience at the conclusion of *As You Like It*:

If I were a Woman, I would kiss as many of you as had beards that pleased me, complexions that liked me, and breaths that I defied not: And I am sure, as many as have good beards, or good faces, or sweet breaths, will for my kind offer, when I make curtsy, bid me farewell. [Epilogue, 17]

First the nouns: "woman," "beards," "complexions," "breaths," "faces," "offer," "curtsy," "farewell." These fall into two categories: tangible and conceptual. The tangible nouns bring to mind an immediate mental image: a woman, different kinds of beards, different complexions, different breaths, a curtsy. An offer and a farewell are conceptual. We can translate these ideas into a visual image of someone making an offer or bidding someone farewell, but we can also leave these nouns in the realm of an idea, a concept: people make offers to other people; people say goodbye by bidding farewell. As a sub-category of nouns we have the pronouns: I/me/my and you. The ratio is nine of me to one of you. Although the speech is very much about the men in the audience, the pronouns are almost entirely variations on the first person singular.

Now for the verbs:

- "were" (following "if," suggesting only a possibility),
- "kiss" (following "if" plus "would"; another possibility),
- "had" (still influenced by "if," a condition of the kiss),
- "pleased" (hidden in a phrase that tells us more about the beards),
- "liked" (another verb within a phrase telling us about complexions; also, an unexpected turn of phrase. Wouldn't you expect Rosalind to like the complexions rather than the complexions to like her?),
- "defied" (another condition, here negative through the use of the word "not"; note how once again we are surprised by which noun is doing what to which noun. Wouldn't the bad breaths defy Rosalind rather than the other way around?),
- "am" (after that long possibility, we're back to the present situation, as it concerns Rosalind),
- "have" (now the present situation, as it concerns at least some of the audience),
- "will . . . bid" (this is what Rosalind predicts for the future; note how the first part is separated from the second by two phrases, to keep us in suspense), and

- "make" (hidden in the prepositional phrase that tells us when something else will happen).

In this single sentence there are no adverbs, but several significant adjectives: "good" (beards and faces), "sweet" (breaths), "kind" (offer), and "sure" (what Rosalind is). The other words in the sentence serve to link idea to idea:

- "if" introduces a phrase that sets up the conditions under which possibility offered by Rosalind would occur;
- "as many of you as" includes the repeated preposition "as" to set up the comparison ("Many" is an adjective that marks the amount, here limited by the specific conditions that occur following the second "as." The noun that "many" should modify is absent; in its place we have another prepositional phrase, "of you." Since she is addressing the men in the audience, we assume that she is thinking of an unspecified but relatively large number of men. The second time the phrase is simplified to "as many as" and we supply the longer meaning by implication.);
- "and" and "or" allow Rosalind to create lists and to link ideas together, and
- "that," "for," and "when" are three linking words that allow Rosalind to tell us more about the nouns and verbs she uses by introducing modifying phrases.

Armed with this basic vocabulary, we are ready to venture into an examination of the immense achievement of Shakespeare's plays.

❧ 2 ❧
An Actor's Guide to Shakespeare's Verse

Nay then God buy you, and you talk in blank verse.

Jaques [*AYLI* 4.1.31]

The greatest paradox at work in the rehearsal halls of Shakespeare productions is the combination of horror and awe with which inexperienced actors regard the dramatic poetry they are required to speak when playing a significant role. Everyone acknowledges the importance of the verse to the enduring power of Shakespeare's plays, but those who are entrusted with the public delivery of the most famous passages struggle to reconcile their task of presenting a compelling character to a contemporary audience, with all that they have been told is at work in the language they have memorized.

The modern Shakespearean actor must avoid the excesses of bombastic declamation and such overtly poetical acting strategies as putting on a fake "Shakespeare" accent and posturing to indicate heightened sensibilities in keeping with the heightened language. But she must also avoid the temptation to reduce Shakespeare to the language patterns of our contemporary script writers, whose conventions for suggestion of deep emotion and complex relationships feel "true" simply because they are familiar and reflective of a unified attitude to language that permeates the vast majority of cultural artifacts that surround us.

Even if we wanted to, there would be no escaping the necessity of coming to terms with Shakespeare's verse when rehearsing and performing his plays. Even if we do not suffer from the intimidation that might result from earlier worshipful encounters with the poetical devices that he uses with such skill, simply speaking a passage of Shakespeare's dramatic poetry floods the actor with the sensation of difference. The sequence of sounds launches an intuitive sensory reaction. The balance of words and phrases in complex patterns suggest hidden significance that puzzles the intellect even as it arouses the emotional centres of the body. The markers for breathing shift and change so rapidly and radically that it seems impossible to speak and breathe naturally as one does in ordinary conversation or in the naturalistic plays of our contemporaries. Overall, there is the sensation of sitting on the surface of something powerful and compelling, but not something that you could imagine "owning" readily.

It is always possible to break the massive chunks of language apart into digestible units, and then to do something while speaking each bit, thus creating a mosaic of understood and understandable speaking. As soon as I know what I'm going to do in that moment, says such an actor, I'll be able to figure out how to say those words so that they support what's happening with my character.

The alternative is to let the language teach you what is happening in that moment. Further, you can allow the language to shape what you do in any given moment of the play *before* you understand what that might be. In order to allow such discoveries, in order to partake of such a rehearsal process, you need to prepare yourself to let the language work on you as richly as possible.

This requires that you not only break apart speeches into component language elements in order to understand meaning, but also that you reassemble the speeches and allow the submerged power to act on your senses intuitively. If you have ever waded into the ocean during a strong tide, you will know the combination of awe and terror that the submerged power can have on your experience of a role. We all admire the skill of the master surfer who uses that power to move with apparent ease back and forth across the face of the wave. Just so, we can all learn from the master actors who have found ways to use the power of the verse to do a great deal more than simply say the words so that the intellectual meaning can be understood.

BILL THE DIRECTOR

Because Shakespeare has become more central to the experience of English students than to the training of actors, it is all too easy for us to forget that every single strategy he employed was an actor's strategy. There was not a single poetical trick up his sleeve that was used because it might appeal to scholarly readers. Everything that is embedded in the language of his plays, whether or not it provides the basis for literary analysis, is there to assist the actors of his company in their day-to-day task of creating popular entertainment for a wide audience.

If Shakespeare had no interest in publishing his plays, why were they written in verse? If no one but the actors is ever going to see them, and if there is no real difference between the sound of verse and the sound of prose, then why bother? The only answer is that the verse is in some way linked to the success of the plays. The sound of the verse must somehow accomplish most efficiently and effectively the pleasing of the diverse audience, and the activity of the actors speaking the words in verse form must somehow allow them to do what best pleases an audience.

We do not know a great deal about how actors were trained in Shakespeare's theatre, except that there was an apprentice system that allowed for the passing on of concrete strategies of proven success. But the theatre was not so wealthy a guild as to allow junior apprentices to avoid public performance until sufficiently trained and experienced. Every member of the company whose material needs were met by the profits of the company had to appear regularly on stage and do an adequate or better job in revealing the events of the play.

Although the companies lacked so much of what we take for granted today—lighting, complex sets and costumes, time for extensive rehearsals, and actresses—clearly they had sufficient skill in pleasing large numbers of patrons to generate financial stability and even wealth in the shareholders like Shakespeare. Given that there was so little time for rehearsal, and that the company offered repertory entertainment, is it possible that the format of the script facilitated the memorization of lines? Is it possible that the insights that today are discovered in rehearsal emerged directly from whatever the actors were given?

The theatre company was a profit-sharing organization. Profits, then as now, were computed as income from productions minus expenses. Greater expenses meant fewer profits. Paper was expensive. Each actor received his "side," and only the bookkeeper, who controlled exits and entrances, organized props and costumes, and kept the show running from backstage in the tiring house, would have a complete copy of the play.

Given that everyone wanted to use as little paper as possible, why were the lines not written out in huge paragraphs filling the entire page? Why were the speeches in blank verse written with wasteful margins? We must assume that the pattern of verse lines was a significant aspect of the transmission of the play text to the actor who would speak those words with minimal rehearsal in front of a large and knowledgeable theatre-going audience.

We know very little about how Shakespeare functioned in his company, but we do have clear evidence that he ranged far and wide in search of other plays to adapt for his actors. He thought nothing of reworking popular stories and lifting speeches as well as plots from just about anywhere. He was a playwright. The root verb is "to wrought," defined in the Merriam-Webster dictionary as "to bring into desired form by a gradual process of cutting, hammering, scraping, pressing, or stretching." His job was to shape the work of the actors; his instruments were the language strategies available to him within the conventions of his theatre. Like any great artist, he explored different ways to shape the fire and mettle of his actors, with varying results. We can look upon the language of the plays as the supporting structure created to assist actors in doing what they do best. We can look upon the language as the guidance a skilled and experienced surfer of giant waves might offer a beginning paddler at the ocean's shore.

The conventions of theatre have changed radically more than once in the four hundred years since Shakespeare earned his fortune shaping and acting in plays. Some of the structures he used are suitable only for the conventions of his theatre. Some of the shapes he was interested in creating hold little or no appeal to audiences today. Some of the guidance he built into the language of the plays is counterproductive to actors who are members of quite a different artistic profession than his own.

However, if there is an unbroken continuum of human experience that produces the immense power we attribute to these plays, then we must conclude that there is also an unbroken continuum linking the excellence of Shakespeare's first actors to the best Shakespearean actors working today. The packaging has changed, but the essential imaginative and emotional experience of acting at work in Richard Burbage is significantly similar to that working in Anthony Hopkins or Emma Thompson, Gwenyth Paltrow, or Leonardo DiCaprio.

If we can learn to read the encoded messages, perhaps even today we can receive directly from the playwright the subtle and overt shapings of our intuition and our senses that will allow us to benefit from the theatrical genius who conducted these experiments so long ago.

THE IAMBIC CODE

Shakespeare and his contemporaries made use of very specific rhythmic patterns in order to shape the emotional content of the verse. I call the set of conventions, observed and described by scholars, the Iambic Code. In order to understand how the code works, we must first comprehend the medium through which this code was communicated. This is the blank verse, or unrhymed iambic pentameter, the standard verse form in use in Shakespeare's theatre. Before we can access the Iambic Code, and all of the actor-friendly hints and suggestions waiting there, we must learn the language in which the code is written. First we will encounter the "alphabet" and then some "vocabulary."

Unlike Stanislavsky, Shakespeare did not leave behind any writing on his thoughts on the connection between his use of dramatic poetry and the craft of the actors in his company. It has been left to scholars to examine the conventions of dramatic poetry that actors had helped to shape and audiences had come to expect in the theatres for which Shakespeare wrote his plays. These exhaustive studies have resulted in a variety of theories and some heated debates which do not concern modern actors, save as they point the way to recovering the purely theatrical guideposts and actor-friendly techniques that can be of use in today's theatres.

The Iambic Code is an observable pattern of manipulations of the basic verse forms that reveals a direct connection between shifts in rhythm and shifts in emotion. These patterns can be charted in the plays of Shakespeare's contemporaries, and seems to have been the raw material that any of the playwrights could use as a sort of shorthand indicator.

Inherent in the use of such a code is a shared familiarity with the tonal quality of subtle shifts in variation. The code isn't going to be much use if there is no one who can "read" the markers and make use of them to understand what is being communicated. In offering the Iambic Code to actors as a means of exploring Shakespeare's language, I have assumed that Shakespeare shared with the actors in his company a facility with the rhythmic patterns that came from much experience in speaking them as actors, rather than overt indicators of emotion, such as might be found in a modern script:

Ben: [*with real anger*] Don't you EVER try that again. [*He slams the coffee cup onto the counter. It shatters.*] Oh, god. I'm . . . I'm so . . . sorry. [*There is a long silence as they look at each other, facing the finality of this moment.*]

In contrast, Shakespeare's instructions take the form of subtle shapings of rhythm and sound patterns that evoke shifts in the flow of emotion. Once identified, these can serve as messages from Bill the actor/writer/director to the actor saying the lines, messages that can still affect you, even across four hundred years.

REHEARSAL CONDITIONS

Here's a marvellous convenient place for our rehearsal. This green plot shall be our stage, this hawthorn brake our tyring house, and we will do it in action, as we will do it before the Duke.

Quince [*Dream* 3.1.2]

The Elizabethan theatre was conducted under less-than-ideal work conditions. Actors had to have a large number of roles at their mental fingertips: either seven or eight major roles or three or four characters from seven or eight plays. To prepare their roles they received "sides" made up of the lines their characters were to speak and a cue line. And, to top that, the younger actors blessed with tenor voices and slender frames carried the women's parts. They performed a different play each afternoon, and mounted a brand new or pirated play with minimal rehearsals. In the month of January 1596, the Admiral's Men performed fourteen different plays over twenty-seven days of performance. Six of the plays were performed once; no play was performed more than four times. The shortest interval between the repetition of a play was three days; the next shortest was five days. All but one of the fourteen were revivals of old scripts. This is the working reality of the professional actor in Shakespeare's theatre.

And yet, as we know from reports of eye witnesses, these plays moved people deeply, and allowed the actors to develop the craft that has been handed down, unbroken, to us today. Actors who had apprenticed under Burbage, Bill's leading man, helped to reintroduce the theatre after the Puritan interregnum, when theatres had been closed. The great actors of the Restoration saw those performances, and built upon them. The great actors of the eighteenth and nineteenth centuries regularly served lengthy apprenticeships under older actors who had witnessed and learned from still older actors. Even today, it is possible to trace the influence of Laurence Olivier on contemporary Shakespearean stars, and of Lawrence Irving on Olivier, and of Henry Irving, the great late-nineteenth-century star and first actor knighted, through all of them, onto actors today.

The Iambic Code was the means by which Shakespeare and his contemporary playwrights shaped acting performances during a time when rehearsing as we know it just never took place. There was simply no time to explore how best to evoke the most powerful delivery of a highly charged speech. There was also no director sitting out front to suggest, respond, reject, or demand a certain emphasis, shaping, or shading. Instead, the emotional "journey" was traced directly into the rhythms of the speech, handed, as it were, on a platter to the actor. Shakespeare was particularly skilled at this, being an actor himself and writing for actors with whom he acted on a regular basis. This familiarity, shared by the majority of the other working dramatists of this period, allowed him to match actor to role, to create optimum conditions for the showcasing of the actor's craft and unique talents. Moreover, knowing firsthand just what an actor needed to pull off different types of speeches, Shakespeare could shape the most user-friendly prompts to striking delivery.

The Iambic Code is the reason why the traditions for acting Shakespeare remain vibrantly connected despite radical changes in acting and play-writing conventions in four hundred years. It is difficult for us to imagine, but Shakespeare was not the playwright voted most likely to survive the test of time. That honor was awarded Ben Jonson, a more prolific and better-educated writer who took great pains to ensure that the plays he wrote were published as he wished. However, brilliant as Ben was, he was not as profoundly connected to actors as was our Bill, and as a result, though his plays continued to amuse and move audiences for years after his death, eventually, as acting styles changed, the plays no longer came alive in quite the same way. Shakespeare, however, continued to connect to each new generation of actors, despite complete revisions in casting, including the introduction of women, of staging, including the introduction of the proscenium, massive illusion-creating scenery, and a darkened auditorium, and of the medium itself, with the introduction of film, radio, and television Shakespeare.

It is as if Shakespeare's sensitivity to an actor's experience cuts through the various forms such an experience might take, to some essential element that remains constant, whether the actor is working within the conventions of eighteenth-century heroic tragedy or twentieth-century realism. A sensitivity to the code and the clues it contains allows for the ghostly hand of old Bill himself to guide the actor toward the heart of the moment and the character.

REHEARSING WITH THE CODE

In offering the Iambic Code, my goal is to prepare the actor to use the language of the plays for the purpose of playing. I have no interest in suggesting any specific shaping that might be deemed "correct." Rather, I view any shaping that emerges from a rich, intuitive interaction with the language of the plays as a valid and worthwhile interpretation, whether it repeats or challenges scholarly or traditional views.

One of the most dangerous aspects of any system is that it is all too quickly transformed from a tool to a rule. A suggestion that one might benefit from a certain type of exploration becomes an instruction that one must undertake specific sorts of preparation in order to act Shakespeare. What was created to be an inspiration and an aid to creative intuition has been turned into a restriction and a burden.

When I point out the rhythmic shifts of a speech, to demonstrate how they support the actor's entry into the emotions of the character, it is the rare young actor who will not say, "But do I have to say it like that?" My answer is always more than the simple negative that they seek. On the one hand, of course not, they can say the words whatever way they like. And they definitely should never pronounce them in front of an audience the way I might say them when attempting to demonstrate the rhythms at work, because I will naturally have slowed down and exaggerated those rhythms so that they are clear to a modern ear that has not been tuned to the code by extensive encounters with the verse in performance.

However, the modern actor does not have as much freedom in delivery of verse as he might be used to in modern prose. It is remarkably easy to shatter poetry, to undercut its potent sound patterns and transform it into prose. The striking imagery will remain, and the intellectual content of the speech will be undamaged, but the inner music will be silenced, and the actor will be cut off from the inspiration and instruction contained therein.

There is no need to retain a conscious awareness of the Iambic Code at work as you deliver these speeches in rehearsal or performance. In fact, such self-consciousness would be inappropriate. Rather, the intellectual analysis of the language is an activity best suited to your work on the text between rehearsals. Scansion is something you do when you're learning your lines. Occasionally, when a line feels wrong, perhaps because you sense or are told you've said it incorrectly, you might pause in rehearsal and gently tap out the rhythm. Ideally, however, you would do all of the work required to understand the language in order to be able to forget it, or rather to replace that sort of awareness with a more intuitive, connected ownership of the act of speaking the language.

The time required, and the onorous mental effort scansion requires when one is first mastering the basics and applying them to the complexity of Shakespeare's verse, does not represent the manner in which Shakespeare wrote the speeches or his first actors memorized them. The only reason we have to work so hard, and so cerebrally, is because we are forced to acquire with conscious effort what the actors and actor-writers of Shakespeare's theatre acquired through regular contact and extensive familiarity. This is the language that surrounded them, and the system of communication in which they flourished as intuitive creative artists.

A modern actor's goal is to master the elements of the Iambic Code in order to be able to go into rehearsal and truly play with the language of the plays, because she is open to all of the riches contained therein, and knows that all of her work is invited by, supported by, and fuelled by the language she speaks and hears.

PREPARING TO ENCOUNTER THE CODE

In exploring the Iambic Code with actors, I employ several strategies that have proven successful in shifting the modern actor's awareness away from the familiar toward the unfamiliar code. These are simple activities, suited to private study and coaching sessions rather than the rehearsal hall. They help an actor to open intuitively to the language of the play, perhaps in combination with memorization, but also effective when returning to a well-known piece seeking fresh insights and inspiration.

I am a great believer in the intuitive, and wish that modern actors could partake of the fruits of the Iambic Code without study and intellectual effort. However, this is simply not to be. The best that can be hoped for is that, after tuning one's inner ear to the subtleties and richness of Shakespeare's use of dramatic verse, the actor spends less and less time in conscious scanning and analysis, and more and more time speaking the lines in a mental and physical state that is entirely open to the subliminal messages their hard work has trained them to hear.

Speak Aloud

The first strategy is a simple one. These words were written to be spoken aloud. Never read Shakespeare silently. Never let a day go by without speaking huge chunks of Shakespeare in a full and richly expressive voice, not caring if your interpretation is right or not. Shakespeare's blending of sound and rhythm is only appreciated when heard by more than the imagination and rolled off the tongue, stretched through the jaw, felt in the breath.

Read Slowly

Never race through the plays. Never try to speak as quickly as you can read. Take a piece of paper and cover the rest of the speech, so that your eye takes in just the one line of verse. Don't move on to the next line until you've slowly and carefully given voice to every single sound in that one line.

Honor Sensation

Yes, you must figure out the sense of what you say. But always balance that activity with attention to the sensory quality of the sounds of the verse. Because we are top-heavy and sensual-illiterates, count on it taking two or three times the effort to let the sensations of the verse work on your intuition as to let the thoughts of the verse work on your imagination.

Never Cadence

In ordinary spoken language we convey sentence structure by cadencing. We drop our voices to suggest the end of a thought, what would be a period in a written script. One of the conventions of contemporary script writing is the use of many and short thought units, either short and relatively simply constructed sentences, or sentence fragments. These get us in the habit of cadencing often, of creating many self-contained bubbles of energy emerging rapidly in a stream of dialogue. Complexity is created by the contrasting shape and texture of the many short shapings. Shakespeare's dramatic language worked in quite a different way. It will take a considerable effort to break the habit of cadencing, and as a start, discipline yourself to avoid it at all costs. Assume that every speech, no matter how long, is one sentence, and that every phrase, even if it ends with a period, exists to set up the one that follows.

ꙮ 3 ꙮ

Scansion

Celia: Didst thou hear these verses?
Rosalind: O yes, I heard them all, and more too, for some of them had in
them more feet then the Verses would bear.

[AYLI 3.2.163]

What is scansion, anyway? Why should I waste my time learning how to
scan? What does poetry have to do with theatre? What is iambic pentameter?
What is blank verse? Is the only difference between prose and poetry the way
they divide the lines? If I scan it, I don't have to say it like that, do I? These
are just some of the many questions that actors ask when embarking on the
mastery of the rhythmic patterns of Shakespeare's verse.

There is no shortcut. You cannot unlock the clues that might assist you in
acting Shakespeare if you do not master scansion. You cannot master scansion
if you do not understand not only iambic pentameter and its variations but
also some essential aspects of how the English language works and how Elizabethan poets made it work for them.

The good news is that, sooner than you might believe when you first start
learning about scansion, the Iambic Code becomes a subliminal stethoscope
directly to the heartbeat of the emotional life of the language. Words have
changed meaning, the punctuation is up for grabs, but the human experiences
that are captured in these plays are universal. Learn to use this sensitive and
actor-tuned listening device and you will begin to sense the intimate, visceral
connection between yourself and your experiences and those of the characters
of the plays. A quick check of scansion will simply confirm your instincts rather
than puzzle your intellect, once you have cracked the code.

IAMBIC PENTAMETER

Scansion is the activity of reading the score of the music which permeates the literal meaning of the words. This music provides the speaker with a significant amount of information about the emotional forces at work in what a modern actor might call the "subtext" of the scene.

Scansion requires first the understanding of the expected patterns of rhythm, in order to hear the significance of the variations upon those expected patterns, which are in fact the music of the score. This is comparable to the relationship between the scale of notes and a song written in that key. Here is a list of the classical Greek terminology for rhythms. This is a good example of the sort of thing that we all know intuitively, because we *feel* the rhythm as we speak words aloud, but which we hesitate to describe, in part because the vocabulary is archaic and foreign, but also because we sense that dissection threatens our access to the emotional potency of great poetry for the sake of mere intellectual comprehension.

Iamb, Iambic	de DUM	as in "before"
Trochee, Trochaic	DUM de	as in "after"
Dactyl, Dactylic	DUM de de	as in "cantaloupe"
Anapest, Anapestic	de de DUM	as in "unabridged"
Spondee, Spondaic	DUM DUM	as in "heartburn"
Amphibrac	de DUM de	as in "potato"
Pyrric	de de	as in "so so"

Iambic pentameter is the key of music that Shakespeare most frequently used for his dramatic verse. It was the key that dominated his theatre, and the key in which his actors were most accustomed to presenting their characters and which his audience was most attuned to hear the melody with which he was experimenting. Pentameter refers to the number of iambs, also known as feet. As each foot had two syllables, and pentameter requires five such feet, the standard line had ten syllables, alternating unstressed with stressed. The regular iambic pulse of light/strong/light/strong echoes the beating of the human heart as it fills with blood, then pushes blood out to the extremities. This is the sound that we first hear, *in utero*, and to which we respond in two-part music and other rhythmic activity. In the theatre we often refer to the iambic pulse as the heartbeat of Shakespeare's dramatic poetry.

The Greeks used the word iamb not only to describe a rhythm, but also as a military term meaning to assault, to drive forth, to attack. The forward-moving, upward-lifting quality of a series of iambs was, to their ear, an aggressive, masculine meter, in contrast to its sister rhythm, also based on the heartbeat, but which falls away in a graceful release of energy, in keeping with the "strong/light/strong/light/strong/light" cadence.

From the perspective of an actor, the forward-moving energy of the iamb is the perfect vehicle for the creation of speech acts. The character wants something, needs something, is fighting for something, not just passively expressing emotion. An understanding of the essentially dramatic nature of the rising line will answer the question, why iambic?

The question, why pentameter, leads us to a consideration of each line of poetry as the perfect unit for an actor to absorb and deliver. You can acquire the sensation of this by working on a speech line by line, being sure to reveal it to yourself one line at a time. As each new line appears, murmur it silently to yourself, letting the five-foot pattern work on your emotions even as you use it as a hook for memorization. Then, take in a full breath, and deliver the line in full voice, allowing the rising energy of the iambs to lift you from the beginning of the line toward the end.

What actors have consistently reported is that the five-foot line turns out to be the perfect unit for memorization, and the perfect amount of text for full-voiced and supported delivery suitable to an outdoor theatre. No wonder the new professional actors of Shakespeare's theatre made iambic pentameter their dominant pattern of language!

Creating Iambic Pentameter

The English language contains many two-syllable words with the stress on the second syllable. These lend themselves to iamb rhythms. Our language also has many two-syllable words with the stress on the first syllable, which are easily fitted into the iamb rhythm by the inclusion of a relatively less important word. It is the natural ease of the iambic rhythm that makes a line of iambic pentameter so easy to create.

The poet's task is picking words that convey thought and fall into the rhythm at the same time. It's not so difficult. Try it yourself! "Before" is a perfect iambic foot. "Window" can be used to create two iambic feet, by adding an unstressed word before it and a stressed word after. "A window pane" makes two iambic feet.

English lends itself to strict rhythm patterns like iambic pentameter for one simple reason: it is a *big* language. There are so many ways of saying the same thing that the poet can, with a little manipulation and a good thesaurus, find a word with accents in just the right spot to make the line regular.

When Shakespeare was working as an actor-playwright, the language was even more flexible than it is today. If he needed a word to fit a certain rhythm, then he could feel free to change the work, to invent a new word, to take a word from Latin or French and create a brand new English word, if that was what would work for the verse. Shakespeare had great fun with the "un-" preface, which he added to all sorts of words to create a new word meaning the opposite of the original. He also enjoyed creating new applications for well-known words by adding the suffix "-ness."

Elizabethans had some conventions that helped them to blend thought and rhythm at a very sophisticated level. The most important of these has to do with word order. Today, we hesitate to reposition the parts of a sentence in any way that severely damages the expected structure of subject, verb, object. It is almost immediately apparent, when reading Shakespeare's plays, that he did not feel any restrictions on his poetry that might ask him to sacrifice dramatic effect for something as mundane as good grammar.

When we combine the flexibility of vocabulary with the freedom of poetic sentence structures, iambic pentameter is very easy to create. If, in the first attempt, your line came out: "But see what light upon the sea now glimmers," a substitution for "glimmers" can quickly be found, so that the last word is "shines" or "gleams." Since you are allowed to rearrange the parts of the sentence, then the line might read, "Now glimmers there the light upon the sea," or "What light upon the sea now glimmers here?"

When iambic pentameter is written to be spoken, and sometimes even when it's just written to be read, the poet can compress two syllables into one the way the people do when they speak. "I'd like to take you out to see a show," is a perfect iambic line, because "I would" is not something I would say unless the situation were fraught with tension. Poets can push this trick to the extreme, and you will often see printed strange hybrid poeticisms like "e'en" for "even" or "th'angel" for "the angel." Spoken English lends itself to the addition and subtraction of syllables for a wide range of word variations. "Hold" and "ahold" mean the same thing, as do "between" and "tween." English is full of these, and Shakespeare and his contemporaries felt free to manufacture new ones as needed.

Another even more subtle aspect of the spoken form of iambic pentameter has to do with the double vowel sounds that we call diphthongs. Let us consider the word "fire." This can be stretched out into two full syllables, so that it sounds like "fie-errrr" or, just as easily, clipped into a one-syllable version. The capacity of the spoken sound to expand to fill out the line of poetry is not as easily marked in the written line, which is another reason for reading aloud when exploring Shakespeare's poetry.

There were other ways in which Shakespeare's English was more flexible than ours is today, because the English language was in a state of transformation. Shakespeare and his contemporaries were particularly fortunate in their poetry making with regard to the pronunciation of verb forms created by the addition of "-ed." Sometimes the "-ed" would be pronounced and other times, with the same verb, it would not. This seems to have been what was occurring in ordinary conversation, and it was definitely happening all the time in poetry. Today, we don't have that option. "He's a marked man!" can never be correct iambic pentameter, but Richard III could proclaim:

And this is Edwards Wife, that monstrous Witch,
Consorted with that Harlot, Strumpet Shore,
That by their Witchcraft thus have marked me. [3.4.70]

By pronouncing the "-ed," "marked" becomes a two-syllable word and holds the iambics firm in the final line.

Modern editors conveniently mark these for us so that we, as modern readers, can jump immediately onto the iambic band wagon and feel its firm beat at work. There are two customary styles of doing this, one of which draws attention to the unexpected pronunciation of the final syllable, so that, if pronounced it would be printed "marked" and the other that creates a contraction, so that when the final syllable is not pronounced it appears as "mark'd." The former style helps a modern reader with unfamiliar pronunciations, but the latter style matches the first printings, suggesting that the two-syllable version of the word was expected.

English contains words that mean something different if the stress falls on the first or second syllable. "I'll proceed now with the legal paperwork," says the lawyer to the fundraiser, "if you take charge of the proceeds of the charity ball." We have no trouble hearing these words, and usually only a momentary uncertainty reading them. Elizabethan English was even more flexible. Some words could be stressed on either syllable and mean the same thing.

Perfection

For all these reasons, I think we have to conclude that creating "pure" iambic pentameter would have been well within the capabilities of even a second-rate poet of the English language. Therefore, what are we to conclude by the relative scarcity of clean, regular, "correct" iambic pentameter lines in Shakespeare's plays?

One of the comments made about Shakespeare by his friend Ben Jonson is that he "blotted nary a line," suggesting that he did not slave long and hard rewriting, tinkering, searching for the perfect word, but rather that the plays emerged with ease and rapidity. If we combine this insight with our discovery of the ease with which "perfect" iambic pentameter can be written, and the rarity of such perfection in Shakespeare's dramatic poetry, then perhaps it is time to redefine what we mean by "perfect" dramatic poetry.

Clearly, perfect iambic pentameter, for Shakespeare's purposes, was not an attribute he valued. For his purposes, the imperfections were far more useful, adding as they did variety to the rhythms of the spoken text. The ripples in the flow, created by these variations, are like the ripples that mark the movement of fast-running water over rocks. We do not see the rocks, but we know they are there.

It is the imperfections in the pure iambic pentameter that make up what we call the Iambic Code. What we discover, on the basis of a careful scansion of the dramatic of poetry of all of the Elizabethan playwrights, is that certain specific variations were used regularly to break up the regular iambic rhythm, and that it is the careful balance between an ongoing evocation of the heartbeat and the unexpected shifts, jolts, lengthenings, and shortenings that gives this poetry its theatrical vitality.

Variations

It is with the variations on the Iambic Code that Shakespeare wrote the emotional music unique to the specific moment in the play. Some of the variations occur so frequently as to become common, almost expected, while others are rarer and represent Shakespeare's experimentations within his task of shaping actors into characters and speaking into dramatic action.

Taken all together, these variations provide us with a fairly clear-cut emotional shorthand, a series of clues that excite the unique sensitivities of an individual performer. Although they place demands on the speaker of the verse, in that the voice and breath must negotiate the making of this particular sequence of sounds, they do not lock an actor into a specific delivery. In that, they are less of a straightjacket binding an actor into an uncomfortably bombastic or "poetical" approach, and more of a stethoscope providing insight into the living energy that attracts us to these plays.

The Feminine Ending: "To Infinity, and Beyond!"

The most common variation is the addition of an extra, unstressed syllable at the end of the five-foot line. This is called the feminine ending, and it results in two specific and almost automatic shapings. Because the use of a stressed syllable to end the line is the more common (by three or four to one), the unstressed syllable is unexpected and gives the sensation that something more must be hovering in the air, waiting to be expressed in what comes next. Because the syllable is unstressed, it is a soft, drifting sound, suggesting that the thought or feeling the line contains is just that little bit too long, too complex, or more open-ended and ambiguous than a firm, accented final foot would suggest. That extra syllable suggests that things are not over, somehow, and that the following line is needed to wrap things up. On the one hand, this arouses a sensation of opening up to the possibilities of what has just been expressed. On the other hand, this arouses a desire to move on, to push forward to what is about to be said, whatever it may be. If the actor takes notice of this psychological clue and moves right on to the next line of verse, a fascinating variation in the iambic heartbeat signals an undercurrent of heightened intensity. Two lines together create: da DÚM da DUM da DUM da DUM da DUM da, da DUM da DUM da DUM da DUM da DUM.

For some reason, an older generation of scholars associated the feminine ending with a womanly weakness, and the more traditional ending on a stressed syllable as a strong or masculine ending. Although I do agree that the

extra, unaccented syllable removes some of the weight of a final stressed syllable, I'm not sure from what myth of womanhood they received their concept
of womanly weakness. The Greeks found the Trochaic beat to be the more
graceful and delicate, but also they call a line of trochees a "falling" line, and
used it for moments of grief and despair. For our purposes there is something
to be said for comparing the two different line-endings to male and female
images. The male involves a final thrust that suggests one type of power or
certainty. The female involves an opening, perhaps into uncertainty, perhaps
into infinite possibility. We would be wrong, however, in assuming that this
is weakness, when it is just as likely to suggest an alternative power.

A physicist might remind us that sound waves, if sent off into space, make
their way out into the vast expanse just as light does. Next time you are on a
hilltop on a dark and starry night, far away from the light and noise pollution
of an urban setting, give in to the temptation to shine your flashlight up into
the night and imagine that beam travelling out to those stars. Then raise your
voice and say some of Shakespeare's great dramatic poetry, knowing that those
sounds will do the same.

This is, for me, the opening to mystery suggested by the feminine ending.

The Inverted First Foot: "Attack!"

One of the benefits of slowing down your reading and switching your attention from the thoughts (encoded in sentences) to the emotions (encoded in
sounds and rhythms) is that you begin to get a strong sense of the double time
system at work in the verse. On the one hand, there is the varied length of
sentences, stretching between lines, starting and ending mid-line, or matching
verse lines. On the other hand, the constancy of the five-foot verse line serves
as a more ritualized ebb and flow of emotional energy.

Just as a line of regular iambic pentameter ends on a stress, allowing the
contrasting rhythm of an extra, unstressed syllable, so too each regular line
begins with an unstressed syllable, allowing for a striking contrast when the
writer reverses our expectations by starting with a stressed syllable. This variation happens frequently enough to be a familiar indicator of heightened emotion, but rarely enough to catch the ear and make a striking point.

For those lines wherein the first foot is inverted, it is as if the emotional
energy contained in the line requires an extra burst of energy to start it off.
Rather than the more familiar unstressed syllable serving as a springboard
taking us immediately into the first stressed syllable, the inversion pounds out
a stress, followed by two unstressed and another stressed. This distinctive
pattern gives us just a taste of an alternative to the iamb, reminding us that
there is another way to express human experiences, another key in which
emotion can be expressed. In this, the inverted foot can be likened to the use
of additional sharps and flats in a major scale of music, giving a hint of a minor
key or modulation into a completely different key before returning to the
familiar major sequence of notes.

Shakespeare often allowed his characters to get a strong, attacking start to a line of verse by reversing the usual iambic foot (soft-HARD as in "before") and creating a striking pattern when combined with the second, regular iambic foot: HARD soft soft HARD. "Always before" is just such a rhythm pattern. The other rhythms that are echoed are the anapest and dactyl. These are often used in poetry of another sort, and are not that difficult to sustain in the English system of stressed and unstressed syllables.

> Ride a cock horse, to Banbury cross
> See a fine lady upon a white horse
> With rings on her fingers and bells on her toes
> She shall have music wherever she goes.

The anapest, dactyl rhythms, which place two unstressed syllables before or behind a stressed syllable, are somehow more energetic, more charged than the regular unstressed, stressed, unstressed, stressed pattern of the iamb. And so, when a foot is inverted, it is as if Shakespeare offers the actor a small charge of energy at the beginning of that emotional unit.

Looking for five iambs, spotting feminine endings and inverted first feet, and opening ourselves to a growing awareness of the sensory power of the Iambic Code through some simple scansion exercises will prepare us to move on to the infinitely varied and immensely complex use of the Iambic Code in Shakespeare's mature dramatic language.

The Rising Line

The single most important aspect of the iambic pentameter line is the rising energy of the iambs which march inexorably to the final word of the line. This, however, is the aspect of the dramatic verse that most readily drops away when a modern actor seeks to own the language and transmit it credibly to a modern audience. This creates a very real barrier between the messages conveyed through the Iambic Code and the actor's instinctive and intellectual encounter with the poetry, because Shakespeare made great use of this rise and of his actors' and audience's sensitivity to the pentameter line by placing key words at the ends of lines of poetry. He also made use of a variety of striking first sounds of lines, and he had great fun playing variations with the mid-line break. The combination of position within the line and emotional and/or intellectual significance leads to a natural pause or savoring or emphasizing: poetical equivalents to the musician's rest, fermata, or accent.

Modern playwrights, and through their work modern actors, strive above all to reproduce the rhythms of contemporary conversation. In doing this they do not, in fact, transcribe or replicate precisely the actual exchanges that might be overheard on a bus or in the mall. Instead, they make use of a limited repertoire of conventional linguistic tricks that have become encoded by frequent use so that they are acceptable indicators of the way real people talk every day.

The speed with which these conventions change can be observed by comparing the screenplays of thirty years ago with those of today. The shift in vocabulary indicated by the introduction of expletives has run parallel to a language rhythm that privileges incomplete sentences, sentence fragments, and highly repetitive speeches making use of a strikingly limited range of words. Complex sentences, polysyllabic words, and lengthy and logically structured speeches now strike the ear as "unnatural," unless the speaker is a university professor, a con artist, or a politician.

The "natural" delivery of a modern dramatic speech begins in the medium range, includes a slight build to the penultimate phrase or word, and then cadences down, with room for a tiny flip upward if the line is framed as a question. Shorter units might begin with a burst of linguistic energy, perhaps in the form of a curse word, but it is very rare to find any sort of significant variation on the familiar pattern that has become the norm.

"I really have to go to the *bath*room."

"Look out for that *truck*, you idiot."

"And where have *you* been, young man?"

The result of these norms of behavior is that modern actors, committed as they are to judging the validity of their acting choices within a standard of truthfulness, seek, above all, to avoid the fake, the contrived, the stagy (possibly meaning old-fashioned or any theatrical trick used to grab the attention of the audience divorced from any consideration of character or situation).

Nothing could be more contrived than the carefully structured wave-effect of the iambic verse line. Each five-foot unit, although it can absorb countless variations in subtle shift of emphasis, is constructed to partake of a rising energy that culminates in the final word of the line, whether or not that word is the end of the intellectual grouping.

The contrast between the choices for emphasis between iambic pentameter and modern prose can be illustrated if we rewrite some verse into sentences and compare the alternative patterns of emphasis suggested by (a) the verse structure, and (b) the meaning, using contemporary "normal" strategies for the second.

(a) We have strict Statutes, and most biting **Laws**, (the needful bits and curbs to headstrong **weeds**,) which for this fourteen years, we have let **slip**, even like an o'er-grown Lion in a **Cave** that goes not out to prey: now, as fond **Fathers**, having bound up the threatening twigs of **birch**, only to stick it in their childrens **sight** for terror, not to use: in time the **rod** becomes more mocked, than feared: so our **Decrees**, dead to infliction, to themselves are **dead**, and liberty, plucks Justice by the **nose**; the Baby beats the Nurse, and quite **athwart** goes all decorum.

(b) We have strict Statutes, and most **biting** Laws, (the needful bits and curbs to **headstrong** weeds,) which for this **fourteen** years, we have let slip, even like an o'er-grown **Lion** in a Cave that goes not out to prey: now, as fond Fathers, having bound up the threatening twigs of birch, only to stick it in their childrens sight for terror, not to use: in time the rod becomes more **mocked**, than feared: so our Decrees, dead to **infliction**, to themselves are dead, and liberty, plucks **Justice** by the nose; the Baby beats the Nurse, and quite **athwart** goes all decorum.

With the exception of "athwart," there is no concurrence in the two versions. Some of my choices in (b) are, of course, arbitrary, and "laws," "weeds," "decrees," "dead," and "nose" might work quite well for a modern actor. But it is very unlikely that the *sense* of the lines would have an actor finding "cave" a more interesting word than "lion," and "birch," "sight," and "rod" simply don't seem worthy of any sort of heightened significance.

By cross-checking our predilection for the penultimate against the regularization of emphasis at the last word of the iambic line, we note some interesting subtleties of meaning. The significance of the overgrown lion is not in the choice of animal, but rather that the beast remains in a cave instead of coming out to hunt, as would be natural in a mature predator. When we link "birch," "sight," and "rod" with the strongly positioned "fathers," we are reminded of the biblical injunction that became the well-known aphorism, "Spare the rod and spoil the child."

Returning to our original blank verse example, we can see how the entire line has been shaped to feed into the final word. In half the lines there is something early on that forms a striking link to the final word, either in meaning or sound, the first lightly emphasized, the second profoundly significant for the speaker.

> We have strict *Statutes*, and most biting **Laws**, [synonym]
> (The *needful* bits and curbs to headstrong **weeds**,) [antonym]
> Which for this fourteen years, we have let **slip**,
> Even like an o'er-grown Lion in a **Cave**
> That goes not out to prey: Now, as fond **Fathers**,
> Having *bound* up the threatening twigs of **birch**, [alliterative]
> Only to *stick* it in their childrens **sight** [alliterative]
> For *terror*, not to use: in time the **rod** [association]
> Becomes more mocked, than feared: so our **Decrees**,
> *Dead* to infliction, to themselves are **dead**, [repetition]
> And liberty, plucks Justice by the **nose**;
> The Baby beats the Nurse, and quite **athwart**
> Goes all decorum. [*Measure* 1.3.19]

As soon as we spot this pattern, we look for similar key words in every line.

> And liberty, plucks Justice by the nose

Both liberty and justice seem important. The vivid verb "pluck" also seems significant. And yet to make every one of these words equally dramatic would result in a slow, ponderous, muddy reading of a line which otherwise moves off the tongue fairly quickly. But "liberty" is, as we have seen, a double indemnity word, and sets up the import of the line powerfully.

> Which for this fourteen years, we have let **slip**,
> Even like an o'ergrown Lion in a **Cave**,
> That goes not out to prey: Now, as fond **fathers**,

In two of these three lines there seems to be an obvious choice: "fourteen" is powerful in its significance (compared to, for example, "many," an obvious alternative). "Prey," which allows for a triple significance: the verb to prey, meaning to prey upon weaker animals; the victims themselves, who are also known as "prey," and the punning "to pray," which sets up the biblical images in the next sentence and also marks the end of the current thought unit.

As we have seen, "lion" is an appealing choice for emphasis. But is the animal as important as the fact that it is still in a cave even at that advanced age and physical development? I would argue for "o'ergrown" as the more interesting word, because it also marks, in the contraction, a potential pressure-cooker word worth thinking about. Has perhaps the entire city overgrown itself to the point where it is not easily governed?

> Becomes more mocked, than feared: so our **Decrees**,

The final example is relatively easy, because the sentence is set up to impress upon the listener that the activity of mocking is more than the activity of fearing, and emphasizing "mocked" over "feared" is a natural choice to reinforce that meaning.

This then is how the primary (ending) and secondary (leaping off) emphases work in the speech we have been examining.

> We have strict *Statutes*, and most biting **Laws**,
> (The *needful* bits and curbs to headstrong **weeds**,)
> Which for this *fourteen* years, we have let **slip**,
> Even like an *o'er-grown* Lion in a **Cave**
> That goes not out to *prey*: Now, as fond **Fathers**,
> Having *bound* up the threatening twigs of **birch**,
> Only to *stick* it in their childrens **sight**
> For *terror*, not to use: in time the **rod**
> Becomes more *mocked*, than feared: so our **Decrees**,
> *Dead* to infliction, to themselves are **dead**,
> And *liberty*, plucks Justice by the **nose**;
> The Baby *beats* the Nurse, and quite **athwart**
> Goes all decorum.

Now, contrast this pattern of emphasis with what I call the "penultimate temptation:"

> We have strict Statutes, and most **biting** Laws,
> (The needful bits and curbs to **headstrong** weeds,)
> Which for this fourteen **years**, we have let slip,
> Even like an o'er-grown **Lion** in a Cave
> That goes not out to prey: **Now**, as fond Fathers,
> Having bound up the **threatening** twigs of birch,
> Only to stick it in their **childrens** sight
> For terror, not to **use**: in time the rod
> Becomes more mocked, than **feared**: so our Decrees,
> Dead to infliction, to **themselves** are dead,
> And liberty, plucks **Justice** by the nose;
> The Baby beats the **Nurse**, and quite athwart
> Goes all decorum.

Emphasizing the second-last word makes just as much sense of the meaning of the lines but undercuts the music of the iambic pentameter. Learning to trust the rising line requires honoring both the sense and the sensation of the line.

⤜ 4 ⤛

The Sonnets

Assist me some extemporal god of Rhyme, for I am sure I shall turn
Sonnet. Devise Wit, write Pen, for I am for whole volumes in folio.
                                              Don Armado [*LLL* 1.2.183]

Shakespeare's sonnets provide important tools for understanding the Iambic
Code. Some actors and coaches of voice and acting swear by them as acting
exercises as well. Because they are poetry, not dramatic verse, they offer no
examples of Shakespeare's quite remarkable craft in shaping sound and emotion in service of theatrical character and event. But they do demonstrate his
ability to manipulate words and to capture human experience.

The strongest justification for actors using the sonnets to explore the speaking of Shakespeare's verse is the fact that they, too, were written to be read
aloud. The convention of this sort of writing was that the poet/lover created
the sonnet, imagining it being spoken aloud by the patron/lover. Then the
sonnet was sent, and the patron/lover did, very likely, read it aloud, but in
turn imagined the poet/lover's voice saying the words. It was this convention
that made the exchanging of sonnets an intimate event.

Shakespeare and his contemporaries enjoyed the widespread literacy that
resulted from the Tudor policy of free schools in every small town in England.
But three years was the extent of the education of the majority, including, we
think, Shakespeare, and more than likely every member of his acting troupe.
Therefore, when you read his writing, please read at the grade three level.
This means slowly and out loud. You must work hard to put aside your
twentieth-century adult facility: our silent, rapid skimming of words does more
harm than good when attempting to listen for the Iambic Code.

Read aloud the following sonnet. The only rule you need to follow in this sort of a sight reading is to fight any tendency to cadence (i.e., drop the voice at the end of a line as it were the end of a sentence) until you reach a period. Other than that, just emphasize whichever words or syllables invite or require emphasis.

> No longer mourn for me when I am dead,
> Than you shall hear the surly sullen bell
> Give warning to the world that I am fled
> From this vile world, with vilest worms to dwell:
> Nay if you read this line, remember not,
> The hand that writ it, for I love you so,
> That I in your sweet thoughts would be forgot,
> If thinking on me then should make you woe.
> O, if (I say) you look upon this verse,
> When I (perhaps) compounded am with clay,
> Do not so much as my poor name rehearse;
> But let your love even with my life decay.
>   Lest the wise world should look into your moan,
>   And mock you with me after I am gone. [LXXI]

To begin, we must make sure we understand every word. Double check that you have an accurate and precise meaning of the beautifully evocative words "surly," "sullen," and "vile." You might already know the noun "compound" from chemistry; here it appears as a verb. Be sure that you know exactly what it means to be compounded with clay. Shakespeare pulls a similar trick with the word "woe" which is usually a noun, something you feel, but here is a verb, something that you can be made to do.

Now, we must reorder the phrases so that they make grammatical sense, remembering that Shakespeare puts things out of order to draw attention to what is most important emotionally. First, link "no longer" with "than" to clarify the sense of the first three lines, which mean, "Do not mourn any longer than you are going to hear the funeral bell announcing I'm dead." Not a very long period of mourning! The image of death makes two uses of the word "vile" to suggest two different interpretations of death: we flee this vile (sinful) world by going to heaven, and we are buried in the ground where the slimiest (vilest) kind of worms, maggots, eat us. What a terrible image!

Now the poet/lover flashes forward to an imaginary future when the patron/lover reads the poem after the poet/lover's death. Don't think about the hand (now rotting in the ground) or say aloud to memorize (rehearse) the name of the author. Love decays over time, just like bodies, and the patron/lover is advised to let love die at the moment of the poet/lover's death, so that the patron/lover will not be mocked by the wise world.

We must be specific, however, rather than general with the final couplet. What does it mean, "mock you with me" and "look into your moan"? Both are things that the world would do, because it is wise and can see into the real cause of grief, and because patron/lovers should not groan in mourning (moan) for poet/lovers who have died.

Is the poet/lover as humble as the surface of the poem suggests? Or is this a challenge to the patron/lover, a suggestion that the regard for the poet is not going to stand the test of time? I've never found that abject humility makes for interesting theatre, so let's decide that the piece confronts the patron/lover with these serious accusations of superficiality and unreliability.

Now we have a place to start with our exploration of this sonnet as an example of iambic pentameter. Let's see what happens when we read it aloud slowly, trying to stay connected with the iambic heartbeat. For this, I will remove all punctuation and capitalization in order to suggest the contrast of stressed and unstressed syllables.

> no LONGer MOURN for ME when I am DEAD [this works fine]
> than YOU shall HEAR the SURly SULlen BELL [fine]
> give WARNing TO the WORLD that I am FLED [great]
> from THIS vile WORLD, with VILest WORMS to DWELL [it all fits!]
> nay IF you READ this LINE reMEMber NOT
> the HAND that WRIT it FOR i LOVE you SO
> that I in YOUR sweet THOUGHTS would BE forGOT
> if THINKing ON me THEN should MAKE you WOE [this is a bit of
>   a problem, for surely "me" is more interesting and important than
>   "on"?]
> o IF i SAY you LOOK upON this VERSE
> when I perHAPS comPOUNDed AM with CLAY
> do NOT so MUCH as MY poor NAME reHEARSE
> but LET your LOVE even WITH my LIFE deCAY ["even" creates a
>   bit of a problem, unless we reduce it to e'en to fit the rhythm]
> lest THE wise WORLD should LOOK inTO your MOAN [it seems
>   very strange to emphasize "the" and "inTO" seems wrong]
> and MOCK you WITH me AFter I am GONE [it also seems strange to
>   emphasize "with" rather than "you"]

In addition to the "glitches" in the last two lines, there is a problem throughout if we say these words giving every capitalized syllable the same amount of increased intensity. Clearly, if we mechanically speak the meter of the verse, we destroy the sense. The connection between emphasis in the verse rhythm and intensity in spoken delivery is not a simple correspondence.

We will soon discover that the solution to the problem with "inTO" and "you WITH me" is that none of the syllables need receive particular emphasis, because the emotional meaning can be more clearly conveyed by emphasizing other words or syllables in those lines:

LEST the WISE WORLD should LOOK into your MOAN
and MOCK you with me AFter I am GONE

Changing the emphasis from "the" to "Lest" is a common variation that Shakespeare and his contemporaries used frequently; whenever we encounter it we must inject the line with something of the energy of "attack!"

This same phrase demonstrates another problem: both "wise" and "world" are interesting words and need to be emphasized for the richest speaking of the phrase. Why not? If we give ourselves the freedom to emphasize four instead of five syllables per line, letting uninteresting words sink to a natural delivery, and also allow a natural emphasis on an interesting additional word, then we have the best of both worlds: emphasis for sense and the downbeat of the iambic heartbeat. We will find that some lines of verse have us tossing away a downbeat and increasing the emphasis on a different, more interesting, word, so that we end up with five again!

Let's work through another, more difficult example.

Take all my loves, my love, yea take them all,
What hast thou then more than thou hadst before?
No love, my love, that thou mayst true love call,
All mine was thine, before thou hadst this more:
Then if for my love, thou my love receivest,
I cannot blame thee, for my love thou usest,
But yet be blamed, if thou thyself deceivest
By wilful taste of what thyself refusest.
I do forgive thy robbery gentle thief
Although thou steal thee all my poverty:
And yet love knows, it is a greater grief
To bear loves wrong, than hates known injury.
    Lascivious grace, in whom all ill well shows,
    Kill me with spites yet we must not be foes. [XL]

Now spot the iambic pentameter in the verse.

Take ALL my LOVES my LOVE yea TAKE them ALL

This is probably the way you said it, though you likely didn't give all of the capitalized words equal weight. You probably emphasized the first ALL and the last ALL, but gave LOVES only a slight emphasis, and then LOVE a bit more, and TAKE a bit more. This would be a natural ebb and flow of intensity that falls in line with the heartbeat provided by the iambic rhythm built into the language.

Let's look at the eleventh line.

And YET love KNOWS it IS a GREATer GRIEF

The first line was made up of single-syllable words, but here we have a two-syllable word and the accent on the first syllable lines up perfectly with the emphasis provided by the heartbeat. Probably you would not give a simple word like IS any great intensity, yet there is no discomfort from it sitting in that position within the rhythm of the poetry. Instead, you probably "traded off" an emphasis on IS for the significant word LOVE which sits in an unemphasized position but seems to cry out for emphasis:

And YET LOVE KNOWS it is a GREATer GRIEF.

Even so, "YET" and "KNOWS" are emphasized more than the "LOVE" that sits between them, preserving the iambic feel to the line.

These two lines of the sonnet have the flow we associate with the iambic heartbeat. But every other line of the sonnet contains some sort of friction between the iambic rhythm and the words chosen as the best expression of the emotions that inspired the poet. Because of the remarkable flexibility of the English language, we know that alternative words could have been found and arranged so that every line was as "perfect" an example of five iambs as these two lines are.

Clearly, perfection is *not* what iambic pentameter is about. Instead, it is about the friction. We want to explore as richly as possible the sensation of that friction, as the heartbeat remains in our inner ear even as our sounding apparatus pushes against that regular rhythm. There is no better way to undertake this exploration than by, once again, reading the sonnet aloud. Use the first and eleventh lines to anchor the heartbeat in your inner ear, but read all of the other lines simply as the words demand. Don't alter your pronunciation of any word. Don't switch your emphasis from an interesting word to a boring word to speak in iambics. They are present, in the heartbeat, in the inner ear. When your words battle that rhythm, the words must win.

Let's try another example.

> Since brass, nor stone, nor earth, nor boundless sea,
> But sad mortality o'er-sways their power,
> How with this rage shall beauty hold a plea,
> Whose action is no stronger than a flower?
> O how shall summers honey breath hold out,
> Against the wreckful siege of battering days,
> When rocks impregnable are not so stout,
> Nor gates of steel so strong but time decays?
> O fearful meditation, where alack,
> Shall times best jewel from times chest lie hid?
> Or what strong hand can hold his swift foot back,
> Or who his spoil or beauty can forbid?
> > O none, unless this miracle have might,
> > That in black ink my love may still shine bright. [LXV]

If your inner ear is developing, you should have felt as you read this aloud
that the iambic heartbeat and the words were more frequently connected in
this sonnet. Remembering that the capitalized syllables do not imply that the
emphasis is exactly the same strength for each, look again at the following
lines:

Since BRASS nor STONE nor EARTH nor BOUNDless SEA

How WITH this RAGE shall BEAUty HOLD a PLEA

Nor GATES of STEEL so STRONG but TIME deCAYS

Or WHAT strong HAND can HOLD his SWIFT foot BACK

Or WHO his SPOIL of BEAUty CAN forBID

That IN black INK my LOVE may STILL shine BRIGHT

It might be that your mind was attracted to the word "black" as much as the
word "ink" in this last line, and there is no reason why, even in keeping with
the iambic, you cannot say and feel black, but it is there to modify ink, and
ink is the more important word. To test this, ask yourself: is it more important
to communicate, "black ink, not red or blue ink" *or* "black ink, not a sword
or building or monument or anything else I might construct that would with-
stand time."

Let's look at the second, fourth, and tenth lines, which contain the words
"power," "flower," and "jewel." The words contain diphthongs, vowels that
can fit into the poet's rhythm as one or two syllables, as needed. The first two,
which are used to create a rhyme at the end of lines, have a special function
for that reason. But "jewel," which can so easily become the one-syllable sound
"jule" must be fully two syllables or the line has only nine beats. But it is clear,
if you say the tenth line aloud, using a natural emphasis of those words that
contain meaning for the poet, that the line is never going to be one of the
smooth merging of emphasis and rhythm like the examples above.

ENACTING THE SONNETS

Some actors can access strong emotions just by saying strong words. Other
actors need to connect through physical actions, and others through eye contact with another human being. We need to expand our explorations of sonnets
to include everyone's strengths. I am a great believer in connecting spoken
rhythms with simple physical actions and getting actors up on their feet and
moving around a room. This is an excellent exercise after a time of sitting and
talking about sonnets, and I strongly recommend it for classroom explorations.

To prepare, everyone must have a sonnet and a highlighter. It is almost
better if the students encounter the sonnet for the first time as the exercise

begins, but of course it can also work on a sonnet that the student has already read, studied, or discussed.

The student reads the sonnet aloud and highlights every syllable that is emphasized. If the students are working in pairs, one can read and the other can highlight. Remember to read slowly and highlight "honestly"; in other words, do not highlight the syllables you think you should have emphasized, but rather the ones that you really do emphasize. Also, highlight with precision. You *must not* highlight an entire word if it is more than one syllable. Set yourself a rule: you must find no less than four and no more than six highlighted syllables per line.

It is possible for the teacher to introduce the students to this exercise by providing a sample of a highlighted sonnet. It might look something like this:

> SOME GLORy in their BIRTH, SOME in their SKILL
> SOME in their WEALTH, SOME in their BODies FORCE
> SOME in their GARments, THOUGH NEW FANGled ILL
> SOME in their HAWKS and HOUNDS, SOME in their HORSE
> And EVery HUMour hath his ADjunct PLEAsure
> WhereIN it FINDS a JOY aBOVE the REST
> But THESE parTICulars are NOT my MEAsure
> ALL THESE i BETter in one GENeral BEST
> Thy LOVE is BETter than HIGH BIRTH to ME
> RICHer than WEALTH, PROUDer than GARment's COST
> Of MORE deLIGHT than HAWKS or HORSes be
> And HAVing THEE, of ALL MEN'S PRIDE i BOAST
> WRETCHed in this aLONE, that THOU mayst TAKE
> ALL THIS aWAY and me most WRETCHed MAKE. [XCI]

You can see from this example that the highlighting is neither an accurate indication of iambic pentameter nor a perfect representation of words that must be emphasized to clarify meaning. Whenever a two-syllable word occurs, I have to highlight the accented syllable. Sometimes I find myself highlighting a word, not because it is important, but because it contrasts an unaccented syllable on either side, though the word itself is not all that important emotionally. Sometimes the highlighting has missed a word that probably would be emphasized, such as "be" in the eleventh line and "me" in the last, because I just can't bring myself to say such unimportant words with any emphasis. There are lines where I've selected an entire phrase for emphasis, because they are all important to me. If I could make some of the highlighting relatively darker, I could suggest a hierarchy of emphasis within the phrase that corresponds to the way I actually say it.

Once everyone has a highlighted sonnet, everyone stands up and prepares to walk around the room, taking one step for each of the highlighted words. The idea is to speak slowly and without emotion, just stepping exactly on the accented syllable. What happens, as soon as students begin to explore the exercise, is that they experience these subtleties in overt form. They find their feet demanding that a step be taken when they have missed a word that receives a natural emphasis within the iambics of English, such as the "be" and "me" in my example. They also find that when they step on a string of words, they want to step "harder/softer/harder" or "softer/harder/softer" but very seldom with exactly equal emphasis.

The students can return to their seats, make a few changes in the highlighting, and try it again. The point isn't to smooth the highlighting out so that every other syllable is emphasized, because, in fact, the sonnets do *not* represent perfect iambic pentameter, perfection not being the point of the verse form, as we have seen.

After a few walks around the room, the sonnets can be spoken aloud to the class, with a natural emphasis to convey meaning. The pulsing rhythms emphasized so overtly in the walking should disappear into relaxed delivery, but the iambic should now be settling into the inner ears of the class, and everyone should hear clearly those lines where emphasis and rhythm match up effortlessly, as in "WhereIN it FINDS a JOY aBOVE the REST" from my example above.

Here is an exercise for actors who connect through eye contact. It is also an effective way of bringing together all that you have discovered while working on the sonnets.

Work in pairs, each of you bringing to the work a sonnet you have chosen and read through aloud several times. It works best if you can avoid duplication in the class, so that everyone encounters as many sonnets as possible. Of course, in your preparation, you've figured out what you're actually saying, right? No shortcuts here. Look up the words you don't understand, and stay away from the ones with terribly convoluted lines of thought unless you can follow the meaning effortlessly.

Now, because you've worked on the sonnet, you know it better than your partner. Find a quiet spot, give your partner a copy of the sonnet written out in your handwriting, and then sit behind your partner, where you cannot be seen, only heard. Read the sonnet aloud, slowly, with a natural emphasis on words so that the meaning is clear, but do not give a huge emotional performance. That's for later. If you are the one receiving the sonnet, ask to have it read to you as many times as you need to understand the emotions it contains, as expressed by these words in this form. Don't be shy to ask for several readings. It doesn't mean that your partner has failed, just that the sonnet form is currently foreign to you, and you want to familiarize yourself with how it sounds, in your partner's voice. Assume that your partner won't mind reading aloud to you as many times as you would like.

Now, before you reverse the procedure, reconvene with the entire class. The one who received the sonnet goes to the front of the class, and the one who chose the sonnet, wrote it out, and spoke it over and over should sit as far away as possible. The receiver now speaks the sonnet, and this is where the strongly emotional delivery should occur. Why? Because the receiver is offering the sonnet back as a gift, trying to communicate as powerfully as possible the feelings the sonnet has aroused as well as the thoughts it has conveyed.

After everyone has listened to half the sonnets, it is time for the gift to be returned. Don't spend time discussing what happened in the first round. Just get to work and focus entirely on the second sonnet, following the same procedure. You might very well find that the second sonnet can serve as a sort of answer to the first, but don't push that. And remember, as you are reading the sonnet over and over to your partner, sitting behind where you cannot be seen, it is *not* your job to convey feeling, just meaning.

It can be fun to take the sonnet exchanges one giant step further toward a theatrical presentation. By doing this, the complexity of the emotional event that the sonnet captures can become clear, and the striking links between the rhythms of the language and the heart of the speaker can be felt by speaker and listeners. Let me give you an example.

> Thou art as tyrannous, so as thou art,
> As those whose beauties proudly make them cruel;
> For well thou know'st to my dear doting heart
> Thou art the fairest and most precious jewel.
> Yet in good faith some say that thee behold,
> Thy face hath not the power to make love groan;
> To say they err, I dare not be so bold,
> Although I swear it to myself alone.
> And to be sure that is not false I swear
> A thousand groans but thinking on thy face,
> One on anothers neck do witness bear
> Thy black is fairest in my judgment's place.
> > In nothing art thou black save in thy deeds,
> > And thence this slander as I think proceeds. [CXXXI]

Take this example and walk through the process whereby I would help an actor unravel the meaning of the sonnet. First, let's see what meaning is illuminated by the heartbeat of the verse, line by line.

> Thou art as tyrannous, so as thou art,

"Tyrannous" dominates the line. We must accent the first syllable, and after a quick scan of the rest of the line we realize that the final syllable, though not emphasized for meaning, fills the position of the third downbeat of the line. We can also see immediately that the final word of the line, as is always the case, is accented. But what about the rest? Would we say, "THOU art as tyrannous," making the point that the patron/lover to whom we are writing must be contrasted to others, including the poet/lover? Or would we say, "It's true, thou ART as tyrannous," using the emphasis to overcome denial on the part of the patron/lover of what we have observed.

And what about the phrase that follows the accusation of tyranny? Do we say, "so AS thou ART" or "SO as thou ART" perhaps to match the rhythm of the beginning of the line if we emphasize THOU? The actor could try out the various rhythms, because with so many single syllable words and without a clear sense of what should be emphasized at this point in the sonnet, any of these variations seems viable.

Wouldn't the patron/lover have the same problem when first reading this sonnet aloud, having received it from the poet/lover? Try saying the line aloud with only the word "tyrannous" touching a deep chord, and every other word as neutrally as possible. Perhaps that is the best way to understand the line. But what does "so as thou art" mean? We won't know for a while, but nor would the original reader. Maybe that's the point of the first line! On to the second.

As those whose beauties proudly make them cruel;

Hurray! This line reads firmly and clearly and flows without any glitches.

As THOSE whose BEAUties PROUDly MAKE them CRUEL

We notice of course that "cruel" and "jewel," which is used two lines later, are diphthongs and even if we try to put them into one syllable it's such a tight squeeze that the emotion contained in the word seems to break out of the box created by the iambic pentameter. This probably reflects the feelings of the poet/lover. Notice also how you have to slow down to say the unaccented syllable in "beauties" as compared to the "-ly" in "proudly make" which can be said more quickly. A bit more feeling seems to be contained in "beauties," but of course the diphthong in "proud" fills out the word with feeling. Next line.

For well thou know'st to my dear doting heart

The eye is immediately caught by "dear doting heart" and the mouth longs to explore the alliteration, but when you say the line aloud, the mind and the mouth collide a bit, because of the very difficult sequence of sounds of "know'st to" which sit in the middle of the line. These are not important words for feeling, we might think, but when we say them we must slow down. Although there is no comma, we must stop to separate the two "t" sounds. And although the punctuation suggests that "knowest" has been collapsed into a single syllable, there is no way the word "know'st" can be said quickly.

In saying "my dear doting heart" with sensitivity to the iambic heartbeat, we find that although the heart is dear, the fact that it is doting, in other words besotted with love, a little crazed with it, is more important. So we hit "dear" but we *top* it with "DOTing" to create the heartbeat.

On to the next line. Clearly, it's going to take a bit of time just to work through the riches of the sonnet that are signalled by the code, and only then are we able to see if we have a better understanding of the meaning of the whole thing. Don't give up just yet. Onward!

> Thou art the fairest and most precious jewel.

This line feels much easier. We've already had "cruel," and now "jewel" seems right in its position at the end of the line, as a more-than-one-, but not necessarily two-, syllable word. If we want to emphasize MOST, we realize that it modifies "precious," which must be accented on the first syllable, and the sensation of growing intensity naturally has us emphasize MOST but emphasize PREcious more. Should we emphasize THOU or ART? We've explored this possibility in the first line. Do we echo the rhythm we chose there or contrast it? We have to see what feels right, as we proceed with unlocking the emotional complexity in the sonnet.

However, before we move on, let's have another look at "precious." Today we say this as a two-syllable word, and there's no mystery. But the spelling suggests that at one time it was said as a three-syllable word, and that, at the very least, we should honor the power of the word by making the "-ious" a diphthong. The minute the actor "drops in" on the word by saying it over and over, making full use of the elongated sound in the final syllable, the potential of the word comes alive. By endowing it with its fullest sound, the fullest meaning begins to come clear. Next line.

> Yet in good faith some say that thee behold,

The rhythm is easy, but what on earth does it mean? Don't worry about that, just say it aloud:

> Yet IN good FAITH some SAY that THEE beHOLD

or possibly, if you like,

> YET in good FAITH some SAY that THEE beHOLD

and quickly on to the next to see if we can figure out meaning in the continuation of the sentence:

> Thy face hath not the power to make love groan;

This is simple enough, except for the word "power," which is supposed to fit into a one-syllable box in the verse but is at the very least a lengthy dipthong and maybe even a two-syllable word, resulting in

Thy FACE hath NOT the POWer to MAKE love GROAN

Clearly, the word power has emotional significance, like cruel and jewel, but can't be allowed to expand or contract at the end of a line, because it's held in the middle of the line. Now watch for an even more subtle diphthong in the next line, which otherwise falls into an easy iambic rhythm:

To say they err, I dare not be so bold,

It's natural to emphasize "say," "dare," and "bold," and even "be" feels comfortable in the emphasized slot, though it receives no particular punch when spoken aloud. But what about "err"? This is the subtle diphthong that is not easily said and understood. What a simple word, and how much more feeling it can contain if one says it and allows the "air" sound to expand slightly against the demands of the single-syllable "box" of the verse. This sensation is heightened by the internal rhyme created by "err" and "dare" which is almost but not quite perfect. We don't say the two words with exactly the same vowel sound, because dare has no diphthong. Next is the wonderfully flowing,

Although I swear it to myself alone.

At this point we have worked our way through the first two quatrains, and if the poet/lover uses the form conventionally, we should have the argument or point of the sonnet before us. Read through these eight lines with whatever emphasis comes out naturally, taking care to read slowly and to savor the words that we've discovered along the way.

Thou art as tyrannous, so as thou art,
As those whose beauties proudly make them cruel;
For well thou know'st to my dear doting heart
Thou art the fairest and most precious jewel.
Yet in good faith some say that thee behold,
Thy face hath not the power to make love groan;
To say they err, I dare not be so bold,
Although I swear it to myself alone.

Here is how it might sound. I've capitalized emphasized syllables and put in italics entire words that have come to have special meaning. Remember that this represents the instinctive choices that one actor might make. Another actor might go in a different direction.

> THOU art as *TYRannous* so AS thou ART
> As THOSE whose *BEAUties PROUDly* MAKE them *CRUel*
> For WELL thou *KNOWst* to MY dear *DOTing* HEART
> THOU art the FAIRest AND most *PRECious JEWel*
> YET in good FAITH some SAY that THEE beHOLD
> Thy FACE hath NOT the *POWer* to MAKE love GROAN
> To SAY they *ERR* i DARE not BE so BOLD
> AlTHOUGH i SWEAR it TO mySELF aLONE.

So, the sonnet is something about tyranny, proud cruelty connected to beauty, knowing and doting, a precious jewel, power, and erring. Let's see how the sonnet develops in the third quatrain, and how it resolves in the final couplet.

> And to be sure that is not false I swear

Although "And TO be SURE" would be in keeping with iambic rhythm, I prefer the bouncy rhythm of "AND to be SURE" which matches the emphasis our imaginary actor gave to "Yet in good faith," the phrase that begins the second quatrain. The extra pulse of energy seems a good way to launch each new quatrain.

It's easy to see that "false" and "swear" are going to be key words. But what about the mess in the middle of the line, where the meaning seems to become vague and it's difficult to tell which word to emphasize? The problem word is "that." What does it mean? If we emphasize it or not, the problem remains. Think what would happen if the line were written out as, "And to be sure that I am not swearing falsely" as compared to, "And to be sure that which I am swearing is not false." Suddenly we realize that the meaning must be the second, because of the verb formation, and that the meaning is clearest of we emphasize the IS in the sentence. Fortunately, the next line flows easily and the meaning is clear:

> A thousand groans but thinking on thy face,

What about the next?

> One on anothers neck do witness bear

Almost as clear a rhythm, although I would argue strongly for emphasizing ONE instead of ON at the beginning of the line. But what on earth does the phrase "One on another's neck" mean? We must look to the straightforward conclusion to the quatrain:

Thy black is fairest in my judgment's place.

And on to the rhymed couplet which should make everything clear:

In nothing art thou black save in thy deeds,
And thence this slander as I think proceeds.

The "s" sounds in the last line provide a hissing sound, and notice also the little pause that must occur between "this" and "slander" if the speaker pays careful attention to clarity. So "slander" joins the special words "tyrannous," "beauties," "proudly," "cruel," "jewel," "doting," "precious," "power," and "err" from the first two quatrains.

Now that the rhythm is worked out, there remain some problems with meaning. In particular, what is meant by "so as thou art" in the first line, and "one on another's neck" in the eleventh line? The argument centers on a debate about the slander of tyranny. The poet suggests a connection between the cruelty and the beauty, and then says that others do not think the patron/lover's face has that power. Now we can zoom in on another subtle diphthong that we missed earlier, the word "swear," which the poet/lover uses twice, spanning two quatrains. Something is sworn that is not false, and that is sworn in a silent thousand groans, when thinking on the face (that others say has not the power).

Now it is time to link the two problem phrases. "So as thou art" means just as you are, in just such a way. And how is the patron/lover? Image the poet/lover looking at the patron/lover's face and having a thousand groans confirm that the patron's dark beauty is, in the poet/lover's judgement, "fairest." How could that face be on another's neck? Does it help to remember the custom of wearing a miniature portrait of the beloved on a chain around one's neck? Is the poet/lover looking at that face because it is in the possession of a rival?

Back to the first line of the sonnet. The poet/lover is standing, talking to the rival, and catches sight of the locket containing the picture of the patron/lover. Suddenly we realize that "so as thou art" means "on another's neck" and the bitter irony of the twelfth line becomes clear. When the poet/lover confirms the validity of his judgment by labelling this particular blackness the fairest, what is meant is simultaneously the greatest compliment and the greatest insult. Yes, the patron/lover is the fairest, most beautiful, most precious jewel, but because this jewel hangs around the neck of a rival, the patron/lover is also the proudest, cruelest tyrant. That is the source of the patron/lover's power, and suggests that poet/lover's error, though his judgment is true and his swearing never false.

By locating the meaning of the sonnet through the words whose special significance is revealed by the Iambic Code, the actor unlocks the connection between the music of the words and their sense, both intellectually and emotionally. Problems will remain in communicating this to an audience, but perhaps some staging might help. Another actor could play the patron/lover, who gives the locket to the rival. The actor playing the poet/lover can encounter the locket, recognize it, and then confront the patron/lover. It's no insult to be addressed as a tyrant if that state is linked to one's beauty. That was a commonplace lover's image. So the patron/lover might quite enjoy the first quatrain. Then, an unpleasant truth: there are many who say the patron/lover isn't sufficiently beautiful to have that power. The poet/lover believes otherwise, but isn't about to come forward to say so. Not so pleasant a feeling for the patron/lover. The poet/lover cannot stop there!

At this point, the sonnet could go in quite a different direction. The poet/lover could use the rest of the poem to do the very thing that is not dared, to boldly proclaim the beauty of the patron/lover. That is what should occur for this to be a love poem. Instead, almost as if questioning what has just been sworn, the poet/lover offers proof. The evidence: the terrible pain of seeing the locket around the rival's neck. Proof undeniable. A compliment? Can the patron/lover be sure?

And then, brutally, the terrible closing couplet. The meaning of "black" changes from hair coloring to morality. The patron/lover's dark beauty is most fair, but at the same time this black is worth nothing, because the patron/lover is capable of such black deeds, "And thence this slander, as I think, proceeds." Which slander? The opinion of those who say that the patron/lover does not have the power? Or the cruel accusation of black deeds from the poet/lover? Or both?

Here are two more sonnets that cry out for a vivid sense of complex relationships as a means of following the complexity of the language:

> Beshrew that heart that makes my heart to groan
> For that deep wound it gives my friend and me;
> Is't not enough to torture me alone,
> But slave to slavery my sweet'st friend must be?
> Me from my self thy cruel eye hath taken,
> And my next self thou harder hast engrossed,
> Of him, my self, and thee, I am forsaken,
> A torment thrice three-fold thus to be crossed:
> Prison my heart in thy steel bosoms ward,
> But then my friends heart let my poor heart bail,
> Who e'er keeps me, let my heart be his guard,
> Thou canst not then use rigor in my jail.
>   And yet thou wilt, for I being pent in thee,
>   Perforce am thine and all that is in me. [CXXXIII]

> So now I have confessed that he is thine,
> And I my self am mortgaged to thy will,
> My self I'll forfeit, so that other mine,
> Thou wilt restore to be my comfort still:
> But thou wilt not, nore he will not be free,

> For thou art covetous, and he is kind,
> He learned but surety-like to write for me,
> Under that bond that him as fast doth bind.
> The statute of thy beauty thou wilt take,
> Thou usurer that put'st forth all to use,
> And sue a friend, came debtor for my sake,
> So him I lose through my unkind abuse.
>   Him have I lost, thou hast both him and me,
>   He pays the whole, and yet am I not free. [CXXXIV]

The image at work in both of these sonnets is a prison. The sonnets each contain several words that were in common usage in Shakespeare's time, but that will not make any sense unless you do a bit of homework. "Ward," "bail," "guard," "rigor," "gaol," and "pent," along with "prison" and "torture" in the first sonnet, and "confess," "mortgage," "forfeit," "surety," "bond," "statute," "usurer," "use," "debtor," as well as "sue," "pay," and "free" in the second have to do with being in prison. The first prison seems to be connected with treason and the torture that would drive someone to betray friends to the interrogator. The second prison is clearly for debtors.

To enact the love triangles, we need the poet/lover, the patron/lover, and the rival. And let us imagine that these poems were written to a woman who was having an affair with both Shakespeare and Southampton, his beloved patron. Let's pursue the prison metaphors to imagine a type of "staging" that illuminates the language and the relationships.

First, the poet is groaning and cursing the torturer, who has caused such great pain to the poet and his dear friend. Both men are not only in great pain, but the friend is actually a slave to the subjugation. Perhaps you can imagine the nature of the torment, betrayal, and horror as the friend bows in submission.

The next image echoes the blinding of political prisoners, but here the eyes that have been taken belong to the woman, and a comparison is suggested between removing her eyes, by looking away, and removing his through blinding. She has withdrawn her fond regard and it feels like he's had his eyes ripped out. But the friend is the poet's "next self," so whatever happens to the friend hurts the poet, and the friend has been engrossed harder. What does that mean? Does it help to know that "eye" was a euphemism for the testicle? That genital mutilation was used in torture chambers? Is it an effective metaphor for lovesickness? I think so.

The poet has named the torment, and suggests that the triangle means that each of them will experience three types of loss, once of the self, and once of each of the others. This is the pain that must be endured (as one crosses a bed of hot coals) because they are at cross purposes in their terrible triangle.

Now the poet suggests an alternative to torture: prison. If the woman locks up the poet in her prison, the poet will have to free the friend's heart, which the poet now cherishes. Is he offering to switch places, or acknowledging that he, too, is capable of imprisoning, and possibly even torturing, others? As if in acknowledgment of that terrible truth, the poet now addresses both of his lovers, indirectly, by suggesting that whoever might imprison him in a castle keep (like the Tower of London), he would offer to stand guard of that person's vulnerable core. But guards serve two purposes, to keep horror out, and keep prisoners in. With a guard at the jail door, no more torture (rigor) could be used, but the heart of the beloved would never be free.

The next sonnet starts with the sort of confession that would be the result of a session of torture, but immediately we shift to another type of prison, in which debtors are imprisoned and the crime is civil, not capital treason. Remember, please, that "will" means what it does today, and also sexual desire. The poet has taken out a mortgage from the woman's sexuality, receiving, we can assume, great pleasure as payment. But he's willing to forfeit on the debt, in other words lose whatever it was that he mortgaged (his property? his selfhood?) in order to bail out his friend, who is also now the possession of the woman. But he doesn't want to be free. It's as if the poet arrived at debtor's prison, having given up so much of himself to come up with the necessary cash to bail out his friend, only to find that the friend would rather stay in prison, or the woman won't set him free because she wants more money. How did the friend get there in the first place? He learned from the poet to stand surety for the poet's debt and then was bound just as tightly in the legal bond of the poet's original mortgage. Put this another way, he fell in love with a woman the poet was crazy about because he had first-hand knowledge of the poet's obsession, and now he's equally obsessed. A statute is the full amount mentioned in a bond. Most usurers, people who take a mortgage in exchange of the loan of ready cash, are willing to accept less than the full amount rather than send a debtor to prison and risk getting nothing at all. But the woman stands to collect the full amount because it is her beauty, which has not been diminished one jot, and which she is willing to put out on the open market for usage (like lending money to make money), and that is how the poet came to lose his best friend, who only got involved with the woman to free the poet from his obsession. So he loses his friend, the woman possesses both of the men, the friend has paid the complete and terrible price and yet the poet is still not free of the obsession.

Quite a terrible portrait of the female apex of the love triangle! Let us hope that Shakespeare did not hold this misogyny too closely to his heart. It's interesting how he paints the woman in such horrible terms—torturer, usurer—but exonerates his friend of the terrible betrayal of having an affair with the woman. Oh well, it makes for good poetry.

A word of advice in selecting sonnets. Pick a sonnet that you can understand the first time you read it aloud. Some of the sonnets are linguistic puzzles, designed to be read over and over, each time coming closer to understanding the complex meaning contained in the pattern of the words. In Shakespeare's dramatic verse you will also find such tangled webs that require careful deconstruction before they can be communicated, but these were intended to be spoken and understood on first hearing. The sonnets are not and some of them defy even the most skilled actor. Let's look at an example.

> When most I wink then do mine eyes best see,
> For all the day they view things unrespected,
> But when I sleep, in dreams they look on thee,
> And darkly bright, are bright in dark directed.
> Then thou whose shadow shadows doth make bright,
> How would thy shadows form, form happy show,
> To the clear day with thy much clearer light,
> When to un-seeing eyes thy shade shines so?
> How would (I say) mine eyes be blessed made,
> By looking on thee in the living day?
> When in dead night thy fair imperfect shade,
> Through heavy sleep on sightless eyes doth stay?
>   All days are nights to see till I see thee,
>   And nights bright days when dreams do show thee me. [XLIII]

After two or three readings the sense begins to come clear, but for the purposes of exploration this sonnet is not a good first choice.

For experienced students, however, it demonstrates how the iambic pentameter of the verse supports the complexity of the thoughts. Because the convoluted sentences reflect the complex feelings of the poet, these difficult sonnets, once understood, challenge an actor emotionally as well as intellectually, but they are very difficult to convey on a single hearing. If working toward a presentation, it would be best if everyone in the class read the sonnet silently as the speaker delivers the words aloud, explaining meaning by that delivery, while giving the class a chance to see the words on the page at the same time. Have a look at the fourth line.

> And darkly bright, are bright in dark directed.

If you have the sonnet in front of you, and time to "fill in the blanks," then the meaning of the line comes clear: eyes that gleam bright in the dark are directed toward that thing that brightens up the dark night, the dream of the beloved. Shakespeare seldom creates this sort of a dense ellipsis in this dramatic dialogue, though he often creates phrases like the following line:

> Then thou whose shadow shadows doth make bright,

By reordering the sentence the meaning is clear, but we have lost the effect of "shadow shadows" which seems like nonsense but makes perfect sense because we easily understand it to mean "even your shadow is capable of turning the shadows in my darkened bedroom bright."

In the next line, Shakespeare uses the same effect, and we can understand it because of the different ways we use the word:

How would thy shadows form, form happy show,

The word "form" can mean shape when it is used as a noun, but as a verb it means to create. So Shakespeare can repeat his trick of repetition, this time without inverting the natural word order. The patron/lover's form (shape) would form (create) a happy show.

And then something very strange happens, for the words shift their meaning as we move to the next line:

How would thy shadows form, form happy show,
To the clear day with thy much clearer light,

Something needs to be shown to the clear day. Show, like form, can be both a noun and a verb, but instead of repeating the word it is placed at the end of one line and serves as a double-hinged double meaning: the shadow's shape creates a pleasant entertainment, which is visible to the clear light of day thanks to that part of the lover/patron which shines a light to create the shadow. These slippings and slidings of meaning are all possible with the words in front of us, and it is a trick Shakespeare uses often in the sonnets but rarely in the theatre, where the spoken words come only once to the listener, and fall into a single shape in the mouth of the speaker.

For our purposes, sonnets are ideal for acquiring an inner ear tuned to the Iambic Code. Scan them. Observe the tricks of the trade. If you are adventureous, try writing your own sonnet: fourteen lines of precise iambic pentameter which follow the specific rhyme scheme: ABAB CDCD EFEF GG. Don't worry if your rhymes are predictable and your word choice mundane. Strive to keep as true to iambic pentameter as you can. You don't have to show them to anyone, just see if you can work out the puzzle. If you do this, then read aloud some of Shakespeare's, then come back to your own efforts, then return to Shakespeare's. You will be solidifying your sensitivity to the Iambic Code, and preparing to use that sensitivity when speaking Shakespeare's dramatic verse.

After all of these explorations of the Iambic Code using Shakespeare's sonnets, it is time to return to his plays, and what better transition than the shared sonnet spoken by his most famous young lovers:

Romeo: If I profane with my unworthiest hand,
        This holy shrine, the gentle sin is this,

My lips two blushing Pilgrims did ready stand,
To smooth that rough touch, with a tender kiss.

Juliet: Good Pilgrim,
You do wrong your hand too much.
Which mannerly devotion shows in this,
For Saints have hands, that Pilgrims hands do touch,
And palm to palm, is holy Palmers kiss.

Romeo: Have not Saints lips, and holy Palmers too?

Juliet: Ay Pilgrim, lips that they must use in prayer.

Romeo: O then dear Saint, let lips do what hands do,
They pray (grant thou) lest faith turn to despair.

Juliet: Saints do not move,
Though grant for prayers sake.

Romeo: Then move not while my prayers effect I take:
Thus from my lips, by thine my sin is purged.

Juliet: Then have my lips the sin that they have took.

Romeo: Sin from thy lips? O trespass sweetly urged:
Give me my sin again.

Juliet: You kiss by th' book. [1.5.93]

Notice the perfect simplicity created by the high correspondence of word to iambic heartbeat:

This HOLy SHRINE the GENtle SIN is THIS
My LIPS two BLUSHing PILgrims READy STAND
Good PILgrim You do WRONG your HAND too MUCH
For SAINTS have HANDS that PILgrims HANDS do TOUCH
And PALM to PALM is HOLy PALmers KISS

And now, what about the delicacy of those moments when there is a tension between the iambic heartbeat and the naturally spoken emphasis of the line? Let's start with the first line. Should Romeo say, "IF i proFANE" or "if I proFANE?" I'd advise the first option, because it gives such a wonderfully energetic beginning to the sonnet, a trick Shakespeare often uses as you will see if you look at the following first lines from an index of sonnets:

Music to hear, why hear'st thou music sadly? [VIII]

Weary with toil, I haste me to my bed, [XXVII]

Being your slave what should I do but tend, [LVII]

Cupid laid by his brand and fell asleep, [CLIII]

The accent must fall on the first syllable of the first word of these sonnets, but in other sonnets the choice is between two single-syllable words. Sometimes either word could be the more important, but in the following first lines, it's much more likely that the first word is the one to be emphasized:

Look in thy glass and tell the face thou viewest, [III]

Lo in the Orient when the gracious light, [VII]

Lord of my love, to whom in vassalage [XXVI]

How can I then return in happy plight [XXVIII]

When in disgrace with fortune and mens eyes, [XXIX]

Like as the waves make towards the pebbled shore, [LX]

Thus is his cheek the map of days out-worn, [LXVIII]

Love is too young to know what conscience is, [CLI]

I trust that these examples give you permission to consider that Romeo emphasizes his first word rather than his second. When Juliet says, "Saints do not move" the first word is far more interesting than the second, as when Romeo says, "Sin from thy lips?" and "Give me my sin again."

Other choices are more difficult. "Have not saints lips" would be equally effective as "HAVE not saints lips" as "have NOT saints LIPS," and it would depend on the flow of feeling and the intuition of the actor to discover which works best on any given running of the scene. Several other lines seem to have two equally interesting first words: "Then move not," "Thus from my lips," and "Then have my lips" could be used to create a marvellous urgency if all three of the first words are emphasized. But the second word could also be emphasized to make sense of the lines. What is required for an actor to make his choice is the delivery of the line with, and then without, the "attack!" energy and rhythm. Whichever delivery best suits whatever the actor is exploring, is the "correct" meter for that line.

There are a few lines in this sonnet in which the eye catches two words side by side that seem of equal significance. In the fourth line we find "rough touch" and the next line has "Good pilgrim." As we have found already, there is nothing wrong with giving both words an added intensity. But in this sonnet we find that the iambic rhythm is correct for the meaning. In the first example, "rough" sits in the downbeat position of the iambic heartbeat. Clearly, the adjective modifying "touch" is important. It's a rough, unworthy touch, contrasted by the tender kiss to come. Juliet's "Good pilgrim" offers the actress a lovely first word, but the second word demands an emphasis that solidifies the line around the heartbeat, so that it becomes "good PILgrim" even if "good" is filled with feeling. The same happens a few lines later, when she says, "Ay, pilgrim." Of course the "yes" conveyed by "Ay" is important, but the downbeat gets connected to the accented syllable of the next word. The secret? Don't rush this moment. Say "Ay." Mean it, then move on with the rest of the line, accenting the first syllable of pilgrim as you must.

Another interesting puzzle is found in the twelfth line of the sonnet. If we followed the heart beat we'd have:

the PRAY grant THOU lest FAITH turn TO desPAIR

This makes perfect sense, and makes for a cooly intellectual presentation of a theological argument. But it seems a bit of a waste of a downbeat to emphasize "to" instead of the more interesting "turn." If we trusted that intuition, we'd have:

they PRAY grant THOU lest FAITH TURN to desPAIR

We have seen many examples of Shakespeare playing with the first foot of the pentameter, but here it seems as if he might be playing with the fourth foot, creating a tiny glitch or burst of energy midway through the line. We discover this with great frequency in his dramatic poetry, and so I recommend it here. Notice how it creates a tiny break between "faith" and "turn" as the flow of the iambic rhythm is broken. That is the secret of its usefulness. We call this midline break the caesura, and Shakespeare and his contemporaries made great use of a range of variations at the midline break in order to create variety in long passages of verse.

We've seen examples of the diphthongs that allow a word to be one or two syllables in the verse. In this sonnet we have the hugely significant word "prayer," used three times. First, it is set up to rhyme with "despair" so we can give it a full two-syllable value. That is the value it has when next it appears, or else the iambs of the line will fall apart.

SAINTS do not MOVE though GRANT for PRAYer's SAKE

However, in the next line, the same word is boxed into a single syllable

Then MOVE not WHILE my PRAYER'S efFECT i TAKE

A word like prayer is never quite a full two syllables, and cannot really be reduced to a crisp clean single syllable. Clearly, the word is too big *and* too small for the emotions conveyed in the heartbeat.

Similarly, words like "unworthiest" and "mannerly" jar against the rhythm of the heartbeat, suggesting a tension between the intellect and the emotions. Here are two well-educated young adults having a theological debate with their minds while their hearts and souls cope with the implications of the immediacy of their love. In Romeo's first line, the "iest" sound must be compressed into something like "yest" to fit, but that extra little half-syllable remains, like a quiver in the muscle of the heart. In Juliet's second line, "MAN-ner-ly" is spoken while the heart pounds out, "da DUM da DUM." Of course she doesn't say, "MANnerLY" but nor can she rush the word. The extra downbeat must sit in there somewhere, in some sort of heightened significance of a word. For that reason, flag "unworthiest" and "mannerly" as being significant, perhaps in a way that even the characters don't understand just yet, and say *and hear* them open to the richness of their sound and meaning.

One last anomaly in the sonnet. What do we do with a word like "O," given the immense potential of any sort of open vowel to express sustained deep feeling? Let's have a look at the open "O" in this line:

O then dear Saint, let lips do what hands do,

What is so amazing about this line is that every single word could be emphasized. Try it. Say it slowly and don't give any word more or less emphasis than the next. What do we discover?

O THEN DEAR SAINT LET LIPS DO WHAT HANDS DO

"O" can be filled with the breathing out of deep feeling. "Then" can be another in the chain of time words that heighten the sensation of immediacy in the experience of the first kiss:

THEN move not WHILE my prayer's effect I take:
THUS from my lips, by thine my sin is purged.
THEN have my lips the sin that they have took.

"Dear" is as wonderful and rich a word as "saint," just as "let" can be filled with such a strong sense of longing that it becomes as important as "lips" and "hands." And yet "hands" *cannot* be in the stressed position of the iambic line, because that is reserved for "do." The power of the second "do" is prefigured in the first, leaving only the word "what" as relatively uninteresting!

Here is my "solution" to the way the words intersect with the heartbeat:

O then dear SAINT let LIPS DO what hands DO

The actor playing Romeo needs to let his "solution" emerge in the exploration of the line during rehearsals and performances. If his explorations are informed by a sensitivity to the Iambic Code, he will have little difficulty in finding a delivery that serves the emotional and poetic requirements of the lines he has been given to speak.

Developing the Inner Ear

I pray you mar no more of my verses with reading them ill-favouredly.
                                        Orlando [*AYLI* 3.2.261]

Now it is time to fine-tune your inner ear to the very specific use of the Iambic
Code that Shakespeare developed for use in his plays. During the ten years
of Shakespeare's apprenticeship in the theatre, when we assume he was in
London (he'd disappeared from public record in Stratford and had not yet
presented his first accredited play and thus reentered our line of vision), the
craft of the playwright evolved radically. It was actually Christopher Marlowe,
who died tragically young in a barroom brawl (if he had lived, he might well
have taken old Bill's place as the greatest English language playwright), who
took the stilted, predictably rhymed iambic pentameter and transformed it into
the flexible, quintessentially theatrical blank verse we find in Shakespeare. On
the surface, all Marlowe did was jettison the restriction of rhyming couplets,
where lines are linked in pairs by the fifth foot creating a rhyme. But in fact,
the rhymed couplet convention of the early Elizabethans contained other restrictions. Ideas were parcelled neatly into paired lines, so that all thoughts
were the same length and started at the beginning of a line and ended, neatly,
ten feet later. Human experience is simply not so tidy. Marlowe began the
experimentation with expressing thoughts that were longer or shorter than the
ten-foot allotment, and Shakespeare pushed this irregularity still further.

Irregularity is the single most important inheritance from Marlowe. Once
the rhyme was eliminated, except when it might best serve the dramatic event,
and the tidiness of two-line thoughts rejected, other irregularities were suddenly
possible and, in fact, invited. An examination of Shakespeare's use of blank

verse, as scholars call unrhymed iambic pentameter, is, in fact, the charting of his increasing use of irregularities. It is almost as if he pushed against the convention of iambic pentameter, injecting more and more breaks in rhythm and stress, until the iambic was barely preserved.

And the gentle hand of Bill, the director of actors, is found in his subtle and overt manipulation of the Iambic Code. This is the great pay-off for all your hard work in mastering regular iambic pentameter. Please remember that the actors and the audience were trained (through constant exposure) to hear and expect iambics in five-foot units. The heartbeat that is the iambic rhythm was deeply ingrained into their inner ear. Any irregularity ran like an emotional electrical shock through the actor and the audience: a small jolt or a large attack.

Every application of scansion to the actor's experience of a Shakespearean role must be specific rather than general, because the variations in irregularities are tied to sound patterns and meanings as well as to the structural progression of the speech and the play. Therefore we now look at quite a few examples, and then you must begin to apply these ideas to any and every bit of Shakespeare you encounter.

SUBTLETIES OF THE CODE

> Why thy verse swells with stuff so fine and smooth,
> That thou art even Natural in thine Art.
>
> Timon [*Timon* 5.1.84]

The two most common variations on regular iambic pentameter are the most obvious of the encoding that Shakespeare's verse structures allowed. There were other, less common, but not rare, variations that assisted Shakespeare in the shaping of theatrical events. Some of these have already been spotted in the sonnets, and become central to our experience of his dramatic poetry.

Midline Inversions and Feminine Endings

The inverted first foot and the end-of-line feminine ending were techniques that could be moved into the middle of the line, particularly in connection with the beginning and ending of a thought midline. Here is the rhythm of such an inversion: da DUM da DUM//DUM da da DUM da DUM. Here is the rhythm of such an addition: da DUM da DUM da//da DUM da DUM da DUM.

These two strategies do not work exactly the same way midline, however, as they do at the beginning or end of a line. The driving force of the emotional wave pushes the energy on to the end of the line, so the midline shift in rhythm is less abrupt than when the first foot is inverted. Similarly, the midline feminine ending has a quality of opening up, but it is, of necessity, quickly over-taken by the forward-moving energy of the line. On the other hand, when these rhythmic variations are united with striking changes in thought (marked by, perhaps, a period in a modern edition) we can see immediately how the emotional rhythm supports the intellectual shift.

This midline shift is known as the caesura, and is a common feature of all verse. One of the exciting attributes of a five-foot line, as compared to a four- or six-foot line, is that the location of the break can vary from line to line, sometimes occurring after the end of the second foot, sometimes after the third, sometimes halfway through the second. This gives much more variety to the delivery of lines. If you'd like a comparison, have a look at a passage from classical French theatre, which customarily used the hexameter, or six-foot, line, and which established a highly ritualized and almost hypnotic rhythm by the regularization of the caesura, or midline shift. This is the title character of Racine's *Phèdre*, sharing her passionate love of her stepson with her confidante:

> Je t'ai tout avoué; je ne m'en repens pas,
> Pourvu que de ma mort respectant les approches,
> Tu ne m'affliges plus par d'injustes reproches,
> Et que tes vains secours cessent de rappeler
> Un reste de chaleur tout prêt à s'exhaler. [I, iii, last lines of the scene]

Compare that more regular caesura with the flexibility afforded Shakespeare by the five-foot line:

> The Crow doth sing as sweetly as the Lark
> When neither is attended: and I think
> The Nightingale if she should sing by day
> When every Goose is cackling, would be thought
> No better a Musician than the Wren? [*Merchant* 5.1.102]

The first line does not have a strong caesura, though there might be the slightest of shifts after "sing," which is the end of the second foot. The second line has a clear caesura, midway through the third foot, a placement that is echoed in the fourth line. The third line also has a grammatical shift midline, this time at the end of the second foot.

The conventions of the Iambic Code allowed the playwright to manipulate the starting and completing of thought patterns with regard to the beginnings and endings of lines of poetry, with maximum flexibility. Although many sentences begin at the beginning of lines and end as a line ends, this is by no means the standard format. Sometimes, a far more exciting tension between thought and feeling is created by the repeated use of midline shifts to start and conclude phrases. It is almost as if the five-foot unit, representing the emotional ebb and flow of rising energy, sets up a counterpoint with the grammatical structures that contain the intellectual thought. Here is an excerpt from the debate between Isabella and Angelo in *Measure for Measure*. Isabella's speech demonstrates the counterpoint in action, as her thoughts race forward from midline to midline, while the lines of poetry build to the key words "alas," "once," "took," "be," "should," "that," and "lips." Angelo's response, in contrast, demonstrates what happens when thought and line correspond. His is the cooler voice, heart and mind working together in parallel patterns.

Isabella: Alas, alas:
    Why all the souls that were, were forfeit once,
    And he that might the vantage best have took,
    Found out the remedy: how would you be,
    If he, which is the top of Judgment, should
    But judge you, as you are? Oh, think on that,
    And mercy then will breathe within your lips
    Like man new made.

Angelo: Be you content, (fair Maid)
    It is the Law, not I, condemn your brother,
    Were he my kinsman, brother, or my son,
    It should be thus with him: he must die tomorrow. [2.2.72]

You will notice, in this dialog, that I adopted the format used by the majority of modern editors, in suggesting that Isabella and Angelo actually share a five-foot line as she ends her speech and he begins his. In fact, Angelo's line immediately before Isabella's "Alas, alas" creates the same effect:

Angelo: Your Brother is a forfeit of the Law,
    And you but waste your words.

Isabella: Alas, alas.

These shared lines create an immensely powerful stage energy, as the two characters work to a single pulse, so closely connected that a single heartbeat serves them both. Here are the Macbeths, immediately after the murder of Duncan:

Macbeth: I have done the deed: Didst thou not hear a noise?

Lady Macbeth: I heard the Owl scream, and the Crickets cry.
    Did not you speak?

Macbeth: When?

Lady Macbeth: Now.

Macbeth: As I descended?

Lady Macbeth: Ay.

Macbeth: Hark, who lies i' th' second Chamber?

Lady Macbeth: Donalbain.

Macbeth: This is a sorry sight.

Lady Macbeth: A foolish thought, to say a sorry sight. [2.2.14]

The first publications did not use this format, but printed all speeches starting immediately after the character name. Different editors have designated the lines in the Macbeths' exchange slightly differently, but what is clear from the breaking up of the verse lines between two speakers, regardless of exactly how it works out, is that they are very much in tune with each other at this moment.

Short and Long Lines

Sometimes, in contrast to giving a line an extra syllable, the line has only nine syllables. Where is the missing beat? Sometimes it is in the middle of the line, and sometimes at the beginning. Here are two examples from *Richard II*. In the first, the Marshal signals for the start of the trial by combat and then, unexpectedly, brings it to an abrupt stop. The second is Northumberland's response to Richard's observation that he has not been addressed as King.

Sound Trumpets, and set forward Combatants:
Stay, the King hath thrown his Warder down. [1.3.117]

Your Grace mistakes: only to be brief,
Left I his Title out. [3.3.10]

It is quite easy to clarify the absence of sound by marking the place it should occupy with an audible intake or expulsion of breath, so that the Marshal's second line takes the shape of "[gasp] Stay, the King hath thrown his warder down" and Northumberland's first: "Your Grace mistakes: [ha] only to be brief." We call these sorts of variations, of which there are sufficient number for this to be considered a customary aspect of the Iambic Code, the headless line or the broken-back line.

When a headless line variation is combined with a feminine ending, we have what seems to be a line that reverses the iambic rhythm of light/strong/light to create what the Greeks would call a trochaic line: strong/light/strong/light. Saying such a line aloud instantly reveals that the line falls naturally. Consider, for example, Lear's last speech:

And my poor Fool is hanged: no, no, no life?
Why should a Dog, a Horse, a Rat have life,
And thou no breath at all? Thou'lt come no more,
Never, never, never, never, never.
Pray you undo this Button. Thank you Sir.
Do you see this? Look on her? Look on her lips,
Look there, look there. [5.3.306]

The second, fifth, and sixth lines each begin with an inverted first foot; the sixth also has an extra syllable that rocks the heartbeat midline, fracturing it into three sharp commands. And in the middle, we have the word "never" five times.

Clearly, Lear's poor old heart is breaking, and the tortured rhythms reflect his emotional state. The danger of the fourth line, however, is that the falling meter cuts across the iambic rhythm to the point where the rising line will be lost. However, if we add a sigh to the beginning of the line, and fill that feminine ending with an opening out of feeling, we can retain the careful balance between the foundation and the variation. The word "never," said five times, need not fall away into mumbled passivity, but can convey the full power of despair, and ensure that the voicing of that emotion is an active, dramatic event.

We have already discovered the potency of the eleventh syllable, at the end of a line or at the end of a phrase midline. Shakespeare also played with a variation which we might call the running start, where the first foot of the line has an extra syllable, creating an anapest, or "da da DUM," rhythm. Here is an example of this effect. Read this speech aloud and watch for the sensation of extra syllables as you reach the end of the third line and launch into the fourth:

> You were to blame, I must be plain with you,
> To part so slightly with your wives first gift,
> A thing stuck on with oaths upon your finger,
> And so riveted with faith unto your flesh. [*Merchant* 5.1.166]

Imagine the little *frisson* of excitement that ripples through Portia as she says these lines. It is important to let such fibrillations work upon your heart even as they ripple across the heartbeat of the speech.

Some lines of poetry expand to contain twelve syllables. We call these Alexandrines, which is the name given to the six-foot, or hexameter, line used in French classical theatre. Here is Shakespeare's manipulation of such a variation, which sticks out in the midst of a set of pentameters, drawing attention to itself as an extra-long line. Here is Isabella, again debating with Angelo, and finding herself in a situation where what she needs to express overflows the limitations of the five-foot line:

> Oh pardon me my Lord, it oft falls out
> To have, what we would have,
> We speak not what we mean:
> I something do excuse the thing I hate,
> For his advantage that I dearly love. [*M for M* 2.4.117]

The second and third lines, separated in the folio, are printed as one line in most modern editions. There is something about these words that rings of a proverb or aphorism. The two halves work so perfectly to express the dichotomy she is expressing, that it reminds us of such lines as those associated with the caskets in *Merchant of Venice*. This is what is written on the inscriptions: "Who chooseth me, shall gain what many men desire," "Who chooseth me, shall get as much as he deserves," and "Who chooseth me, must give and hazard all he hath" [2.7.5]. Shylock also has an Alexandrine when he confronts Antonio with the latter's anti-Semitism, and mockingly paints of picture of abject servility: "Shall I bend low, and in a bond mans key / With bated breath, and whisp'ring humbleness, / Say this: Fair sire, you spat on me on Wednesday last" [*Merchant* 1.3.123]. Although modern editors like to separate "Say this" from that which follows, in the folio this appears all on one line.

In contrast, Shakespeare is also fond of suddenly cutting a line short, not so that another person can pick up the energy and complete the five-foot pattern, but so that silence sits for a moment and the heart just beats until language kicks in again. Here is Hamlet responding to what he has learned from his father's ghost:

> O most pernicious woman.
> O Villain, Villain, smiling, damned Villain! [1.5.105]

When he speaks of Claudius, Hamlet can fill out the line of poetry, but when he speaks of his mother in the line before, he can only give voice for three and a half. In the space created by a foot-and-a-half silence, his heart gives forth a silent scream of pain and horror.

More Subtle Variations

Now that you have begun to internalize the simple, strong heartbeat of the Iambic Code within your inner ear, it is time to start heightening your awareness of the subtle variations of rhythm with which Shakespeare and his contemporaries loved to play using the sounds of words as well as their relative stress. This type of scansion is comparable to the acquiring of more sophisticated musical skills. Up until now you have done the poetic equivalent of reading music in strict 4/4 time, using quarter, half, and whole notes. It is now time to introduce dotted eighth and sixteenth notes, held notes, triplets, and all the tricks that composers use even when working in good old 4/4 time.

Double Stressed and Under-Stressed

One of the most common complaints of actors who first attempt to master scansion is that the mechanical delivery of the iambic weightings of light/strong/light/strong forces them to violate the emotional meaning of a line. Even after they have learned that the tensions between what they would like to emphasize and the heartbeat are intentional, they continue to find lines that every theatrical bone in their body demands they say in apparent violation of the heartbeat.

A flexibility that we must allow ourselves, even in creating these "correctly" shaped iambic pentameter lines, is to vary the levels of intensity in our contrasting stressed and unstressed syllables. Over the course of a line, some words are going to be more interesting or significant than others. The Greeks had a term for a two-beat unit where neither beat receives particular emphasis, the "pyrric." In fact, when we speak Shakespeare's dramatic poetry aloud, there is scarcely a line that does not demonstrate his remarkable capacity for subtle shadings of intensity, an ebbing and flowing of energy shaped by rhythm and sound or emotion coupled with the intellectual content of the speech. It is this subtle shaping that makes so many of the best-loved speeches so compelling and memorable. Here is Othello's obituary, spoken by himself as he acknowledges his terrible crime in murdering his wife:

> Speak of me, as I am. Nothing extenuate,
> Nor set down aught in malice.
> Then must you speak,
> Of one that loved not wisely, but too well:
> Of one, not easily Jealous, but being wrought,
> Perplexed in the extreme: Of one, whose hand
> (Like the base Indian) threw a Pearl away
> Richer than all his Tribe. [5.2.342]

What is remarkable about this speech is that Shakespeare makes every word count, even as some of them, such as "extenuate" and "perplexed," are heavy, powerful, even strange words, while others, like "pearl" and "hand," have a simple honesty and clarity. Each line has a hierarchy of weight, distributed through the ten or eleven syllables, so that the five stronger are not all equally strong. The gentlest of the five stressed syllables is just slightly stronger than the unstressed syllables on either side. Generally speaking, in a five-foot line, there are at most four strongly stressed syllables.

Shakespeare was also interested in putting together phrases that build on quite a different approach to the unstressed syllables in a line. Rather than serving as functional contrasts to the stressed syllables, such words take on a special power all their own. The Greeks also had a word for a two-beat unit, both parts of which were stressed, "spondee," and Shakespeare made great use of the special power of such rhythms. Here is Orsino musing on the power of music:

> O, it came o'er my ear, like the sweet sound
> That breathes upon a bank of Violets;
> Stealing, and giving Odour. [*12th Night* 1.1.5]

It is clear, if one says the first of these lines aloud, that "sweet" and "sound" are almost equal in importance. Rather than viewing the iambic rhythm as a law that forbids "sweet" to be richly sounded, the actor must recognize still another variation in the Iambic Code.

Remember that the unstressed position in the line does not necessarily indicate lack of importance. Whenever two interesting words occupy the light/ strong positions of the iamb, the actor needs to imagine the heart at work. With the strong word, the heart pumps the blood outward, to the far reaches of the imagination. Such is the role of "sound" in Orsino's line. However, the other word corresponds to the moment when the heart *fills* with blood or feeling, and such is the role of "sweet."

Here is another example that contains a highly charged example of a blood-filling and a blood-pumping pair of words. This is Ophelia, mourning the apparent madness of her beloved Hamlet:

> O what a Noble mind is here o'er-thrown?
> The Courtiers, Soldiers, Scholars: Eye, tongue, sword,
> Th'expectancy and Rose of the fair State,
> The glass of Fashion, and the mould of Form,
> Th'observed of all Observers, quite, quite down. [3.1.150]

Clearly, each of "eye," "tongue," and "sword" is equally significant. The rising line keeps the rising emotion on track, so that the ladder created by the list of three is apparent; this effect would be diminished if "tongue" dropped out of the three-step ascension. However, if we consider that the heart fills with feeling as she thinks of his capacity to speak, we might remember that she earlier confessed to her father, "He hath importuned me with love, / In honourable fashion. . . . And hath given countenance to his speech, / My Lord, with all the holy vows of Heaven" [1.3.111]. This might lead us to consider the difference in how Ophelia feels about, and therefore says, each of these important words.

There is a very special sort of line that Shakespeare creates with some regularity, one composed entirely of single-syllable words. Sometimes the words fall into an obvious pattern of important and unimportant words to match the heartbeat, such as these two lines from Hamlet's most famous soliloquy: "For in that sleep of death, what dreams may come," and "For who would bear the Whips and Scorns of time" [3.1.65,69]. Other times, the single syllables, any one of which might receive emphasis, lend themselves to one of the common variations of the code, as in Ophelia's last line of the "eye, tongue, sword" speech, "T'have seen what I have seen: see what I see."

Sometimes these single-syllable lines are called Anglo-Saxon lines, because of a notable pattern in the English of Shakespeare's era: new words, created from Latin or Greek roots or adopted from French, tended to be polysyllabic, while the words that could trace their roots back to the middle and old English of the Angles and Saxons tended to be single-syllable words. This is not an absolute rule, but representative rather of the difference between simple, striking words of one syllable and complex and intellectual words of many syllables.

Consider, for example, Desdemona's plea to the Senate. Read this aloud and feel the difference in texture between the long, complex, sophisticated words of many syllables, and the simple, clear, direct words of one syllable. As you make these sounds, explore the possibility that the single-syllable words represent a more primitive, grounded connection between language and experience, while the bigger words represent an educated, intellectual, recently acquired capacity to make sense of the world.

> That I did love the Moor, to live with him,
> My down-right violence, and storm of Fortunes,
> May trumpet to the world. My heart's subdued
> Even to the very quality of my Lord;
> I saw Othello's visage in his mind,
> And to his Honours and his valiant parts,
> Did I my soul and Fortunes consecrate.
> So that (dear Lords) if I be left behind
> A Moth of Peace and he go to the War,
> The Rites for why I love him, are bereft me:
> And I a heavy interim shall support
> By his dear absence. Let me go with him. [1.3.248]

Yes, this young woman can use words like "consecrate" and "visage" but she can also put together a sentence like "Let me go with him" as the purest, best expression of her thoughts and feelings. Look also at the first and ninth lines, entirely single syllables, and the eighth and tenth, almost entirely single syllables. What a contrast these are to the second and third lines, and the sixth and seventh, with the more complex concepts used to express essentially the same emotions.

Now that we have started to consider words of three and more syllables, we need to consider how Shakespeare and his contemporaries molded these words into the heartbeat of the Iambic Code.

Tri-Syllabic Dislocations

Many three-syllable words would be called "amphibracs" by the Greeks, meaning that they contained the rhythm "de DUM de," which easily fits into an iambic line with the addition of stressed words on either side, so that "potato" becomes "sweet potato pie." It is the anapest (de de DUM) and dactyl (DUM de de) rhythms that cause disruptions to the contrasting light and strong of the heartbeat. Although Shakespeare could do a great deal with single- and two-syllable words, and poly-syllabic words that lend themselves to the unstressed/stressed pattern, it is difficult to find a speech of any length that does not have a three-syllable word that strikingly does not lend itself to iambic pentameter.

Remembering that the vast vocabulary available to Shakespeare would enable him to avoid such awkward words, we must consider just what might be gained by their inclusion in such speeches as this by Isabella:

> Then Isabel live chaste, and brother die;
> More than our Brother, is our Chastity. [*Measure* 2.4.183]

Not only is the word "chastity" pronounced to create the rhythm "DUM de de" instead of the "DUM de DUM" required by the heartbeat, it is at the end of the line, so the full force of the rising energy builds toward the final syllable of the word, a syllable that cannot be stressed without mispronouncing the word. Why on earth did he not simply have her say, "More than our brother is our very soul," an equally powerful thought and one that would make use of the rising line more effectively?

What is actually at work when the mouth says "chastity" while the heart pumps, fills, and then pumps again? It is as if the heart beats twice as the mouth whips out the word. I consider these moments to be ones in which the mind and the heart are at odds. The word is easy to say, hard to experience.

The placement of an unaccented syllable in the position of the downbeat of the iambic rhythm, the "-ty" of "chastity" against the second "DUM" of "DUM de DUM," and further, a syllable that can be said so quickly together with the previous syllable, opens up a quick stab of silence. The word "chastity" hangs in the air, demanding the full weight of the double pulse of the heart as the mind and body come to terms with the concept that the mouth has voiced.

In order to give these words sufficient emotional content to justify the double heartbeat, an actor must invest into the content of the word the richest possible associations, both intellectual and emotional. What does "chastity" mean to Isabella, as a young unmarried woman, as a postulate in a strict religious order, as a woman pleading to save the life of her lecherous brother before a man who has demanded sexual favors from her, to win the pardon she so desires? What does it feel like to say that word, knowing all that you mean by it, and all that it has come to mean to the events unfolding around you? By dislocating the iambic rhythm to this extent, Shakespeare has drawn your actor's ear to a key word, and offered you an opportunity to let it work upon you, and upon the audience as you deliver it in just this disruptive way.

These lines, when spoken aloud, reveal actual gaps in the rhythm, comparable to rests in bars of music. To answer your question before you ask it, no, I do not suggest that the "-ty" be emphasized in the modern theatre. That would be ridiculous. Surely the very least you can do is give the word its full three syllables. Avoid at all costs the modern actors' tendency to throw away the third unstressed sound, to swallow it into the back of the throat or let it drop out of the mouth onto the floor at their feet. And if the word sits at the end of a rising line of verse, remember that it has the *weight* within the line of two stresses, even if you do not actually stress two syllables when you say it. Therefore you must give it the time it deserves within the steady rhythm of the heartbeat.

In contrast to those words that create a silence by the way their polysyllabic shapes slice across the iambic rhythm, Shakespeare also regularly overloads his lines, creating a sort of condensing that is not easily accomplished by the spoken voice. The result is the sensation that the structure of the line serves to squeeze in the extra syllable into a running, racing, pressured energy. Here is Angelo, putting the pressure on Isabella that drives her to the realization that she must place her chastity above her brother's life:

> My unsoiled name, th'austereness of my life,
> My vouch against you, and my place i'th'State,
> Will so your accusation over-weigh,
> That you shall stifle in your own report,
> And smell of calumny. I have begun,
> And now I give my sensual race, the rein,
> Fit thy consent to my sharp appetite,
> Lay by all nicety, and prolixious blushes
> That banish what they sue for: Redeem thy brother,
> By yielding up thy body to my will,
> Or else he must not only die the death,
> But thy unkindness shall his death draw out
> To ling'ring sufferance.[2.4.155]

As we have already discovered, Shakespeare could collapse words to remove unwanted syllables to match the way that they might be spoken. "The austereness" becomes "Th'austereness" to create a smooth "de DUM de" rhythm and also because that is how it would be said on stage. But what about "place i'th'state?" Can this really be reduced to three syllables and still be understood? Even if you said exactly what is printed in the folio, "place i'th State," you would have to separate the "th" from the "s" of "state" to be understood.

I like to call this subtlety of the Iambic Code the pressure-cooker words. Pressure cookers are not much used these days, but my mother swears by hers. The heavy, aluminium pot is put on the heating element. Inside is a tough side of beef and a little bit of water. The lid is twisted on to seal it and a pressure gauge is attached to the top. Before you know it, the meat is being cooked under pressure, though the pot looks quite ordinary from a distance. I am always curious, when I encounter a pressure-cooker word, just what has lit the fire under this word, and what is cooking away, perhaps about to explode, under the surface of intellectual control.

The extra part-syllables of the diphthong and the contraction upset the smooth flow of the iambic line, like rocks under the surface of a fast-moving river. Say this line, giving the word "sensual" its full diphthong:

And now I give my sensual race, the rein:

Or, try to let the next line roll off the tongue:

Lay by all nicety, and prolixious blushes

Clearly, there are large rocks under the surface here, and Angelo is very definitely giving himself over to the ripping, tearing, searing dislocation of her former persona of calm clarity and rational honor.

Modern actors must train themselves to spot the ripples created by these subtle manipulations of sound because the vast majority of them have been lost to us in our modern vocal laziness. We seldom give vowels their full weight, and if a complex sound can be reduced and still understood, we are not likely to enunciate it without feeling phony.

For example, take the word "accusation." We say the "-ion" suffixes as single syllables. The Elizabethans gave them the weight of two full syllables. It is possible to give them a subtle diphthong today and not sound pretentious, but only if you are very careful and practice on creating the exact sound. The diphthong is a softer, more lyrical sound than the firm, hard "shun" we are used to. But more importantly, as with the examples directly above, you must give these words the full weight that their multiple stress warrants.

Shakespeare and his fellow dramatic poets made freest possible use of contractions, some of which are in common usage today and others of which are not. The greatest danger is in the most familiar, particularly in the common "I'll." We say this so often that it has become a single syllable word. But it should be considered, at the very least, a diphthong. The "will" that is implied must be given a small space in which to resonate.

The contraction-as-diphthong is readily apparent in such contractions as "o'er" and "th'invisible" (lest the actor appear to be saying "or" and "thin visible"). It requires a little more conscious effort, however, to honor the extra half-syllable in "I'll" or "they're." However, unless the actor sounds out the real shape of the line, he will remain cut off from the guidance offered by fellow-actor and master-wordsmith Shakespeare.

❧ 6 ❧

The Flow of Thought and Feeling

The Lady shall say her mind freely; or the
blank Verse shall halt for't.

Hamlet [Hamlet 2.2.324]

We do not have a single edition of Shakespeare's plays that contains the punctuation he used. Every comma, period, colon, semicolon, question mark, and exclamation mark is suspect. Further, such markers, which stress grammar and the intellectual component of the verse, play into our tendency to sacrifice the mysteries of emotion to the solidity of ideas. Therefore, let us agree that the punctuation in any edition of Shakespeare is dangerous and something to be fought against.

Although there is also some doubt about the actual sequences of words, this uncertainty is limited to a few problematical passages. Therefore, if an actor wants to trust Bill's craft as a playwright, better to trust the clues in the subtle rhythms of the poetry than in the markings on the score by a non-actor editor. At least Bill acted himself, and wrote for actors, and seemed to have an ear for what actors need to capture authentic human experiences using the voice alone. If we remove all punctuation and leave ourselves just the Iambic Code, then scan for Bill's overt and subtle variations on the verse form, do we have the sort of clues we need for sense as well and emotional substance?

SIGHT READING SHAKESPEARE'S VERSE

In order to prepare, we must first adapt the text as it might be found in a published edition of the play. Because punctuation is such a powerful means of shaping speech, it is important that you never encounter the test passage in a punctuated version, at least not until after you've seen what might be there in the poetry itself. As an example of a modern editor's heavy hand, here is Isabella's soliloquy as punctuated in *The Riverside Shakespeare*:

> To whom should I complain? Did I tell this,
> Who would believe me? O perilous mouths,
> That bear in them one and the self-same tongue,
> Either of condemnation or approof;
> Bidding the law make curtsy to their will,
> Hooking both right and wrong to th' appetite,
> To follow as it draws! I'll to my brother.
> Though he hath fall'n by prompture of the blood,
> Yet hath he in him such a mind of honour.
> That, had he twenty heads to tender down
> On twenty bloody blocks, he'ld yield them up,
> Before his sister should her body stoop
> To such abhorred pollution.
> Then, Isabel, live chaste, and, brother, die;
> More than our brother is our chastity.
> I'll tell him yet of Angelo's request,
> And fit his mind to death, for his soul's rest. [*Measure* 2.4.171]

Now let us strip away the extra-textual markings, and see what is left.

The first removal is every punctuation marker at the end of a line of poetry. Since we are placing such emphasis on the verse line as an important emotional unit, if it also marks the end of a section of intellectual thought, the congruence is immediately apparent, and the exploratory delivery with the rising cadence, the emphasis on the last word, and the slight pause before the exploration begins on the next line, supports all of the punctuation that we are removing.

Next, look at the commas that have been inserted into lines. They are very useful for a reader figuring out meaning, but are they necessary when the words are spoken? An excellent example is the line:

> Then, Isabel, live chaste, and, brother, die;

If every one of those punctuation marks were removed and the line simply said with attention to the alternating stress of the iambs and the rising line, the sense is perfectly clear. Other midline commas turn out to be equally unnecessary, as the words themselves convey the shift from one phrase to another. "That" and "for" serve as audible markers of the syntax of the sentence.

Having removed those, all that remain are two question marks and one exclamation mark at the midline. In each case, the rhythm of the line has been shifted to suggest a change of thought at that moment. Let us look at each.

"To whom should I complain?" is a regular iambic phrase, but it is followed by the four-word phrase "Did I tell this," which is composed entirely of single-syllable words all calling out for emphasis. Moreover, it is not at all clear that these are two separate sentences. A modern script writer might punctuate them separated by a dash: "To whom should I complain—did I tell this, who would believe me?" A question mark followed by a capital letter sends a signal that two separate questions are presented, when really it is one question with two parallel and integrally joined implications.

"Who would believe me?" which features a powerfully inverted first foot, is followed by "O perilous mouths," one of those lines that is difficult to scan. The open vowel of the "O" invites an elongated emotional release, while "per-ilous" could just as easily be a contraction, "per'lous" or a dactyl (da da DUM). If the former, then the "O" would seem to be unstressed, so that "O perilous mouths" has the rhythm of "da DUM da DUM" and perilous is a pressure-cooker word. But how could that powerful "O" be unstressed? Also, that leaves the line one syllable short, and the absent syllable is a stressed one that should appear between the unstressed "me" and the unstressed "O."

Our alternative would have "perilous mouths" form a midline inversion, creating the distinctive "DUM da da DUM" rhythm. "O" then sits firmly in the stressed position following "me" and the line has ten syllables. Either way, "O perilous mouths" marks a change in the rhythm. In addition, the word "O" is a clear marker of a new thought. Therefore, the question mark is not really needed.

"I'll to my brother," which follows the exclamation mark, is a typical midline inversion marking the beginning of a new pulse of energy along with a new thought. The rhythm alone is sufficient to provide the marker, and far more subtle a shaping than the line reading suggested by an exclamation mark.

To mark a change of thought that does not immediately leap off the page, I use a slash. This allows the sight-reading actor to know that one thought is ending and a new one beginning, without predisposing the nature of that transition. Should it be a period, a colon, or a semicolon? Should it be a question mark or an exclamation mark? Such decisions are better left until the inner workings of the text are clear.

One last set of markings are removed, and those are the contractions that the editor has suggested to keep the line as regular as possible, since we are always interested in irregularity. We want to give full weight to the sounds of every contraction, because these create a pressure-cooker syllable-and-a-half, and so I replace all contractions with the full word, indicated with square brackets: "i'th'state" is written as "i[n]th[e]state." It is important to signal an alternative to the most familiar uses of an apostrophe such as "I'll," which today we say as a single syllable, but which should be pronounced closer to "I y'ull," a diphthong.

There are groupings of words that are so common and familiar today that we no longer give them their full weight and significance. For that reason, when retyping your speech without punctuation, draw attention to such words by revealing the newly created compound word. "Myself" then becomes "my self," two separate words, which asks for some consideration of what your character means by that second word. "Unhappy" becomes un-happy to invite a consideration of what it means to be happy as the key to understanding life without that sensation. "Fearful" becomes "fear-full" reminding us that it can mean full of fear as well as arousing great fear.

I separate compound words to encourage, as much as possible, the reading within the simple iambic rhythms. I remove the apostrophes to indicate the possessive, as there is no difference to the ear between the plural and the possessive, and clarification can then come from the words themselves. Finally, I remove the editor's guidepost of using "'d" instead of "-ed" to clarify that the "-ed" was not pronounced on that verb. I would rather have the actors figure that out themselves. This, then, is how the unpunctuated text looks.

> To whom should I complain / did I tell this
> Who would believe me O perilous mouths
> That bear in them one and the self same tongue
> Either of condemnation or approof
> Bidding the law make curtsy to their will
> Hooking both right and wrong to the appetite
> To follow as it draws / I[wi]ll to my brother
> Though he hath fallen by prompture of the blood
> Yet hath he in him such a mind of honour
> That had he twenty heads to tender down
> On twenty bloody blocks he[wou]ld yield them up
> Before his sister should her body stoop
> To such abhorred pollution
> Then Isabel live chaste and brother die
> More than our brother is our chastity
> I[wi]ll tell him yet of Angelos request
> And fit his mind to death for his souls rest

There is one last thing we can do, to give each line of verse an opportunity to work its magic upon us. We can read aloud, slowly. Remember that the actors of Bill's company, with their limited education, likely read at what today would be the speed of someone about eight to ten years old. Everyone read aloud, always. The unbelievably fast silent reading that allows us to skim the flood of print media every day was completely unknown to Shakespeare's England. By slowing down, reading carefully and thoughtfully, giving oneself over to the natural rhythms of the words while keeping the heartbeat constantly in the inner ear, and by always allowing the line to rise toward the final word, we can encounter the event as shaped by the language, without the intervention of our intellect that instructs us as to what the scene is supposed to be about and therefore how we should say the lines, long before we have ever given them voice.

Let us see, using a single, short speech for each of Angelo and Isabella, from earlier in their confrontation, if the verse without punctuation contains sufficient clues for sight reading. Here is Angelo's first line:

Condemn the fault and not the actor of it

With a line like this, a modern actor has to fight hard against the tendency to drop away, to let the energy out, to let the last two words of the line, seemingly so trivial, rumble deep in the throat. But this goes against everything that the Iambic Code reveals to us. The "it" is the point to which the entire line leads. Words like "condemn," "fault," or even "actor," on the surface, appear to demand the strongest emphasis. In fact, they exist simply to get us to "it," an opportunity for you to fill that crisp sound with a density of feeling. Remember, also, that the speech act is not over. Do not deliver this line as if there were a period after "it." Rise with the energy of the line and leave yourself open, after the last word, for the line to continue, somehow, in whatever direction Angelo's feelings go next. Here is the next line:

Why every fault[i]s condemned ere it be done

It requires slow and careful reading, trusting the heartbeat, to decide whether to pronounce the "-ed" on "condemned." In this case it is not pronounced, but even so it is very difficult to say "condemned" as two crisp syllables. The multiple consonants at the end of the word draw it out, and there is no escaping the pressure sitting under that word when you let it emerge fully sounded from your mouth. Buried in this line are two other words that a modern reader will sling out to fit easily into the rhythm, but that actually disrupt it: "every" and "ere." The first of these is a three-syllable word that can be clipped into two, but remember that even contractions require an extra slight sound where the missing syllable used to be. The second is a diphthong, and cannot be just one quick syllable unless it is pronounced incorrectly.

Say the line again, letting the extra part-syllables suggest the *frisson* under the surface of Angelo's cool judge-like language, and remember not to cadence as if this were the end of a sentence. Instead, rise up in energy toward "done" and then open yourself, unsure where to go next until you move on to the next line:

Mine were the very cipher of a function

Here we have an inverted first foot, that attacking energy, so important to the shaping of the emotional journey of the speech. If you cadenced on the previous line, then you've let all of the energy out, and poor Angelo is forced to pick up steam again with this line. If, however, you resisted the temptation to put in an imaginary period, you are able to cut across the energy that accumulates at the end of the previous line with contrasting energy that builds, moving the energy forward, continuing the action without any wasteful breaks.

Notice also the feminine ending. Be sure to build toward function, and then let that extra, unaccented syllable open you to multiple possibilities even as it demands that you push on, drive forward to the next thought. Note also how the "-ion" requires a diphthong, and therefore contains that pressure-cooker sensation. What conflicted feelings does Angelo experience when he considers his function? How does this tie in with the fact that the Duke left him in charge, even though he expressly stated his unsuitability for the job? Perhaps we will get some clues from the next line, but until then, give that final word its full sound value and its richest possible intellectual and emotional weight.

To fine the faults whose fine stands in record

There are several things that leap out at us from this line. First of all, we repeat the word "faults" from before, and use "fine" twice. Second, the word "record" seems to require an accent on the second syllable, which we can assume to have been an acceptable pronunciation in Shakespeare's day. If you don't want to say it that way, you can split the difference by saying it with an accent of the first syllable, but give the second syllable slightly more weight than ordinarily, and justify this extra emphasis by filling the word with strong emotional associations. However, I have found that modern audiences are not as troubled by such shifts as we are when we first read such a line. In delivery, the context, and thus the meaning, come clear.

Angelo's last line is not complete, as Isabella picks up the second part. Before you decide to cadence, consider that she might be cutting him off, so that he only gets to say:

And let go by the actor

but had intended to build on this point with something more. Notice that his final word serves as a midline feminine ending, and needs the same sort of opening out to possibilities as any other feminine ending, entirely suitable given that he repeats the word "actor," just as he did "fault" and "fine." Now let's look at a speech of Isabella's. Here is her first line:

I would to heaven I had your potency

In this one line we see the sort of pressure-cooker contraction and the "two for the price of one" expansion of the Iambic Code at its most subtle and insightful. Although "heaven" can be scrimped down into something very near one syllable, it can never be a sharp, clean single sound. Clearly, there is an extra little something going on under the surface of that word, that ripples the surface of Isabella's composure. But the line is building toward "potency"; so easy to say but so filled with significance that the actor needs to dig deep into herself and her character to fill it up with associations and resonance. Having thrown that word out, with the rising line and the opening out to possibilities, reinforced by the slight silence created as the heart beats twice, Isabella is ready to continue:

And you were Isabel should it then be thus

Without any punctuation there is a slight glitch as the eye moves from her name to the next word, until the brain catches up with the mouth and the obvious conclusion is reached: there is a caesura after "Isabel." There is an extra syllable there, creating a rushing, racing beginning to the next phrase, that special infusion of uncontrolled energy that Shakespeare likes to use to give his actors a great start to their next bit. He doesn't use this strategy as often as the "Attack!" rhythm of the inverted first foot, but often enough to be a recognizable component of the Iambic Code.

No I would tell what twere to be a judge

You will notice that I write "twere" as a single word, because it can be so easily said that way. What is far more important is how the "t" on the end of "wait" and the "t" that begins "twere" abut against each other. Such doubling of consonants demands that the actor break between the two words, creating the most subtle of caesuras at the midpoint of the line.

And what a prisoner

Like Angelo, Isabella's last line is incomplete, perhaps signalling that she is cut off, or perhaps that the speed of the interaction is such that there is no discernable pause between speeches. Also like Angelo, Isabella's last word is not clean and firm. It is another of those three-syllable words. We don't know if it is squeezed into a two-syllable "slot," with the middle syllable clipped out, suggesting pressure, or if it is a word that needs to expand in significance to fill a small silence, just like "potency" and "chastity." Either way, it demands that the actor consider the greatest number of associations, both emotional and intellectual, and to avoid dropping energy on that oh-so-important word. By looking at the next line, we can guess that it's a pressure-cooker situation, as the next speaker requires three full feet.

Let us move on to a speech of some length, to see if you can try this line-by-line reading aloud on your own. Once you have explored what can be learned directly from the code, we move on to explore other dramatic shapings that are also embedded directly into the language, reducing our reliance on modern punctuation.

> Nought[i]s had all[i]s spent
> Where our desire is got without content
> Tis safer to be that which we destroy
> Than by destruction dwell in doubt-full joy
> How now my lord why do you keep alone
> Of sorriest fancies your companions making
> Using those thoughts which should indeed have died
> With them they think on things without all remedy
> Should be without regard what[i]s done is done [*Macbeth* 3.2.4]

What can be learned about the emotions of Lady Macbeth as she says these words? First, we have the line of poetry itself. Each line rises, and the whole speech rises, line upon line, one flow of dramatic intention or need, until the next speaker interrupts or the need is fulfilled and the moment ended.

If you read through the speech, ignoring intellectual thought, trying to feel your way into the emotional rise of each line toward the last word in the line, and each line building on the energy of the previous, you find that a very powerful impact is created by the words:

spent

content

destroy

joy

alone

making

died

remedy

done

This is the thematic, as well as emotional, heart of the speech, clearly codified for you by the shape of the lines.

Now, something else clearly takes the place of periods, commas, colons, and semicolons. Simple, friendly, familiar joining words that mean the same today as they did then serve to guide us through the larger thought. And, but, or, and if are the beginning, but Shakespeare makes use of other similar joining words. Let us look at some of the linking words in Lady Macbeth's speech.

> Nought[i]s had all[i]s spent
> *Where* our desire is got *without* content
> Tis safer to be *that which* we destroy

Than by destruction dwell *in* doubt-full joy
How now my lord *why* do you keep alone
Of sorriest fancies your companions making
Using those thoughts *which* should indeed have died
With them they think *on* things *without* all remedy
Should be *without* regard *what*[i]s done is done

Explore the simplicity and clarity of the structure of the speech as crafted by the words and rhythms. Read aloud again with the rising line, as rapidly as possible, allowing yourself to breathe only on the highlighted joining words. Sometimes they are used to mark major shifts in thought or focus, other times they signal a short list of key words. The irregularity of the breathing pattern is in itself theatrical, and should signal to you some of the emotional rhythms of the speech even as the conjunctions and prepositions help you to unravel thought patterns.

What other word patterns exist in an unpunctuated piece of blank verse that can guide the actor into Shakespeare's rhythms and structures? How about repetition? In any given speech you can find words used more than once. Some of the repeated words are the familiar conjunctions, prepositions, articles, and so on. These create potential word patterns of a different sort, as we have seen. For now, let us examine other repeated words. Remember to make use of words that share a common root: fearfully and fear, blood and bloody, and so on. And remember that the "-full" suffix was a new tool for describing an emotional state, so that fear-full and awe-full contain a repetition of full, which then might be echoed in the free-standing use of the word elsewhere. Apply this to Macbeth's response to his wife:

We have scorched the snake *not* killed it
She[wi]ll close and be *her* self whilest our poor malice
Remains in danger of *her* former tooth
But let the frame of things dis-joint both the words suffer
Ere *we* will eat *our* meal in fear and *sleep*
In the affliction of these terrible dreams
That shake *us* nightly better be with the dead
Whom *we* to gain *our peace* have sent to *peace*
Than on the torture of the mind to lie
In rest-less ecstasy Duncan is in *his* grave
After lifes fit-full fever *he sleeps* well
Treason has done *his* worst *nor* steel *nor* poison
Malice domestic foreign levy nothing
Can touch *him* further. [3.2.13]

In addition to the interesting pattern in the pronouns (the snake is female and treason is male), and the use of negatives (not, nor), it is the repetition of peace and sleep that dominates this speech. All of the negative words are used only once.

As an exercise to explore these repetitions, mark the first use of "sleep" and "peace" with an arrow pointing up and the second use of the word with an arrow coming down. If this were a longer speech and you were charting more complex repetitions, you could mark a third going up, and so forth. A long speech might contain many groups of repeated words, and this exercise will give you upward and downward arrows in random patterns scattered in the speech.

The first time you say a word, cadence your voice in a rising pitch, as if asking a question on that word. It is as if you throw that word up into the air and let it hang there, significant but as yet unexplained. When you reach the second occasion of that word, cadence down on it, as if finishing a sentence or a thought. You are almost saying, "Remember that idea I introduced a little or a long while ago? Well, here it is again, and isn't that interesting, so there." If there is a third instance, throw it up again, still further, by an even more striking rising cadence. Of course you will be tossing words up and catching them some time later in a complicated interwoven pattern, but you discover many interesting clues about the emotional and intellectual structure and rhythm of the speech.

There is an even more subtle patterning of words at work in these speeches, and that has to do with the repetition of sounds. To pursue this exercise, latch upon a word that, for you, is important as a marker of feeling or thought at work in the scene. For Macbeth, let us take the word "fear." He only says it once, but it is clearly an important emotion here. Now, italicize every word that echoes that sound.

> We have scorched the snake not killed it
> She[wi]ll close and be her self whilest our poor malice
> Remains in danger of her *former* tooth
> But let the *frame* of things dis-joint both the words suffer
> Ere we will eat our meal in *fear* and sleep
> In the affliction of these terrible dreams
> That shake us nightly better be with the dead
> Whom we to gain our peace have sent to peace
> Than on the torture of the mind to lie
> In rest-less ecstasy Duncan is in his grave
> After lifes *fit-full fever* he sleeps well
> Treason has done his worst nor steel nor poison
> Malice domestic *foreign* levy nothing
> Can touch him further.

As you can see, we pursued a pattern of alliteration, but we might want to expand this list of key words to include "suffer" and "affliction," as these have a strong "f" sound in them and also connect powerfully to the emotion we are exploring. Once we move in this direction, a phrase like "After lifes fit-full fever" is revealed in all of its f-full glory.

It is possible now to explore this parallel pattern in the speech, perhaps by moving or making eye contact with your partner while saying each of the highlighted words, or simply by savoring the sound while building strong associations with the word as you come upon it in the speech. You can do this with "s" sounds by whispering the speech, which make the sibilants into hissing.

❧ 7 ❧
Putting It on Its Feet

Suit the Action to the Word, the Word to the Action.

Hamlet [*Hamlet* 3.2.17]

The following are some exercises I use to transform the variations of the code from an intellectual exercise into a movement experience. Students resist them because they do not seem sufficiently serious for use with such inspiring examples of great dramatic poetry. They also dislike the ritual quality of any sort of rhythmic exploration, finding it completely disassociated with their experience of profound and complex human emotions. However, if viewed as a means to an end, which is what they were created to be, these exercises can assist the actor in acquiring an intuitive, nonintellectual sensitivity to iambic pentameter and the variations of the Iambic Code. The goal of all of this work is to tune the inner ear, not train the brain. Remember, you undertake all of your scansion work in order to forget it consciously, having allowed yourself to become open to the possibilities encoded in the text.

RHYTHMS

Even alone it is possible to improvise richly with the rhythms at work in Shakespeare's dramatic poetry. It is even more fun in groups. I bring in percussive instruments: drums, clavés, wood blocks, and so on, and attach to each instrument a role to play in building the rhythmic pattern. The students can exchange instruments and take turns holding different positions in the ensemble.

The loud bass drum sets the heartbeat. I have one that is beaten with a felt-covered stick and that allows a clear, gentle beat to contrast with the strong beat, for the "da DUM da DUM da DUM" of our heartbeat. To acclimatize everyone, I have them feel for their pulse and then beat in time with it, but not for long as that is quite a rapid pace and doesn't allow for improvisation around the beat except by skilled percussionists. When the students begin their improvisation, the person on the bass drum beats in a slow, strict rhythm.

The second instrument I integrate is a chime bar that gives a strong, sustained tone. This is rung at exactly the same time as the fifth strong beat of the bass drum. Because the sound sustains, it carries through each group of five, binding them together into the rhythmic equivalent of the lines of verse.

> Da DUM da DUM da DUM da DUM da DUM
> Chime
> Da DUM da DUM da DUM da DUM da DUM
> Chime
> Da DUM da DUM da DUM da DUM da DUM
> Chime

Next, we add a bell bar to remind us of the climbing pattern of the iambic. Any pattern of rising notes will do, but I've indicated a traditional scale.

> Da DUM da DUM da DUM da DUM da DUM
> Chime
> Do   Re   Mi   Fa   So

Finally, we add a single striking of the wood block that signals change of thought. This person can strike the block at any time, and I encourage whomever has this instrument to bring great variety to the lengths of the sentences, and in particular to strike the block sometimes with the chime and sometimes midway through the five beats of the drum.

We create this basic sound pattern and listen to it or play the various instruments in it until we are quite familiar with the three-part makeup of the sound and the rising line. I encourage them to listen to and/or play the bell bar while thinking of the different lengths of thought they might find in a familiar passage, without attempting to reproduce it accurately. I encourage them to listen to and/or play the chime bar and bell bar while thinking of the driving energy of the verse line units. Throughout this, the heartbeat is difficult to ignore. This musical improvisation provides an immediate introduction to the power of ritualized sound patterns. What is needed next is to experience the infinite possibilities of variation that can be placed against the iambic pentameter.

As a preliminary, open-ended exercise, I have the students pair up and use hands. One hits the knee then claps the hands, to give the contrasting sounds of the unstressed/stressed rhythm. The other claps in a free pattern, sometimes when the partner is clapping, sometimes not. I encourage them to try to work in the most common variations from the Iambic Code, but I also ask them to be free and have fun with whatever comes out. Once they have mastered the basics of this exercise, each taking a turn being the heartbeat, I give them two new challenges: the heartbeat can speed up and slow down, and they can create a dramatic monologue, with a beginning, a middle, and an end.

Next, I have them work in groups of four. One is the conductor, the next the provider of the heartbeat, and the other two are opposing characters having a disagreement. They are free to clap on the knee slap or on the clap of the heartbeat. The conductor points to one, who begins the free clapping in sync with the heartbeat. The conductor points to the other "speaker," who must pick up with the heartbeat as if building on the argument. The heartbeat controls the tempo of the argument, starting from a slow, even rhythm, but slowly speeding up as the disagreement grows more intense.

It is now time to blend the complete freedom of the clapping exercises with the complexity of the Iambic Code. There are two ways to do this, and I have tried them in either order with similar results.

In small groups, the students work out, rehearse, and then perform the score of an existing monologue. Here is an example of what the score would look like. First, the selected text:

> I have almost forgot the taste of Fears:
> The time has been, my senses would have cooled
> To hear a Night-shriek, and my Fell of hair
> Would at a dismal Treatise rouse, and stir
> As life were in't: I have supped full with horrors,
> Direness familiar to my slaughterous thoughts
> Cannot once start me. Wherefore was that cry? [*Macbeth* 5.5.9]

Next, the Iambic Code pounded out by the bass drum, with a chime ringing at the end of each line and a bell struck at each change of thought:

> DUM da DUM da da DUM da DUM da DUM/CHIME/BELL
> da DUM da DUM da DUM da DUM da DUM/CHIME
> da DUM da DUM da DUM da DUM da DUM/CHIME
> da DUM da DUM da DUM da DUM da DUM/CHIME
> da DUM da DUM/BELL/DUM da da DUM da DUM da/CHIME
> DUM da da DUM da DUM da DUM da DUM/CHIME
> da DUM da DUM da/BELL/DUM da DUM da DUM/CHIME

Despite the strange, uniambic beginning, the familiar heartbeat is established and maintained from the second half of the first line through to the middle of the fifth line. The bell marks a transition to a new thought, and the extra energy is brought out also by the change of rhythm and the inclusion of the speech's only feminine ending. The next line, still part of the same thought, also begins with the extra energy of an inverted foot but the rest of the speech is regular, even though there is a complete change of thought halfway through the last line.

It is now time to mark the even more subtle variations of rhythm to be found in rising lines using the different notes of a scale. The rising iambs demand that the final stressed word in any given line be marked by the highest note in that line, and that the general feel of the sequence of notes must be a rising one, but within that general guideline, the group is free to assign note values intuitively. Using "1" to represent the lowest note the instrument plays, they score the "melody" freely. They can play a note for every syllable if they feel ambitious, or they can play notes only for emphasis. Both approaches are indicated with numbers above the text lines.

Version I. Melody

3   2   4 3   3   4   2   5   3 6
I have almost forgot the taste of Fears:

 1   3   1 2   2   3 2   4   3   5
The time has been, my senses would have cooled

 2   4 2   4   3   2   2   3 2   4
To hear a Night-shriek, and my Fell of hair

 3   1 1   3 2   3   2   4   2   5
Would at a dismal Treatise rouse, and stir

2   4   2   3   4 3   4   5   4   6   5
As life were in't: I have supped full with horrors,

5   4   4 5 3   3   3   4   3(3)   5
Direness familiar to my slaughterous thoughts

3   4   4   4 3   5   4   4   3   5
Cannot once start me. Wherefore was that cry?

Version II: Notes for Emphasis

              2   3   4
I have almost forgot the taste of Fears:

   2   1   2   4
The time has been, my senses would have cooled

   3   4   3   3   4
To hear a Night-shriek, and my Fell of hair

<pre>
    2   3   4   5
Would at a dismal Treatise rouse, and stir

    3   2   3   4   5
As life were in't: I have supped full with horrors,

3   2   4   5
Direness familiar to my slaughterous thoughts

    1   2   3   3   4
Cannot once start me. Wherefore was that cry?
</pre>

Before or after this scansion-to-music performance, the students can invent their own eight-line example of the Iambic Code. In this exercise, they make arbitrary decisions of where to place feminine endings or inverted first feet. They continue to mark the ends of lines with the bell chime. They can also make use of midline inversions and midline feminine endings to accompany change of thought, which they indicate with the bell. Then, they can place onto this rhythmic score a free-form climbing note sequence. It is always surprising to me how musical both types of compositions can be, and how striking and powerful the pure-sound compositions almost always turn out to be.

SHAKESPEARE THE CONDUCTOR

A close study of the plays reveals Shakespeare's hand as director. He refers to actions and facial expressions with some regularity, as when Kate addresses the shrewish wives by saying, "Fie, fie, unknit that threatening unkind brow, / And dart not scornful glances from those eyes" [5.2.136], or when King Henry instructs his aunt to rise, and she replies, "Not yet, I thee beseech. / For ever will I walk upon my knees" [*RII* 5.3.92].

I've always assumed, from this evidence, that if the staging was important, Shakespeare ensured that it happened by building it directly into the script. If a specific action wasn't important, then he'd let the actors sort it out, because he could trust them to use the space well, to gesture and move around in a manner that allowed everyone to see and understand the point of the interaction. He'd even describe important facial expressions so that not only would the actor do what was asked, but that the people in the back or standing behind someone with a big hat could see with the mind's eye and understand. By referring to important, large physical actions, like kneeling, and to facial expressions, he shaped two of the three modes of communication, the facial and the kinesthetic. But what about the verbal mode?

His was a theatre of language. The briefest of breaks were sometimes suggested by short lines, but more often than not, the dialog moved back and forth between speakers so smoothly that they could share the same line of poetry. Overt and striking breaks were so rare that they were marked by direct reference, as when Beatrice fills Claudio's stunned silence, upon hearing that his fears were ungrounded and Hero will be his bride, with the wry prompt, "Speak Count, 'tis your cue" [*Much Ado* 2.1.305]. Otherwise, we can assume if *Romeo and Juliet* took two hours, the lines were delivered without our modern dramatic pauses or hesitations. The pure sound flowed like a river, or like a symphony.

Let us, for a moment, pursue that analogy. If the music created by the spoken voices, sometimes many speaking in rapid or measured contrast, sometimes a single voice at length, was the focus of all that writing, then we can look to that writing to see how Shakespeare scored the symphony. Furthermore, just as we don't ask a symphony to "mean" something specific and yet we all agree it conveys something meaningful, we can participate in the creation of this music quite separate from a concern about theme. If we can stop thinking about Shakespeare, and start listening to the emotionally laden score, then perhaps we can bypass the intellectual deadening of our traditional, English-class encounters with the plays and go right to the heart of what makes this language so performable.

Let's have a look at a passage to see how it is scored, a passage about music, spoken by Caliban in *The Tempest*. I've always loved this short passage, because Caliban, who says some pretty rude and crude things most of the time, here is given some of the most beautiful words in the play.

To read the score, we start with the folio punctuation, but with modern spelling and format. Connect the punctuation with the rests that occur in music. A comma is as short as possible, the equivalent of a break in phrasing, but to be sure we make use of the score mark them as sixteenth-note rests. The colon is our quarter-note rest, and the semicolon a dotted quarter-note rest, in other words just slightly longer. We also need a short rest for the end of each line, which is our eighth-note rest. Periods are marked by a half-note rest. As this is music, I'll not mark the verse lines, but you'll spot them by the eighth-note rests.

Read this aloud, slowly, and tap once for [1], twice for [2], three times for [3], four times for [4], and five times for [5]. Don't think too much about it, just try to listen to the score as it comes at you.

Be not afeared [1] the isle is full of noises [1] [2] sounds [1] and sweet airs [1] that give delight and hurt not [3] [2] sometimes a thousand twangling instruments [2] will hum about mine ears [4] and sometime voices [1] [2] that if I then had waked after long sleep [1] [2] will make me sleep again [1] and then in dreaming [1] [2] the clouds methought would open [1] and show riches [2] ready to drop upon me [1] that when I waked [2] I cried to dream again [5]

It's relatively easy to use a regular iambic rhythm as a 2/4 musical notation, but as we have discovered, Shakespeare is seldom so regular. And nor is music.

Triplets, sixteenth notes, and held notes allow a single syllable to expand to fill a bar, or many syllables to compress into a single beat. You might hear a rhythm in the first three words of a quarter note, two eighth notes, and then a half note followed by a rest.

So it's important not to lock ourselves in with iambic pentameter, but explore the intersection of the stressed syllable in any given foot and words that are important because the sense they convey connects powerfully with the desire of the speaker to communicate. If we put those words in the position of the first note of a bar of music, then we begin to take advantage of the power of the downbeat of the conductor's baton. We will indicate this downbeat with a vertical line, like the bar line in music. There is no way to know what is "right," but here is one way I explored this passage.

Be not a|feared [1] the |isle is full of |noises [1] [2] |sounds [1] and sweet |airs [1] that give de |light and hurt not [3] [2] sometimes a thousand |twangling instruments [2] will |hum about mine ears [4] and sometime |voices [1] [2] that if I then had |waked after long |sleep [1] [2] will make me |sleep again [1] and then in |dreaming [1] [2] the |clouds methought would open [1] and show |riches [2] |ready to drop upon me [1] that when I |waked [2] I |cried to |dream a|gain [5]

Don't worry about an exact count at this point. Pick words you naturally hit when you say this aloud, and put a bar sign before them. Your choices might not be my choices. Don't worry about that yet. Just don't feel that you have to mark every interesting word, and definitely don't mark every stressed syllable in the iambic rhythm or your music will plod, not flow.

Let's see if the folio provides another clue. I'm going to put the bar line immediately before any word that received a capital letter or a long spelling. I'll put the bar mark before the accented syllable if it is a polysyllabic word. Because the first word of each line of poetry is capitalized, I'll have to put a bar there, right before the accented word.

|Be not a|feared [1] the |isle is full of |noises [1] [2] |sounds [1] and sweet |airs [1] that give delight and hurt not [3] [2] |sometimes a thousand twangling |instruments [2] will |hum about mine |ears[4] and sometime voices [1] [2] that |if I then had |waked after long |sleep [1] [2] will |make me |sleep a|gain [1] and then in dreaming [1] [2] the |clouds methought would open [1] and show riches [2] |ready to drop upon me [1] that when I waked [2] I |cried to |dream a|gain [5]

Certain interesting things occur. Some of my markings match up with these, others do not. I was prepared to elongate the final five words by putting in three bar marks; these matched up but were revealed as a repetition; Shakespeare had done the same thing with "make me sleep again," creating a beautiful echo. The markings at the beginnings of lines of verse came clearer as I was forced to respond to those capital letters, and now the [2] that marks the end of lines is associated with a bar mark immediately or shortly thereafter.

Let's see what happens when we play with the length of the sounds. When we have a diphthong or a cluster of consonants that demands elongation, we will mark those for longer notes in our score. I am also going to mark the "ee" sound in sleep and dream—an important echo as well as a sound that requires a bit more time.

|Be not a|feared [1] the |isle is full of |noises [1] [2] |sounds [1] and sweet |airs [1] that give de**light** and hurt not [3] [2] |sometimes a thousand **twang**ling |instruments [2] will |**hum** about mine |ears [4] and sometime voices [1] [2] that |if I then had |wa**ked** after long |sleep [1] [2] will |make me |sleep a|gain [1] and then in dreaming [1] [2] the |clouds methought would open [1] and show riches [2] |ready to drop upon me [1] that when I wa**ked** [2] I |cried to |dream a|gain [5]

Now you're ready to sing this piece. Don't worry if you're not a singer. Don't worry about creating a beautify melody. Just sing (not speak) the words. When there's a bar line, the following word is accented. When there's a rest, pause and take a breath, of course. Words that are highlighted have to be held a bit longer. Experiment with using higher and lower pitches, singing faster and slower, louder and softer, whatever appeals.

Immediately after, simply say the words, naturally. See if in your speaking voice you can feel the elongation of those vowel sounds and interesting consonants. See if you can feel the speeding up and slowing down, the rising and falling pitch, which can be so pronounced in singing but can still inform the spoken word.

Here are some additional exercises that bring iambic explorations out of the intellect and into the actor's physical experience.

IAMBIC BRIDGING

I use this in combination with the exercise of hiding all of a speech except for the single line of verse under examination. It reminds students that the five-foot line is just about the perfect unit for uploading into the forebrain, and teaches them a simple trick for memorizing large chunks of text. I like to use it with strong speeches from the lesser-known plays, and set these as sight-reading exercises, just to demonstrate how much the actor can let the words do the work in the scene. I also like to use it to inspire the listener toward active listening with some of the suggestions near the end of the exercise.

I never do this exercise with modern editions. I use unpunctuated editions or versions of the folio punctuation only. The speaker sits close to the listener, who gives full attention and eye contact. The speaker uncovers the first line of the speech. This is read silently with attention to the obvious variations of the code and the elementary guideposts they present. If a foot is inverted, the speaker prepares to commit a surge of energy to those words. If a feminine ending presents itself, the speaker prepares to open to the possibilities, all the while wondering what comes next.

The speaker loads these ten or eleven (or perhaps twelve) syllables into the forebrain, opening herself to the possible emotion and relationship shaped by these words. Then the speaker makes eye contact with the listener, and says the words slowly, accurately, with whatever emphasis seems to come from the sequence of sounds and with a commitment to the rising line and an absolute absence of cadencing, but without attempting to "act" them in any other way.

The listener receives these words and commits the final word to memory. Perhaps, to solidify the connection between them, the listener repeats that final word, also without cadencing, maybe even as a soft question. The two let the final word of the line linger in the air, and then the speaker breaks eye contact, moves the paper to reveal the second line, and repeats the process.

Variations of this basic exercise include adding on the lines, so that it begins with one line, then two, then three, then four, with a pause for the listener to repeat the last word of each line as it is offered by the speaker. The listener is then able to prompt the speaker by feeding the last word of the forgotten line, but only the last word. It always astonishes students, if they take the time to absorb the word and to speak it slowly and with complete awareness, how easy it is, with minimal prompting, to memorize significant chunks of text in one sitting.

Here is another variation that inspires an even richer engagement of the listener, and points out another significant aspect of the pentameter verse line. In this variation, it is imperative that neither the speaker nor the listener know what comes next in the speech.

The speaker uploads the first line as above, and delivers it to the speaker, being sure to make use of the rising line as if asking a question. The listener repeats the last word as a question, and then asks more questions, whatever has been suggested by the line. Some of these will be answered by the next line, some by something else in the speech, some by the play in its entirety, and some are never answered. Of the unanswered questions, some turn out to be unimportant, but a surprising number suggest the mystery at the heart of the human interaction shaped by the language of the play.

Here is an example of how the lines might result in interesting questions. It does require, of course, that both the speaker and the listener understand the meaning of the words they are saying and hearing, so I allow a time out for a quick definition.

Speaker: We will our self in person to this war ... ?

Listener: War? What war? With whom? Were we attacked or are we attacking them? Is it a rare thing for you to go to wars in person? Am I going to the war too?

Speaker: And for our Coffers, with too great a Court ... ?

Listener: Court? Are the courtiers costing too much money? Won't the war cost more money? Has the court grown too large? Or do you mean something else by that, like too much courting, as in begging?

Speaker: And liberal Largess, are grown somewhat light . . . ?

Listener: Light? Do you mean you're broke? How are you going to go to war then? And what is the connection between your open hand, giving away too much money, and the size of the court or the amount of courting going on? Somewhat light? Are you being ironic?

Speaker: We are inforced to farm our royal Realm . . . ?

Listener: Realm? Are things as bad as they sound? How can it be only somewhat light, if you're farming out the entire kingdom? Clearly, you're the king, so you have the power, but aren't you supposed to guard the realm, not squander it? Who is inforcing you? Me?

Speaker: The Revenue whereof shall furnish us . . . ?

Listener: Us? Do you mean you and me, or just your royal kingship? All this money you're going to be getting from farming out the realm, because you're somewhat light, or completely light more like, because of your too great court, and now you're going to war? Could you explain the logic of that?

Speaker: For our affairs in hand: if that come short . . . ?

Listener: Short? You mean the money from farming out the entire kingdom might not be enough? What sort of a war do you have planned? What sort of financial mess are you in? Do I approve of this plan? If so, am I part of the "us" that will benefit, the "our" that joins in the affairs? Or is "our" like "us" just your way of saying it's all for you?

Speaker: Our Substitutes at home shall have Blank-charters . . . ?

Listener: Charters? Like royal powers? Blank? So we can do anything we want, just like a king? Would I be one of those substitutes? Do I get to stay home from war and act like you do?

Speaker: Whereto, when they shall know what men are rich . . . ?

Listener: Rich? Sounds like those are people other than me, right? Am I someone who has no money or power, and you're getting me to buy into this rather tacky financial situation, plus some stupid war, by offering me blank charters and free access to the rich men I've always envied?

Speaker: They shall subscribe them for large sums of gold . . . ?

Listener: Gold? What else would we want? Their lives? That would be the ultimate power, but I guess only kings have that, right? But who are the "they" that will have the blank charters? Do I go to war with you or stay and milk the rich at home?

Speaker: And send them after to supply our wants . . . ?

Listener: Wants? Do you mean someone else will get all the money for our fun and games while we're at war? I still don't know who we're fighting and why, but maybe that's not as important as getting an excuse to leave the court and cover our losses with a couple of blank charters that someone else will use. Better them than us, right?

Speaker: For we will make for Ireland presently . . . ?

Listener: Presently? You mean right away? Don't I get to pack? And why Ireland? Couldn't I stay home and have some fun with those blank charters? [*RII* 1.4.42]

STEPPING OUT

As an introduction to this series of exercises, I have the students walk around the room in a regular step, with each step representing the downbeat of the Iambic Code. They then try to fit the words of the poetry they are reading in and around this pattern. When the words do not fit, they are simply spoken as a counterpoint, but when they do fit, the match between the words and beat is clear. The entire class can march around the room and saying different lines of poetry, in this exercise, create a cacophony of sound alongside the marching beat of many feet in unison.

The next walking and talking challenge is much more difficult. I have students work with passages that they have scanned but not memorized, that have been clearly marked with each stressed syllable, *averaging* five per line. It might be fewer than five if a stressed position in the line is held by a relatively uninteresting word such as a conjunction or preposition. It might be more than five if an emotionally significant word sits in an unstressed position. The student then walks and talks, taking a step on each stressed syllable, but striving to adapt the steps to the actual rhythm of the pattern of sounds, speeding up and slowing down in response to short and long vowels, clipped and dense consonants, as well as all of the subtle variations of rhythm they have noted. The students find this remarkably difficult, akin to patting one's head and rubbing one's stomach. However, they usually find if they focus their attention on sounding the language and marking the actual spoken rhythm slowly and clearly, rather than conveying the sense of the words to an audience, they can master this juggling act.

It is then something of a relief to move on to the next stepping exercise. Here, each line of poetry is sounded with special attention to the rising line, and a step is taken at the end of each line, almost as if the entire weight of the line is needed to move forward toward the object. This works very well if the speaker has memorized the speech and delivers it to someone who serves to provide an obstacle to the goal of the character. As a variation, the speaker remains still and the listener moves toward the speaker at the end of each line. The secret of this exercise is to build toward the final word and to move, not after the word, but as it is said.

A more subtle and interesting stepping out exercise requires that the speaker move as each of the pressure-cooker or double-indemnity words is said, creating a subtle and unexpected pattern of movement and, by linking the stepping toward or away from the goal with the "hot" word, opening the possibility of building a visceral connection with the word.

Here is a short speech that lends itself to this variation on the stepping out exploration. The stepping moments, here expanded to include all of the Iambic Code guideposts, are marked with italics. In the case of an inverted foot, the first word is marked. In the case of a contraction, the primary word in or immediately following the contraction is selected. In the case of a feminine ending, the stressed and unstressed syllables are marked. All double-indemnity and pressure-cooker words are marked, even those created by a diphthong. The final word of every line is marked to keep the actor from losing the feel of the rising line.

The actor playing Angelo *or* the actress playing Isabella may move on the marked words. The actor playing Angelo should not attempt to enact a powerful emotion. Instead, he should simply say the words and open himself to the implications of the marked words, giving them room to work upon himself and his partner.

> *Who* will believe thee *Isabel*
> My *unsoiled* name the *austereness* of my *life*
> My vouch against you and my place i[n] the *state*
> Will so your *accusation* over *weigh*
> That you shall stifle in your own *report*
> And smell of *calumny* / *I* have *begun*
> And now I give my *sensual* race the *rein*
> *Fit* thy consent *to* my sharp *appetite*
> *Lay* by all *nicety* and *prolixious blushes*
> That banish what they *sue for* / redeem thy *brother*
> By *yielding* up thy body to my *will*
> Or else he must not only die the *death*
> But thy unkindness shall his death draw *out*
> To *lingering sufferance* / Answer me *to-morrow*
> Or by the *affection* that now guides me *most*
> *I'll* prove a tyrant to him / As for *you*
> *Say* what you can my false *o'erweighs* your *true*.

It is always possible to substitute more significant actions for the simple stepping. I have seen a terrifying Angelo emerge from a sweet, young student actor when a piece of paper was ripped as each of the above marked words was spoken.

ᘓᴥ 8 ᘓᴥ

Messages in the Code

Let us cast away nothing, for we may live to have need of such a Verse.
                                                    Pandarus [*T&C* 4.4.21]

It would not be appropriate to suggest, even for a moment, that Shakespeare consciously and painstakingly manipulated the rhythmic and tonal qualities of his verse in order to communicate with the actors in his company. He wrote too quickly, and was too busy himself as a working professional, to spend hours fussing with such subtleties. And why would he need to, when he spent every day in the theatre with the rest of the company, and could pass on any important instructions with the manuscript, or steer an actor in the right direction if things weren't going well? Rather, let us assume that all that we today label the Iambic Code was simply the normal, natural flow of dramatic poetry, as spoken and heard in Shakespeare's theatre, and he absorbed subliminally the tricks of the playwright's trade just as a young writer today might be able to churn out sitcom episodes with facility.

These subtle manipulations work in part because they evoke the rhythms of emotional excitement, the sound qualities of sorrow, the brittle sparkle of wit, and the gentle seductive textures of whispered love talk. The vocabulary might have changed, and we might put our sentences together quite differently, but somehow the music of this poetry still stirs the speaker, if she will let it.

Most importantly, the Iambic Code represents a collusion between form and content. Over and over, the key words that emerge from an analysis of variations and patterns are the very words that will most matter to the actor striving to convey the sense as well as the sensuality of Shakespeare's language. Let us have a look at one thrilling speech and link what we find there, using all that we have learned about the code, to the themes contained therein. Here is Mowbray, taking the fall for his king at the beginning of *Richard II*, reproduced here stripped of all signals but those suggested by the scansion.

> A heavy sentence my most *sovereign* liege
> And all un-looked for from your Highness mouth
> A dearer merit not so deep a maim
> As to be cast **forth** in the common air
> Have I deservèd at your Highness hands
> The *language* I have learnt these forty years
> My native English now I must forgo
> And now my tongues use is to me no more
> Than an un-stringèd viol or a harp
> Or like a cunning **instrument** cased up
> Or being opened put into his hands
> That knows no touch to tune the **harmony**
> With in my mouth you have en-*jailed* my tongue
> **Doubly** portcullised with my teeth and lips [Attack! Inverted first foot]
> And dull un-feeling barren **ignorance**
> Is made my jailer to attend on me
> I am too old to fawn upon a nurse [Attack! Inverted first foot]
> Too far in years to be a pupil now
> **What** is thy sentence then but speech-less death [Attack! Inverted first
> foot]
> Which robs my tongue from breathing native breath? [1.3.154]

The first thing that is remarkable about this speech is the absence of a feminine ending. There are several inverted first feet, to give Mowbray the aggressive attacking energy his motivation requires. There is also one midline inversion, or shall we say that I would explore the possibility of such an inversion with the phrase "forth in the common air."

Far more interesting, because more subtle, are the pressure-cooker words that push against the restrictions of the heartbeat, as if there were hidden passions buried there. I have marked these in italics. All three are diphthongs, and all three are hugely important to the sub-text of the speech. The first, "sovereign," takes us directly to the heart of the conflict. Mowbray, out of loyalty to Richard, arranged for, or turned a blind eye to, the murder of Richard's enemy while that man was imprisoned under Mowbray's guard. Now that man's nephew has accused Mowbray of treason and challenged him to trial by combat. Richard, instead of protecting Mowbray, has abruptly stopped the duel and exiled his faithful follower for life. This is the sovereign whom Mowbray has served with such loyalty.

"Language" is what the speech is about. Specifically, Mowbray gives voice to a specific deprivation experienced by the exile that might, at first glance, seem trivial, but that can be seen to embody the essence of homesickness.

Mowbray will never be able to hear or speak English again. During Shakespeare's day, English was spoken nowhere except in England, so anyone travelling off the island had just this experience. But of course, the deeper significance of this word takes us back to Mowbray's story. He had a choice, when accused of murder. He could remain silent, never revealing Richard's hand in the murder, or he could confess all. Either way, he can vehemently avow his innocence of any thought or deed that could be deemed traitorous. Mowbray chooses not to name Richard, and for his silence he pays the price of permanent silence in exile.

"En-jailed" is an even more interesting word. Not surprisingly, it is an invention, the addition of the extra syllable used to push the iambic heartbeat forward, leaving the diphthong of "jail" to expand and put pressure on the rhythm. The fact that the murder took place in a prison setting, and also the fact, known to the audience, if not to the characters on stage, that Richard himself will be murdered while in a prison, draws out the power of this metaphor. Here we are being invited to imagine Mowbray's tongue jailed behind the double gates of the teeth and lips, attended by a terrible jailer named Ignorance. It is remarkable how well this mirrors Richard's situation in his last days. There is, of course, also a strong image of the other sorts of activities that went on in prisons, including torture which was often used to force someone to confess to just such a crime as Mowbray has chosen not to admit. How painful that, after all of his courage and endurance, he faces a lifelong imprisonment and torture as a result of his exile.

Although there are no feminine endings, there are three words that create that very special silence that I call "two for the price of one." These are three-syllable words that are easy to say, the "DUM de de" rhythm rolling off the tongue, but that sit against a heartbeat sounding "DUM de DUM." Two of these are, in addition, the last words of a line, and so are given additional weight and power by the rising line.

Mowbray has been an instrument in the hands of Richard. Because he participated in a soul-destroying act, for the sake of harmony in the kingdom, it is bitterly ironic to find his own life destroyed. He was, for Richard, a very cunning instrument. Now, Richard's clumsy handling of the entire accusation and trial-by-combat demonstrates that Richard's are the hands completely lacking in the touch required to keep England safe and at peace.

Another minor aspect of Mowbray's past, but one that emerges in the imagery of this speech: you might wonder why he brings up an infant's nurse and being a pupil, until you learn that he and Richard were raised together from infancy, living together in the nursery, studying together as young boys, and acquiring all of the skills of the nobility, including a mastery of language and a familiarity with music, together. That this is the man who should now pretend ignorance of the true circumstances of the murder, to say nothing of the shared history and past service and loyalty, suggests just how painful the key words must be to say.

In rehearsing this moment in the play, it is ideal if the people listening also become attuned to the subtle hints encoded into the rhythm of the verse. Everyone on stage, but most particularly Richard himself, can *hear* the subtle frisson under "sovereign," "language," and "jailed," and sense the pressure holding back the depth of feeling underneath each. They can also absorb the weight of significance, even if they don't know for sure why it should be so, in Mowbray's use of "instrument," "harmony," and "ignorance." They can feel the thrust of the attacking inversions, and they can listen to each line build toward the powerful final word, each pounding like a lash across their minds.

The capacity to take in messages from the code, as a character listening to others as well as an actor listening to the playwright, can greatly enrich the journey from page, through rehearsal, to performance, of any Shakespearean play.

TESTING THE CODE

As a further test of the capacity of the Iambic Code to convey the emotional heart of a speech, we can remove not only punctuation marks, but also information provided by the remainder of the play. Here are two speeches, the first spoken by a male character, the second by a woman, which will not be set into dramatic context until after we have attempted to read them "blind."

(a) Hadst thou but shook thy head or made a pause
When I spake darkly what I purposed
Or turned an eye of doubt upon my face
As bid me tell my tale in express words
Deep shame had struck me dumb made me break off
And those thy fears might have wrought fears in me
But thou didst understand me by my signs
And didst in signs again parley with sin
Yea without stop didst let thy heart consent
And consequently thy rude hand to act
The deed which both our tongues held vile to name
Out of my sight and never see me more
My nobles leave me and my state is braved
Even at my gates with ranks of foreign powers
Nay in the body of this fleshly land
This kingdom this confine of blood and breath
Hostility and civil tumult reigns
Between my conscience and my cousins death

(b) Grief fills the room up of my absent child
Lies in his bed walks up and down with me
Puts on his pretty looks repeats his words
Remembers me of all his gracious parts
Stuffs out his vacant garments with his form

Then have I reason to be fond of grief
Fare you well had you such a loss as I
I could give better comfort than you do
I will not keep this form upon my head
When there is such dis-order in my wit
O Lord my boy my Arthur my fair son
My life my joy my food my all the world
My widow comfort and my sorrows cure

Ideally, you will not recognize these speeches, not easily guess the play from which they are taken. With no idea who is speaking, to whom, under what conditions, and to what purpose, you are freed from any necessity to use these words to accomplish your responsibilities as an actor. Instead, you can let these words work on you, and see if the Iambic Code, in combination with the sounds and sense of the words, can guide you into the emotional heart of the action that is being shaped by these lines.

To accomplish this, you need to work your way line by line, always speaking aloud, always avoiding dropping the voice at the end of a line of poetry as if it were the end of the sentence, all the while sensing the heartbeat beneath the line even as your natural emphasis challenges that heartbeat. Let us see what is there to be discovered.

(a) Hadst thou but shook thy head or made a pause

This first line is made up of ten one-syllable words, what scholars like to call an Anglo Saxon line as it makes use of the simplest, most grounded words in the English language. It is also a question. The other speaker is of such an intimacy that "thou" is appropriate. The first word is not easy to say, but the rest of the line seems to flow without impediment. It is easy to resist cadencing, and I'm off to a strong start, even without knowing what I'm saying!

When I spake darkly what I purposed

I have to assume that the "purposed" is a three-syllable word, creating one of those end-line "easy to say, hard to experience" events, and therefore I need to flag that word. What is it that I purposed? Not surprisingly, my mind connects that dislocating rhythm with the word "darkly" earlier in the line.

Or turned an eye of doubt upon my face

I have to remind myself, already, that this is part of a longer thought, that this line is connected to the first, and is also made up of ten single-syllable words, an Anglo Saxon line. In fact, if I read these two Anglo Saxon lines back to back, I not only understand the connection, but feel it even before I know exactly what it means.

>   As bid me tell my tale in express words

The phrase "express words" leaps into my ear, as I find myself emphasizing a different syllable than the one we use today; clearly, this is an adjective rather than a verb. I still don't have a clue as to what my character is saying, but it's something about telling a tale. Does that have anything to do with dark purposes?

>   Deep shame had struck me dumb made me break off

If I have resisted the temptation to read through the entire speech quickly before beginning, this line will catch me in the gut. "Deep shame" is such a powerful phrase, and the line continues to a mid-line inversion, suggesting a surge of feeling at "made me break off." But this is also another of those Anglo Saxon lines, so I try reading the three of them as a unit, and discover an immediate connection with a strong need that my character is expressing to the listener. What's coming next. I have to fight the urge to end a sentence here, but the effort pays off as I continue.

>   And those thy fears might have wrought fears in me

Still another Anglo Saxon line, with a powerful midline inversion on "might have wrought" plus the double "fears," all of which combine to make me feel like things are heating up inside my character's head and heart.

>   But thou didst understand me by my signs

The "but" leaps out at me, and I realize I've reached a turning point in the speech. The "if only" of the first part is over, and now I'm describing what actually did happen. I can't say that I understand yet, which is painfully ironic because the line is about my listener(s) understanding me.

>   And didst in signs again parley with sin

I've now said "didst" twice in two lines, and it's another of those words that slows me down with all those consonants in one syllable. Also, if I say "parley" with the accent on the first syllable, which I think is correct, I get still another midline inversion. And no feminine endings yet. I'm not sure what label I'd put to the feeling this gives me, but there's definitely a feeling at work underneath the surface.

Yea without stop didst let thy heart consent

Another "didst," and in fact the entire line requires me to slow down to get all the sounds out.

And consequently thy rude hand to act

After all of the single syllable words, "consequently" stands out as the longest word yet spoken, and it has the unexpected effect of making what follows hugely significant. Since I have to slow down to negotiate all those consonants, I'm primed and ready to connect with the simple words as they come out of my mouth.

The deed which both our tongues held vile to name

This is giving me a very strong impression of some dark purpose or action, so terrible they don't even want to say it aloud. And here is another Anglo Saxon line, so I try once again to say the five of them back to back:

Hadst thou but shook thy head or made a pause
Or turned an eye of doubt upon my face
Deep shame had struck me dumb made me break off
And those thy fears might have wrought fears in me
The deed which both our tongues held vile to name

I can see that these lines hold the key to the emotional heart of the speech. Once again, I have to resist the temptation to drop my voice and end the thought. If I can manage to drive right through the line before, then I am rewarded with still another Anglo Saxon line emerging directly out of the one before:

Out of my sight and never see me more

I simply have to emphasize the first of these words, creating the surging energy of an inverted first foot. However, it feels so much like the end of a speech that I have to fight myself hard to build a connection between this line and the one that follows:

My nobles leave me and my state is braved

This seems like a change in topic, but I want to trust that there is a connection between where I began and where I now find myself. In a way, it's better that I don't know whether or not there is a connection provided by the plot. It's up to me to make a connection as I say the words.

> Even at my gates with ranks of foreign powers

The first words of this line have the extra syllable creating a nervous chill, perfectly suited to the image of invasion and seige. And here is my first feminine ending, an invitation to open my heart and mind to the vast capacity of that power of which I speak.

> Nay in the body of this fleshly land

Another inverted first foot, creating a surge of energy, and then some confusion. Words like "body" and "fleshly" seem entirely out of place in this situation, but of course I have to place them firmly into the heart of what is going on, even if my intellect rebels.

> This kingdom this confine of blood and breath

Now I'm starting to build a connection between the foreign powers at the gate and the spilling of blood, probably my own.

> Hostility and civil tumult reigns

The first word of this line is another of those "easy to say, hard to experience" words, and so I need to make a connection between whatever it was that I purposed, back in the second line, and the hostility I'm describing now.

> Between my conscience and my cousins death

Until I uncovered and read aloud this line, I'd assumed that the hostility and civil tumult was about the nobles leaving and the foreign power at the gates. Instead, it's about the war between my conscience and my cousin's death. The alliteration makes it impossible to avoid the significance of the pairing. I have something on my conscience, I put the blame for my shame on this other person who is listening; and in addition there are foreign troops at the gates and my nobles have deserted me. Am I a king? Was I responsible in some way for my cousin's death?

At this point, my mind is flooded with questions, all stemming from simple curiosity. But before I read the play, I reread the speech, now knowing where it is going, and let it work its magic upon me. To recreate my suspense, I will now move on to the second speech, before explaining the plot that affects both speakers.

> (b) Grief fills the room up of my absent child

I say these words aloud, and have an immediate response of empathy. Only then do I realize that I have no idea how the line should scan. At the same time, I discover that I want to say "fills up" rather than "fills the room up" and I realize that I have been sloppy in my speaking of the words. I have superimposed a modern rhythm onto the lines, which in fact fall into a very interesting pattern, with an inverted first foot followed by a midline inversion, so that the line reads:

GRIEF fills the room UP of my absent child

It is a strange and disturbing rhythm, and sets me off balance, quite unlike the strong first line of the former speech.

Lies in his bed walks up and down with me

This line works on my emotions with equal power, and the inverted first foot gives me a powerful surge of energy. I feel on firmer footing now.

Puts on his pretty looks repeats his words

I have to say this line twice, because my mouth wants to use "puts" as a springboard to another word, but I realize almost immediately that this is yet another inverted first foot. The alliteration created by "puts," "pretty," and "repeats" is striking.

Remembers me of all his gracious parts

Here "gracious" grabs my attention as I say it aloud. I suspect that the extra half-syllable would have been more pronounced then than now, and so I open myself to this as a possible pressure cooker word. What does "gracious" mean to my character? I don't know yet, but it must be connected with all of the other ideas about grace, both blessed by God and attractive to the general public.

Stuffs out his vacant garments with his form

Another inverted first foot, but a very strange verb, especially after something as beautiful as "gracious." If his room is empty and his clothes are vacant, my guess is that this child is no longer living.

Then have I reason to be fond of grief

"Then" marks a shift, from the first five lines describing the situation to something else. I feel lost, having devoured each line as a self-contained unit, so I go back to the top and read until this point, and it comes much clearer. Grief is keeping me company, even wearing his clothes, so of course I'm feeling quite fond of grief. To be honest I have no idea if this line should have an inverted first foot or not, so I find myself saying the first four words with almost equal weight, which also works for the transition I sense is happening with this line.

Fare you well had you such a loss as I

For the first time I get a clear sense of talking to someone, and it's at the moment I leave, though I don't because I keep talking. This is one of those Anglo Saxon lines, and once again I really don't know which word to emphasize after "fare you well," so I say them with almost equal weight, and I like the sensation of punching out almost every word.

I could give better comfort than you do

There seems to be a pattern in my longing to say a group of words with equal weight, because it happens again with this line. I don't like emphasizing the pronoun, but to hit "could" also sounds wrong. Giving almost equal weight to "I could give" feels just right.

I will not keep this form upon my head

Now I know it's a pattern, because I have another one here. There seems to be such emotional power in minimizing the contrast between stressed and unstressed words.

When there is such dis-order in my wit

This line flows more easily into the expected heartbeat, and it also contains an important clue about what my character is experiencing, namely, "disorder in my wit." I feel I must stop and read the entire speech aloud to this point, trying to make a connection between the sensation of saying these words and feeling disorder. It seems natural to hold onto the words more tightly than usual, trying to keep order, to fight back the disorder that floods my mind. The emotions are almost too powerful, perhaps because of my intensely personal connection with the loss of a child.

O Lord my boy my Arthur my fair son

What a strange experience, to read the speech and savor the rhythms, to feel the tension between the rhythms of the language and the disorder, and then

If this were not the case, intelligent characters would not be nearly as exciting to watch in the theatre.

Of course the appeal to logic is just one of three, and it is the appeal to the feelings of the listener that often wins the day in oratory and the theatre. Rhetoric is much more the art of the public presentation of the private feeling than we might think, if we associate it only with the cool, calm, intellectualism of lawyers and university professors. Here are a few of the rhetorical devices that make overt the emotional basis of rhetoric. Never think that the pure expression of intense feeling has no place in this art:

* * *

Exuscitatio: expression of deep feeling in order to stir listeners to feel the same.

Come weep with me, past hope, past cure, past help. [*R&J* 4.1.45]

* * *

Be prepared for some lengthy "sob stories," also part and parcel of oratory:

* * *

Anamnesis: a recital of past events, usually woeful.

I had an Edward, till a Richard killed him:
I had a Harry, till a Richard killed him:
Thou hadst an Edward, till a Richard killed him:
Thou hadst a Richard, till a Richard killed him. [*RIII* 4.4.39]

* * *

There is a heightened version of this strategy, called the *threnos*, which sits on the boundary between speech and song. These are the lamentations that mark moments of extreme grief. Try saying these words aloud, letting a sing-song speech pattern develop, and you have a taste of threnody. Perhaps then you can imagine a great oratory moving from rational thought into these sounds.

O woe, O woeful, woeful, woeful day,
Most lamentable day, most woeful day,
That ever, ever, I did yet behold.
O day, O day, O day, O hateful day,
Never was seen so black a day as this:
O woeful day, O woeful day. [*R&J* 4.5.49]

If you just look at these words on the page, you might be tempted to giggle at the repetition of such simple words. That gives you an idea of the risks an orator would take when moving into threnody. Without the full force of the almost sung sounds, yes, it is a bit silly. But the "oh" sound in "woe" and the "ay" sound in "hateful" and "day" are like primal moans of grief, if they emerge from that deep cavity in the mouth and soul.

Some emotional strategies had very specific functions, formulated in the earliest Athenian courtrooms:

* * *

Mempsis: complaint against injuries and craving for redress.

> O the blood is spilled
> Of my dear kinsman. Prince as thou art true,
> For blood of ours, shed blood of Montague.
> [*R&J* 3.1.153]

* * *

On occasion the speaker would be moved to address God himself:

* * *

Optatio: emotionally expressed wish or prayer.

> Heavenly Powers, restore him. [*Hamlet* 3.1.141]

* * *

Some of the most powerful rhetorical strategies are designed to arouse intense reactions in listeners:

* * *

Epiplexis: asking questions to chide or reprehend.

> Have you eyes?
> Could you on this fair Mountain leave to feed,
> And batten on this Moor? ha? Have you eyes? [*Hamlet* 3.4.65]

* * *

Other manipulations are more subtle, and structural in nature:

* * *

Epanorthosis: statement followed by a restatement to increase power.

> Such an Act
> That blurs the grace and blush of Modesty,
> Calls Virtue Hypocrite, takes off the Rose
> From the fair forehead of an innocent love,
> And sets a blister there. Makes marriage vows
> As false as Dicers Oaths. Oh such a deed,
> As from the body of Contraction plucks
> The very soul, and sweet Religion makes
> A rhapsody of words. Heavens face does glow,
> Yea this solidity and compound mass,

With tristfull visage as against the doom,
Is thought-sick at the act. [*Hamlet* 3.4.40]

* * *

We can see such a rhetorical figure combines *topoi*, inductive reasoning, and an appeal to the emotions. In the search for all of the different ways of knowing something, one discovers the many different ways of giving voice to what we feel, and then it is an easy and natural development, provided you love language and take the time to let the rush of words come out, to find yourself partaking of rhetorical devices like epanorthosis.

After the *confirmatio* comes the *confutatio*, although, as we can imagine, speakers were not obliged to keep them strictly separate. While confirmatio built up the proof in support of one's own point of view, *confutatio* attacked the opposition as powerfully as possible.

* * *

Apophasis: reject all alternatives but one.

> To eject him hence
> Were but our danger, and to keep him here
> Our certain death: therefore it is decreed,
> He dies tonight. [*Coriolanus* 3.1.286]

* * *

That is the obvious way to go about demolishing an opponent's argument, but rhetoric codified other, more subtle demolitions:

* * *

Metastasis: turning back an objection against the one who made it.

Anne: No Beast so fierce, but knows some touch of pity.

Richard: But I know none, and therefore am no Beast. [*RIII* 1.2.70]

* * *

Or the ever-powerful attack on hypocrisy:

* * *

Inter Se Pugnantia: points out the discrepancy between theory and practice.

> But good my Brother
> Do not as some ungracious Pastors do,
> Show me the steep and thorny way to heaven;
> Whiles like a puffed and reckless Libertine
> Himself, the Primrose path of dalliance treads,
> And reaks not his own rede. [*Hamlet* 1.3.46]

* * *

Modern debaters like to predict dire outcomes if the opponent's recommen-
dations are followed. Rhetoric offered a specific threat:

* * *

Cataplexis: threats of plague or punishment.

> For you fair Hermia, look you arm your self,
> To fit your fancies to your Fathers will;
> Or else the Law of Athens yields you up
> (Which by no means we may extenuate)
> To death, or to a vow of single life. [*Dream* 1.1.117]

* * *

And also a more general prediction:

* * *

Paraenesis: warning of impending evil.

> What will ensue hereof, there's none can tell.
> But by bad courses may be understood,
> That their events can never fall out good. [*RII* 2.1.212]

* * *

Because the best defense is a good offense, rhetoric gave orators many strategies for attaching anyone who held opposing views:

* * *

Antirrhesis: rejection of opponent's argument on basis of error or wickedness.

> Fouler than heart can think thee,
> Thou canst make no excuse current,
> But to hang thy self. [*RIII* 1.2.83]

* * *

Or, if this strategy were inappropriate:

* * *

**Diasyrmus: make opponent's argument ridiculous through comparison with the
ridiculous.**

> You have her father's love, Demetrius:
> Let me have Hermia's: do you marry him. [*Dream* 1.1.93]

* * *

There were also great stylistic tricks that allowed the speaker a variety of "put downs."

* * *

Restrictio: general statement with one exception.

> But it is certain I am loved of all ladies, only you excepted. [*Much Ado* 1.1.124]

* * *

Or this favorite, which allows the speaker to appear to agree, until the other shoe drops:

* * *

Dirimens Copulatio: a statement, then an addition that balances or outweighs.

> I would I could find in my heart that I had not a hard heart, for truly I love none. [*Much Ado* 1.1.126]

* * *

Sarcasm, which tends to be a fall-back position for most of us when we're in the heat of an intense debate about something and losing, was also a rhetorical strategy, but in its most compelling form it was hardly a fall-back, linked as it was to a brilliant sense not only of language and structure but also of the ironic:

* * *

Antiphrasis: irony contained in a single word.

> Seems Madam? Nay, it is: I know not Seems. [*Hamlet* 1.2.76]

* * *

Both Mark Anthony and Iago drive home the power of this device with their repeated ironic use of the words "honourable" and "honest," respectively. Here is Mark Anthony addressing the Roman people at Caesar's funeral:

> Here, under leave of Brutus, and the rest
> (For Brutus is an Honourable man,
> So are they all; all Honourable men)
> Come I to speak in Caesars Funeral.
> He was my Friend, faithful, and just to me;
> But Brutus says, he was Ambitious,
> And Brutus is an Honourable man.
> He hath brought many Captives home to Rome,
> Whose Ransoms, did the general Coffers fill:
> Did this in Caesar seem Ambitious?
> When that the poor have cried, Caesar hath wept:
> Ambition should be made of sterner stuff,

Yet Brutus says, he was Ambitious:
And Brutus is an Honourable man.
You all did see, that on the Lupercal,
I thrice presented him a Kingly Crown,
Which he did thrice refuse. Was this Ambition?
Yet Brutus says, he was Ambitious:
And sure he is an Honourable man. [*JC* 3.2.81]

And here is Iago planting the seeds of murderous jealousy in Othello's mind:

Iago: My Noble Lord.

Othello: What dost thou say, Iago?

Iago: Did Michael Cassio
When he wooed my Lady, know of your love?

Othello: He did, from first to last:
Why dost thou ask?

Iago: But for a satisfaction of my Thought,
No further harm.

Othello: Why of thy thought, Iago?

Iago: I did not think he had been acquainted with her.

Othello: O yes, and went between us very oft.

Iago: Indeed?

Othello: Indeed? I indeed. Discernst thou ought in that?
Is he not honest?

Iago: Honest, my Lord?

Othello: Honest? I, Honest.

Iago: My Lord, for ought I know.

Othello: What dost thou think?

Iago: Think, my Lord?

Othello: Think, my Lord? Alas, thou echo'st me;
As if there were some Monster in thy thought
Too hideous to be shown. Thou dost mean something:
I heard thee say even now, thou lik'st not that,
When Cassio left my wife. What didst not like?
And when I told thee, he was of my Counsel,
Of my whole course of wooing; thou cried'st, Indeede?
And didst contract, and purse thy brow together,
As if thou then hadst shut up in thy Brain
Some horrible Conceit. If thou dost love me,
Show me thy thought. [3.3.93]

Another favored use of irony gave permission, on the surface, to the opposite of what should and could and probably would ever occur.

* * *

Epitrope: ironical permission.

> Ay, do, persever, counterfeit sad looks,
> Make mouths upon me when I turn my back,
> Wink each at other, hold the sweet jest up. [*Dream* 3.2.237]

* * *

If all else failed, rhetoric allowed the speaker to get quite nasty, which comes as a complete surprise to those of us who associate rhetoric with famous leaders. Some of Shakespeare's characters excel at the witty put-down, which turns out to be a well-codified rhetorical strategy:

* * *

Meiosis: using descriptive language to belittle.

> Get you gone you dwarf,
> You minimus, of hindring knot-grass made,
> You bead, you acorn. [*Dream* 3.2.328]

* * *

If that failed, the speaker could raise the stakes:

* * *

Mycterismus: scornful mocking.

> I would I had your bond: for I perceive
> A weak bond holds you, I'll not trust your word. [*Dream* 3.2.267]

* * *

An effective strategy could encompass a short burst of outright invective:

* * *

Bdelygmia: short, powerful expression of hatred or disgust.

> Have done thy Charm, you hateful withered Hag. [*RIII* 1.3.214]

* * *

And, if all else failed, one could resort to extremes and still work within the structured strategies of rhetoric:

* * *

Ara: cursing.

> Here thou incestuous, murd'rous, damned Dane,
> Drink off this Potion. [*Hamlet* 5.2.325]

* * *

Rhetoric, however, was also capable of great subtlety:

* * *

Paralipsis: while pretending to pass over the matter, emphasize it.

> More bitterly could I expostulate,
> Save that for reverence to some alive,
> I give a sparing limit to my Tongue.
> [*RIII* 3.7.191]

* * *

Some of the rhetorical strategies were so subtle, the listener could not figure out the strategy until the speaker was well under way.

* * *

Prosapodosis: reject no alternatives; support each with a reason.

> As I am man,
> My state is desperate for my masters love:
> As I am woman (now alas the day)
> What thriftless sighs shall poor Olivia breathe?
> O time, thou must untangle this, not I,
> It is too hard a knot for me t'untie. [*12th Night* 2.2.36]

* * *

The result of all of this was variety, ingenuity, and pleasure for the speaker and the listeners.

Remember that we began this long list of rhetorical devices as part of an exercise! Now to return to the use of the cards for the exploration of rhetoric. Make up a number of cards, drawing from a variety of types of strategies. Do not feel that you have to understand the figure intellectually, and you are under no obligation to memorize the fancy labels. The goal of the first encounter is not to imitate Shakespeare's style, but to use the rhetorical strategy to provide a structure for modern thought and modern language. This is the way to allow a personal and contemporary ownership of these linguistic shapes. There is a difference in the way things are said and felt if the speaker "owns" not only the individual words but also the patterns of sound and meaning that occur over and over in the plays.

Here is how I use these cards with a medium-sized group. Everyone is dealt two or three cards. Perhaps the participants have some time to find additional examples on their own, from the plays they know well. Perhaps my examples give them a place to start, which is simply saying the excerpt aloud several times, to accustom the lips and tongue and breath to the shape of the figure.

I set a discussion topic, framed in such a way as to give the participants the feeling that they must contribute to the presentation of an argument, in an effort to persuade someone to change a strongly held opinion. For example, I suggested that a group of recently graduated theatre students set out to persuade me, as representative of all loving, concerned, non–theatre-loving parents, that acting was indeed a worthwhile career. Then, we sit in a circle and each person is required to contribute to the discussion, shaping some sort of comment as suggested by the cards in hand. Part of the challenge is to maintain a connection with the previous speaker. Sometimes I force the discussion to travel around the circle; other times I allow students to offer a comment when they spot a connection they can make, given the cards they hold. Each speaker is required to make a comment on the topic, using the rhetorical device on one of her cards. After making her comment, she reads the device name and example aloud, so that we can compare the imitation with the example.

We have great fun with the cards, which can be used to summon a game-playing energy. Participants flip down their cards as they find a way to use them well, and sometimes they are challenged and their cards are retrieved to be read aloud, and they are forced to come up with a better-crafted statement in keeping with the figure on the card. Teams can be formed to heighten the competitive spirit, with everyone still arguing for the same point of view, but challenging the other side to come up with better and better uses of the figures.

We usually have a collection of smokers and nonsmokers, and there are usually rules about where smoking can occur, so I can count on an interesting discussion about the rights of smokers versus the rights of nonsmokers. Here is what someone might say if he had the card labelled "Epanorthosis: statement followed by a restatement to increase power":

I find the assumptions made by smokers, that it's their right and privilege to pollute the air I breathe, deeply disturbing. In fact, I consider it something beyond simple rudeness and inconsideration. It's a sort of passive aggression, a delayed murder. Watching them smoking, makes me aware how little they care for anyone but themselves. To be honest, it enrages me.

The next speaker, who has the card labelled "Hypothetical proposition: if X occurs, then Y will follow," might respond:

I think you're making a mistake to connect the distant and uncertain side-effect of second hand smoke with the intention of a smoker. If someone smokes, then what is most likely going to happen, if anyone is damaged by it, is that the smoker himself will pay the price for his addiction. If someone is addicted, then all sorts of terrible things come from that. If we see a drunk on the street, we think, "What a loser," but if we learn a bit more about alcoholism, we might change our tune, and try to help that person overcome his addiction. If we know someone hooked on heroin, then we try to get them treatment. Did you know that nicotine is more addictive than heroin?

Here we see a speaker being inspired by the rhetorical shape offered by the card, and following the train of thought, blending in other rhetorical strategies such as "Diaeresis: division of subject into all of its specific kinds of variations," in the discussion of different kinds of addiction, or "comprobatio: commending the goodness of the listeners," in ascribing to the others in the group the humane response to alcoholics and drug addicts. There is even a hint of "Anthypophora: asking a question of oneself and then answering it," or "Epiplexis: asking questions to chide or reprehend."

No one in the group would spot the layering of rhetorical strategies, much less ascribe to them a Greek label, even after several rounds with the cards. What does happen, however, is that someone holding the card for Daieresis, Comprobatio, Anthypophora, or Epipliexis, who was at that moment trying to formulate a contribution using that card, suddenly hears the rhetorical shape in the speaker's comments, and might even burst out, "Hey, you stole my strategy!"

For the next round of the game, we might set up teams for a more formal debate, and allow any member of one team to respond to the previous point. This works well when team members become more excited about the topic, have something very important to say, and then try to make use of the rhetorical device to deliver the argument powerfully. But what happens equally often is that the speaker sits looking at her cards, knowing she needs to contribute to her team's part of the debate, and a thought crystalizes in her mind *because of* the rhetorical device on one of her cards.

This is the important discovery: that the familiar shape allows a thought to form, that the shapes are baskets into which otherwise amorphous sensations can flow and be conveyed, that the language systems are required for conscious awareness of concepts and attitudes. What participants report is that the cards actually serve to inspire thoughts they could make, particularly after the first five or six speakers have dealt with all of the primary arguments that leap immediately to mind. The card calls forth a comment because of the shape that comment might take and needs to take. This is a great surprise to many: we are so used to the assumption that we perceive something, then we get a thought, then we look for the language to express that thought. It is perhaps frightening to some that the form actually shapes what we think, that if we did not have the words and the linguistic shapes we would not only be unable to say certain things, we would be unable to think them.

It is also readily discovered, during even the first use of the card game, that rhetorical devices allow for powerful language acts. The listeners respond with enthusiasm when the speaker makes effective use of a shape, laughing at a witty rejoinder, applauding an innovative imitation, admiring the success of the rhetorical strategy, even if disagreeing with the perspective offered.

When the rhetoric cards are used during a more serious discussion, it is easy to see how a passionate commitment to a concept of the heartfelt expression of a personal experience can be both natural and beautiful. Artful language does not have to be artificial.

Once the rhetorical devices have acquired some credibility with the group, it is time to place the individual cards into the larger context of a system of language. Again, as with the Latin labels, this information is not what is being learned. Rather, the actors are placing their newfound excitement about this type of speaking alongside an awareness of a vast, complex, flexible, and variable system. Ideally, their enthusiasm for the skillful use of language will grow, and they will bring that Elizabethan-like thrill to their speaking of Shakespeare.

Throughout these exercises and games, the students are encouraged to use their own words to reflect their own thoughts. All that is "foreign" is the structure, which comes to them from rhetoric. Very soon, however, almost every card has been "solved" in that someone in the group has used the structure to express, spontaneously and effectively, what is clearly a deeply felt, contemporary attitude, and we have seen how modern the structure can be. Each time the cards are dealt, participants turn back cards they've already explored, and soon they have had a go at a significant percentage of the cards themselves, while hearing others tackle the same cards they've tried.

When the group is ready to try a debate, I bring out a second set of cards, so that those speaking for and against the proposition have the same rhetorical resources upon which to draw. I make use of the traditional rules of debate, including strict time keeping, but I never judge the outcome of the debate. Instead, we talk about the use of rhetoric and the sensations of the speakers: emotional, intellectual, and moral. The stronger the opinions, the better, when settling on the topic. When a young actor, in the heat of a debate on a contemporary issue, speaking spontaneously and from the heart, falls unconsciously into a beautiful and strikingly effective rhetorical strategy, everyone in the room is thrilled by the sensation of having experienced the power of language that radiates within the plays of Shakespeare.

TOPOI

> It is no matter how witty, so it be eloquent, and full of invention.
> Sir Toby Belch [*12th Night* 3.2.43]

Of course all the imitation in the world would be worth nothing if there was nothing of merit happening in the brain of the speaker. The schoolmaster used the exercises of *topoi* to fill up the brains of the students with a wealth of ideas upon which to draw spontaneously. Once the topic was assigned, the students explored "topics" of the issue. These topics were actually very specific linguistic tricks that used the structure of language to establish the groundwork from which rhetorical arguments could be created. What we see, more than anything else, is the connection between *topoi* and the exploding English vocabulary. More and more words were being invented to name things. *Inventio* was the name given to this aspect of the art of rhetoric.

When we look at the sixteen *topoi* suggested by Cicero, we see instantly the source of so many of Shakespeare's tricks of language. This gives us a wonderful jolt of recognition, but remains an intellectual exercise, of little use to our acting, unless we can step into the mind-set that corresponds to this linguistic conditioning.

If we take the central impulse of speaking to contain (along with other goals) the desire to communicate ("How can I make you understand? Perhaps if I use these words, then you'll see this thing the way I do?"), then we can see how each of these linguistic tricks serves this primary goal. "How can you know what it is I'm seeing/thinking/feeling unless I define it for you, vividly and in a way that has you seeing/thinking/feeling as I do?" Below, I've tried to suggest the impulse that sits at the heart of each *topoi.*

Definition: If I can define this thing perfectly, then I can change the way you see it.

Division: If I list all of the components of this thing, then you will never see it the same way again.

Naming: If I name it, then I own it somehow, and by having you use the same name, then I tie you to my "take" on this thing, through the name itself.

Conjugates: If I can trace a link between words that have the same root, I can expand your awareness of the power of this thing.

Genus: If I can link this thing to the larger category in which it sits, I can persuade you of the breadth of its significance.

Species: If I can identify all of the subcategories that come under the umbrella of this thing, then I can persuade you of the density of its significance.

Similarity: If I name all of the things that share attributes with this thing, then I create so many comparisons that you will come to know it as richly and deeply as I do, even if you've never experienced it, because I will find similarities with things you have experienced.

Difference: If I name all the ways it is different from what you might expect, or what you already know, then you will see just what a strange and remarkable thing this is.

Contraries: If I name all of the things it is not, then you will not be able to avoid seeing what it is by pretending it is something it is not.

Adjuncts: If I can clarify those associated values that are essential, and those that are superficial or coincidental, then you will never mistake this thing for something else and this thing will not be able to hide.

Consequents: If I name all of the things that will follow from this thing, then you will be aware of the immense impact of this thing, as I am.

Antecedents: If I name all of the things that were necessary to allow this particular thing to be, then you will be aware of the huge significance of this thing, as I am.

Incompatibilities: If I name all of the things that cannot coexist with this thing, then you will see how unique it is.

Causes: If I name with absolute certainty what has caused this thing, then we will know it undeniably, if retroactively.

Effects: If I name with absolute certainty everything that will result from this thing, then we will know it undeniably through time.

Comparisons with things greater, less, or equal: If I demonstrate exactly where it sits on as many scales of value as possible, you will know the true worth of this thing.

As soon as we have a sense of how these *topoi* might work, we begin to spot the trademark word patterns that they produce.

I'm sure you've all spotted the list making that Shakespeare seems to love. So often it doesn't seem enough to make a single comparison, or give a single definition, or give an example of one of the consequences of an action. No, the speaker has to give a huge, long list. But this list making was a natural by-product of the school exercise of *topoi*, where the length of the list demonstrated the excellence of the *inventio*.

Here is Romeo, perhaps just out of the classroom himself, sharing a small portion of an *inventio* on the theme of love.

> Love, is a smoke raised with the fume of sighs,
> Being purged, a fire sparkling in Lovers eyes,
> Being vexed, a Sea nourished with loving tears,
> What is it else? a madness, most discreet,
> A choking gall, and a preserving sweet. [1.1.190]

Why does Romeo go on at such length? Because he is struggling to convince his cousin Benvolio, whom he suspects of mocking him in his lovesick despair, that what he feels is, in fact, true love, and what he feels demonstrates the true nature of love. One comparison is not enough to persuade, to move Benvolio to see the situation as Romeo does. In fact, we get the sense that Romeo could go on in this vein indefinitely. At this point in the scene he already has been talking about the nature of love virtually nonstop since he entered. He's so obsessed that he took in the evidence of the brawl that opens the play, and immediately compared it to the violent nature of the love he feels. The two men continue to discuss love for the rest of the scene, generally and specifically as Romeo reveals his plight with the serenely unresponsive Rosaline, and then they wander off. When they return in scene 3, they're still debating the true nature of love!

The Hunt

I developed the following exercise just before Easter one year, and gave the winning team a basket of Easter eggs. The metaphor of the Easter egg hunt served us well, because the point of the activity is not to set about on some sort of boring homework assignment, but to go back to the plays eager to find the little language gems to share with others. One of the actors also compared this exercise to a scavenger hunt, which works just as well.

Each team is given the scavenger list and is required to fill in an example for each device. The first time we did this, the teams promptly divided up the list, which unfortunately left some team members with easy jobs and others with hard ones. So I added a rule: first everyone on the team took the entire list, went to a few favorite speeches or scenes, and recorded as many examples as they could find. Then the team regrouped and checked off every device for which at least one of them had an example. Then they divided the more difficult examples, and set out to look for specific rhetorical strategies.

Almost immediately the actors discovered that a single quotation could be used as an example for several rhetorical devices. Also, the teams learned that some devices are so common in Shakespeare's plays that every member of the team could think of several examples without going to the plays. Other devices have to be hunted and, when found, marvelled at. Was this the attitude of the audience of first listeners? Rare and marvellous devices suggest rare and marvellous thoughts and feelings. Here is the form we used for scoring the results of the hunt:

I. **Schemes of Grammar**
   A. Schemes of Construction
      1. Hyperbaton: Variations on Ordinary Order for Emphasis
         * **anastrophe**: unusual word order
         * **hysteron proteron**: what occurs later is stated first
         * **hypallage**: subject/verb/predicate are distorted or adverb/adjective/modifying phrases are inserted unexpectedly
         * **parenthesis**: condenses and juxtaposes ideas with sudden striking effect
         * **apposition**: additional modifying phrases that briefly interrupt the flow of the sentence
      2. Schemes of Omission for Compression and Emotional Power
         * **ellipsis**: omission of a word easily understood
         * **zeugma**: one verb serves several clauses
         * **syllepsis**: same as zeugma but if verb were to be repeated its form would have to change
         * **diazeugma**: one subject, many verbs
         * [vs. **hypozeuxis**: every phrase is a complete sentence, with repetition of the subject each time]
         * **brachylogia**: conjunctions left out between words
         * **asyndeton**: conjunctions left out between clauses
         * [vs. **polysyndeton**: every conjunction in place]

3. Schemes of Exchange: Purposeful Errors
   - **enallage**: substitution of incorrect verb form, pronoun, singular/plural, etc.
   - **hendiadys**: two nouns substituted for noun & modifier for increased emphasis
   - **Graecismus**: the confusion of two constructions, as in mixed metaphors
   - **anthimeria**: substitution of one part of speech for another (nouns as verbs, adjectives as nouns, etc.)
4. Errors Made by the Ignorant (Comedy)
   - **solecismus**: grammatical errors (enallage in ignorance)
   - **pleonasmus**: needless telling of what is already known
   - **homiologia**: tedious repetition
   - **periergia**: working too hard to appear elegant when discussing the trivial
   - **bomphioilogia**: bombast (presenting modest achievements as great glories)
   - **cacozelia**: affected vocabulary, especially using Latin (incorrectly); malapropism: using the wrong word, sometimes with more truth than the speaker realizes (acyron: mistakenly using a crude word or the exact opposite to what is intended)

B. Figures of Repetition
   - **climax**: anadiplosis carried on for several clauses
   - **polyptoton**: repetition of words sharing the same root
   - **diaphora**: use of word to name a thing and then to describe it
   - **ploce**: multiple repetition of a word
   - **diacope**: repeating word with only one or two words intervening
   - **epizeuxis**: repeating word with nothing intervening
   - **paroemion**: repetition of sounds, as in alliteration: repeated sound at beginning of words in phrase
   - **anaphora**: beginning series of clauses with same word
   - **epistrophe**: ending series of clauses with same word
   - **symploce**: anaphora and epistrophe combined
   - **epanalepsis**: same word at end as at beginning of phrase
   - **antimetabole**: second phrase begins with what ended first phrase, and ends with what began first phrase
   - **anadiplosis**: repetition of last word of previous clause to begin next clause

II. Topics of Invention

A. Inartificial Argument or Testimony: irrefutable witnesses, often supernatural in the form of oracles, dreams, seers, witches, natural events (storms, astrological portents)

- **orcos**: oath affirming that one speaks the truth
- **euche**: vow to keep a promise
- **eustathia**: pledge of constancy
- **asphalia**: offer of surety for another
- **euphemismus**: prediction of optimistic outcome
- **paraenesis**: warning of evil outcome
- **ominatio**: prediction of terrible outcome
- **apodixis**: the experience of many (resulting in proverbs or adages: the wisdom of generations; can be reshaped for fresh impact)
- **martyria**: one's own experience (resulting in apothegms or maxims: the wisdom of one)
- **diatyposis**: good advice in the form of rules and precepts
- **apomnemonysis**: drawing upon the authority of approved authors
- **epicrisis**: quotation from expert supplemented by personal opinion
- **chria**: short example taken from life of famous person

B. Artificial Argument (developed by investigation, i.e., "art")

- **definition**: explaining nature or essence of subject; stating origins; comparing with other things to establish differences or essential properties of the subject; contrasting shadow and substance of the subject
- **systrophe**: listing many definitions of one thing

C. Division: Genus & Species, Whole & Parts

- **diaeresis**: list of all the subcategories of the subject, with brief description of each
- **partitio**: dividing a whole subject into its parts
- **eutrepismus**: speaker numbers and orders all of the parts of the whole subject
- **synecdoche**: substitution of part for whole or whole for part
- **enumeratio**: dividing subject into various possible outcomes (various effects of the cause, various consequences of the action)
- **restrictio**: make a general statement and then provide exception
- **prolepsis**: amplify general statement by dividing it into many parts
- **epanodos**: prolepsis with repetition of general statement before each statement of a part
- **synathroesmus**: list of details culminating in general statement
- **synathroesmus** (congeries): list of details without general statement
- **epiphonema**: list of details culminating in general statement in form of epigram

- **disjunctive proposition**: state alternative outcomes/choices/points of view arising out of single situation

D. A Subject and Its Essential Attributes (observable/defining characteristics)

   - **peristasis**: list of circumstances affecting person or thing
   - **encomium**: praise of all attributes
   - **taxis**: linking each subject with its proper attributes
   - **epitheton**: adding a new attribute (or two in compound form)
   - **metonymy**: substitution of subject for attribute or attribute for subject
   - **antonomasia**: substitute descriptive phrase for proper name or name for attribute associated with person/place
   - **periphrasis**: use of descriptive phrase for common word
   - **enargia**: lively description for a detailed representation of reality/fantasy
   - **prosopopoeia**: attribution of human qualities to animals or objects
   - **characterismus**: description of body or mind of subject
   - **ethopoeia**: description of abilities, manners, affections of the subject
   - **mimesis**: immitation of subject's way of speaking or gesturing
   - **dialogismus**: framing dialogue suitable to the character of subject
   - **pragmatographia**: vivid description of action or event
   - **chronographia**: a description of the times
   - **topographia**: description of a place
   - **topothesia**: description of imaginary place

E. Contraries and Contradictories: merging of incompatibles and contrasting terms to capture the dramatic conflict (internal or external) and thematic complexity

   - **litotes**: identify subject by denial of contradictory attribute, often with negative terms (not/never) or privative terms (created with addition of suffix "-less")
   - **inter se pugnantia**: pointing out difference between theory & practice
   - **antiphrasis**: irony in a single word (said in a way that suggests an opposite meaning)
   - **paralipsis**: pretending to pass over the matter but actually making much of it
   - **epitrope**: ironical permission, given to someone to do the opposite of what is most desirable
   - **synoeciosis**: blending of incompatible contraries
   - **paradox**: apparent self-contradiction which is nonetheless true *or* a view contrary to the opinion generally held to be true
   - **antithesis**: setting up contraries in opposition

- **syncrisis**: comparing contrary things in contrasting clauses
- **antanagoge**: balancing a favorable attribute with an unfavorable one

F. Similarity and Dissimilarity

- **homoeosis**: any figure that points out similarity
- **icon**: suggests a similarity through a striking image
- **parabola**: suggests a moral or mystical similarity
- **paradigma**: judging the present by finding a similarity with the past
- **fable**: suggesting a complex pattern of similarity through telling a fantastical story
- **onomatopoeia**: suggesting similarity between something and the sounds made to describe it
- **simile**: suggesting a direct comparison using the word "like" or "as"
- **metaphor**: suggesting a direct comparison using the verb "to be"
- **allegory**: metaphor continues through an entire speech
- **catachresis**: implied metaphor through the use of one word usually applied to a specific thing in direct application to something quite different, in a way that draws attention to similarities

G. Comparison: Greater, Equal, Less

- **auxesis**: advancing from less to greater by arranging words or clauses into a sequence of increasing force, intensity, magnitude
- **hyperbole**: suggesting hugely greater magnitude in comparison
- **meiosis**: belittling magnitude of subject
- **paradiastole**: describing in more flattering terms in order to sooth or win favor
- **charientismus**: answering threat with smooth and appeasing mockery
- **catacosmesis**: ordering words from the greatest to the least in dignity
- **epanorthosis**: amend one's first statement by altering it into something stronger
- **dirimens copulatio**: adding a point to balance or outweigh what has already been stated
- **emphasis**: identifying the essence of the subject under discussion
- **synonymia**: restating the same idea in many words to increase the force of delivery
- **exergasia**: repeat the same thought in many different figures
- **paradiegesis**: beginning a speech with a little story
- **digression**: breaking off to tell a little story (and returning with strong effect to the main argument)

H. Cause and Effect, Antecedent and Consequent

- **metonymy**: substituting cause for effect or effect for cause
- **metalepsis**: suggests that present situation is the result of a remote cause

- **hypothetical proposition**: if x occurs, then y will follow, although this has not yet occurred
- **antisagoge**: statement of a precept with the promise of a reward or a punishment if violated

I. Notation (naming things with accuracy) and Conjugates (words having same root)

- **polyptoton**: repetition of words sharing the same root
- **etymology**: suggesting essence by referring to the source of its name (suggesting contrast or similarity between name and essence)
- **antanaclasis**: in repeating word the meaning shifts
- **syllepsis**: word has two meanings simultaneously and is not repeated
- **asteismus**: in dialog, the word is tossed back with an unexpected meaning
- **distinction**: removing ambiguities by stating various meanings of one word
- **enigma**: deliberately obscure use of words with more than one meaning
- **noema**: obscure and subtle speech used for veiled insult, threat, complaint
- **schematismus**: circuitous speech deliberately chosen to avoid, mislead, defuse tension

III. Logos: Argumentation

A. Syllogistic Reasoning: premises are true & conclusions are valid (vs. fallacious reasoning: premises and/or conclusions are false)

- **exposition**: reasoning in a single line through a series of propositions (usually major premise followed by minor premises which follow logically)
- **disputation**: series of contrary or contradictory propositions that result in clear victory for one point of view
- **enthymeme**: some steps in the exposition are omitted
- **aetiologia**: state conclusion of syllogistic reasoning first, then state major or minor premise
- **syllogismus**: single vivid statement that invites the listener to perform syllogistic reasoning that underlies the statement (may be followed with expanded statement of those premises)
- **sorites**: a chain of reasoning involving a series of syllogisms (often enthymemes, some steps missing) usually combined with climax and called gradation—marking the degrees or steps in an argument
- **hypothetical syllogism**: major premise is hypothetical
- **epilogus**: statement of what has occurred followed by hypothetical prediction of future
- **disjunctive syllogism**: statement of alternative points of view followed by confirmation or denial of each, sometimes with surprise ending

- **apophasis**: all alternatives are rejected except one
- **prosapodosis**: none of alternatives are rejected, but each is supported with a reason

B. Fallacious Reasoning (using outward forms of logic to hide specious reasoning, by accident/ignorance or design)

- **equivocation**: material fallacy due to use of word with two different meanings without clarification (often with antanaclasis)
- **fallacy of composition**: assumes that what is applicable to the individual is also applicable to the group of which the individual is a member
- **fallacy of division**: does not acknowledge that what is applicable to the group will be applicable to the individual
- **fallacy of accent**: true significance of word is hidden by style of delivery
- **secundum quid**: hidden/false assumption arising from confusion of absolute and qualified statements
- **fallacy of consequent**: assumption that a statement can be converted simply (if $x = y$ then y must equal x) when it cannot
- **fallacy of false cause**: suggesting something caused something else when it did not
- **fallacy of begging the question**: the conclusion is stated as one of the premises as proof of itself
- **fallacy of many questions**: demanding a simple answer to a complex question

C. Disputation

- **dialectic**: through questions and provocations the opponent disproves self out of own mouth
- **aporia**: doubting or deliberating with oneself
- **anthypophora**: reasoning with oneself, asking questions & answering
- **anacoenosis**: asking for advice
- **paromologia**: admitting something that does not favor one's argument, and then introducing a point that refutes what has just been granted
- **concessio**: granting a point that appears to support but actually hurts the opposition
- **metastasis**: turning back the opposition's point but now used to win one's own argument
- **protrope**: attempted dissuasion through promises, threats, and commands
- **apodioxis**: rejection of argument of opponent
- **diasyrmus**: making the opponent's argument ridiculous through demeaning comparison
- **antirrhesis**: rejection of argument of opponent by pointing out error or wickedness

- **aphorismus**: overthrowing of opponent's argument by questioning proper application of a word

- **commoratio**: attempting to win an argument by coming back repeatedly to one's strongest points

- **epimone**: repetition of same point in same words

- **apoplanesis**: digressing to another matter in order to evade the issue

- **proecthesis**: when one can't win or evade, excusing self by giving reasons why one should not be blamed

- **dicaeologia**: when one can't win or evade, excusing self by reason of necessity

- **pareuresis**: when one can't win or evade, offering an excuse that silences all objections

- **pysma**: asking many questions requiring diverse answers in order to gain attention, to provoke, or to confirm or refute opposition (can become the fallacy of many questions)

- **synchoresis**: because of confidence in rightness of cause, invitation given to listeners to make judgment

IV. Pathos and Ethos

A. Pathos: a form of persuasion using figures of vehemence intended to put the hearer into a frame of mind favorable to one's argument, intensifying the logic of the argument with emotions (which can color judgment)

- **mycterismus**: scornful mocking (can be direct or subtle)

- **sarcasmus**: more bitter and open mocking than mycterismus

- **epiplexis**: asking a question, not to know the answer but in order to criticize or mock

- **onedismus**: criticizing for ingratitude or impiety

- **threnos**: lament

- **categoria**: revealing another's secret wickedness to his or her face

- **proclees**: inciting confrontation through direct & powerful accusation or self-justification

- **bdelygmia**: expression of hatred or disgust, often in just a few words

- **cataplexis**: threat of plague or punishments

- **ara**: cursing

- **eulogia**: blessing the listener

- **optatio**: ardent wish or prayer

- **obtestatio**: intense supplication

- **mempsis**: statement of injuries received while begging for redress

- **paramythia**: consoling in an effort to lessen sorrow

- **medela**: seeking reconciliation for actions of another, actions that cannot be defended or denied

- **philophronesis**: when listener's anger is too great to overcome, using gentle speech and humble submission to mitigate situation
- **exuscitatio**: the speaker is deeply moved and shows it in speaking, thus moving the hearer to a similar feeling
- **aposiopesis**: sudden breaking off of speech
- **ecphosesis**: exclamation
- **thaumasmus**: exclamation of wonder
- **erotema**: powerful statement about which there can be no debate, stated in form of (rhetorical) question
- **apostrophe**: directing speech to a new listener, often combined with figures of exclamation, interrogation, personification of an abstraction

B.   Ethos: persuasion made effective by a demonstration of the personal character of speaker

- **comprobatio**: compliments to good judgment of listeners whose favorable opinion is desired
- **parrhesia**: demonstration of humble respect and/or courage to speak one's mind even if contrary to feelings of powerful listener
- **eucharistia**: giving thanks for benefits received
- **syngnome**: expressing forgiveness of injuries

In developing these games, I was attempting to do no more than awaken the actors' pleasure in these various shapes into which thought could fall, rather than inculcate in them the ability to spot and name the many devices with which Shakespeare and his first actors would have been intimately familiar. Life is too short, we agreed, although it was remarkable how quickly the eye and ear became attuned to the patterns of rhetorical devices, and how familiar the strategies became, even if we could not name them with any precision. In fact, the only name that everyone could remember easily was "Orcos: oath affirming one speaks the truth," which became, after a joke or two, "orcas," and took on the function of a general label for any rhetorical device.

As a metaphor, the black and white whale works well for the newfound pleasure of rhetoric that the actors enjoyed. Sometimes they sensed the presence of that amount of energy and shape, racing under the surface of the flowing language. "There's an orca in here somewhere," they would say, feeling no need to go any further in identifying exactly which rhetorical strategy, but knowing that rhetoric had come to the aid of the character at this moment in the play. At other moments it was comparable to the leaping into the air, and the great splash and crowd-pleasing display of rhetorical genius was clearly as important as carrying forward the argument and giving shape to feeling. The rhetorical devices rely on a few essential principals, and Shakespeare made most use of those devices which repeatedly draw the ear and mind to a conscious awareness of repetition, balance, and contrast. In mastering the skills of delivering complex rhetorical shapes, the actors first learned how to use re-peated words to set up the play of idea against idea, through intonation and phrasing, and how to signal the balance achieved between contrasting ideas by honoring the careful rhythms of symmetrical and asymmetrical phrases. Here are a few examples.

O what a Noble mind is here o'er-thrown?
The Courtiers, Soldiers, Scholars: Eye, tongue, sword,
Th' expectancy and Rose of the fair State,
The glass of Fashion, and the mould of Form,
Th' observed of all Observers, quite, quite down. [*Hamlet* 3.1.151]

This is Ophelia, describing the Prince of Denmark who is, she is now sure, "blasted with ecstasy." The essential marker of repetition is the simple word "the," not a word to be emphasized, but one that in its insistent repeating marks the leaping off points for the shaping of the emotion, which releases in the second and emphasized repetition of "quite, quite down." The balanced phrasing can be heard in several parallel groupings of words. First, we have the compelling rhythm of the three possessive nouns followed by the three objects of possession:

courtiers

soldiers

scholars

eye

tongue

sword

followed by the subtle variations of asymmetrical, linked phrases:

	the	expectancy	
and		rose	of the fair state,
	the	glass	of fashion
and	the	mould of form,	
	the	observed	of all observers

—a pattern that is reinforced by the repetition of sounds: "fair," "fashion," and "form" as well as "observed" and "observers." The playing of word against word does not follow the familiar strategy of contrast through antithesis, but rather of comparison or association, so that we are invited to think of what it is that might link eye and tongue before we leap to sword, to find an associ-ation before the long and intellectual "expectancy" and the metaphor of the rose, and to contemplate the connection between fashion and the mirrors into which the clothes-conscious might gaze, wondering whether fashion shapes the person or the image in the mirror shapes the fashion.

Far too often, Ophelias at this moment simply devolve into weeping masses of injured womanhood, the actresses having forgotten that this young lady has been endowed by Shakespeare with an intellectual capacity to equal Hamlet's. She is capable of giving shape to a complex and sophisticated thought, that being the best way of advancing her argument, which is a demonstration of the horror that she was witnessed and that she feels so acutely. Simple thought, simplistic and uncompelling emotion. Poor little twit, we think. Rhetorically complex thought, and we have the emotional profundity from which tragedy gains its enduring power.

Let's play "Spot the Orcas" in Macbeth's analysis of his situation after the murder of Duncan:

> We have scorched the Snake, not killed it:
> She'll close, and be her self, whilst our poor Malice
> Remains in danger of her former Tooth.
> But let the frame of things dis-joint,
> Both the Worlds suffer,
> Ere we will eat our Meal in fear, and sleep
> In the affliction of these terrible Dreams,
> That shake us Nightly: Better be with the dead,
> Whom we, to gain our peace, have sent to peace,
> Than on the torture of the Mind to lie
> In restless ecstasy.
> Duncan is in his Grave:
> After Lifes fitful Fever, he sleeps well,
> Treason has done his worst: nor Steel, nor Poison,
> Malice domestic, foreign Levy, nothing,
> Can touch him further. [3.2.13]

Start with the repetitions. Macbeth has murdered, in other words sent them to peace, in order to gain peace. This is contrasted with "malice," which is used to describe not only the threat of Macduff and other discontented Thanes but also Macbeth's own murderous ambition, almost personified in the phrase, "whilst our poor malice/Remains in danger of her former tooth." The other significant word that appears twice is "sleep," which we know from earlier in the play is something else that Macbeth has murdered, so that now he knows it's better to be dead than to be plagued by insomnia, that "restless ecstasy." Finally, the double "nor" sets up the list of things: steel, poison, domestic malice, and foreign levy; if not one of these can touch Duncan, then we can safely conclude that nothing can.

The play of word against word carries the argument forward: "scotched," not "killed" is the first and most obvious example. Thereafter, the rhetorical strategies interweave more complexly. "Eat our meal in fear" rings out against "sleep in the affliction" but the second phrase far outweighs the first in length and in significance. Being with the dead is contrasted with lying on the torture of the mind; later, a fitful fever is contrasted with what follows: sleeping well.

There is something about speaking these words aloud that drives home the force of the rhythm, repetition, and playing of word against word, because one instantly feels, through the action of making the sounds, how the repetition of sound qualities supports the rhetorical structure. Even the reader will have noticed "fitful fever" for its alliteration, but the speech rings that sound over and over: former, frame, fear, affliction, foreign, further. Even "grave" into "life" tease out the repeated sound. Then there is the brake that Shakespeare puts on the rush of words with "restless ecstasy." Until that point, it is possible for these words to rip off the tongue and lips at quite a clip, but the insistent hissing of sibilants woven through the first nine lines now stops the entire speech for a musical "rit" or slowing down. The actor probably figured out at first reading that this speech was about the horror of discovering the true price of the crown: perpetual feverish restlessness. An analysis of the rhetoric that gives shape to that feeling reveals just how Shakespeare gave shape to feeling.

COPIA

If so then, be not Tongue-tied: go with me,
And in the breath of bitter words, let's smother
My damned Son, that thy two sweet Sons smothered.
The Trumpet sounds, be copious in exclaims.

Duchess of York [RIII 4.4.132]

Nothing gives a modern actor more trouble than the rhetorical strategy of excess. When the company is looking for a way of trimming thirty minutes off an already trimmed script, actors might be tempted to offer to the knife the middle section of speeches like this, from *Richard II*:

The purest treasure mortal times afford
Is spotless reputation: that away,
Men are but gilded loam, or painted clay.
A Jewel in a ten times barred up Chest,
Is a bold spirit, in a loyal breast.
Mine Honour is my life; both grow in one:
Take Honour from me, and my life is done.
Then (dear my Liege) mine Honour let me try,
In that I live, and for that will I die. [1.1.177]

Surely Mowbray doesn't need that many examples to make his point? And how about Juliet? How many different ways does she need to say what is on her mind? This is one of her shorter speeches, after hearing that Romeo has killed Tybalt:

> O Serpent heart, hid with a flowering face.
> Did ever Dragon keep so fair a Cave?
> Beautiful Tyrant, fiend Angelical:
> Ravenous Dove-feathered Raven,
> Wolvish-ravening Lamb,
> Despised substance of Divinest show:
> Just opposite to what thou justly seem'st,
> A damned Saint, an Honourable Villain:
> O Nature! what hadst thou to do in hell,
> When thou didst bower the spirit of a fiend
> In moral paradise of such sweet flesh?
> Was ever book containing such vile matter
> So fairly bound? O that deceit should dwell
> In such a gorgeous Palace. [3.2.73]

Copia is the natural result of the way rhetoric was taught in the schools. Topics of invention trained the boys to seek multiple examples and associations. The scale of the emotional event sets the size of the rhetorical moment, and *copia* fills that moment to overflowing with a richness of language. A modern audience needs neither the size nor the richness to grasp the depth of emotional turmoil, and so cuts to speeches like these serve to increase the dramatic potency of these scenes in the modern theatre.

I would argue strongly, however, that an actor needs to train the mind, the heart, and the vocal mechanism to a size that can accommodate these copious outpourings, because that is quite simply the intellectual, emotional, and physical muscle that the plays demand. Even if such speeches are cut for a production, in private there is nothing to stop an actor from digging in and finding the blend of modern emotion-based motivation with classical oratorical skills, to make the repeated examples not only credible but powerful and necessary for both the argument and the character.

Recreating an Elizabethan Schoolhouse

Our introduction to the basics of rhetoric requires more than imitation to bring us to the third-grade level. We must move into *invention*, and understand intellectually, as well as intuitively, what is at work in the creation of rhetorical speech events. This allows us to experience them as Shakespeare's characters do.

Let us set ourselves a school exercise in invention, using the standard *topoi* that were used over and over in the little schools. We can select a subject about which we have some knowledge and interest, so that we can draw upon what is readily accessible; we don't want to turn this into a research project!

Each student takes one topic and develops for his team some thoughts on the subject chosen for debate; for example, abortion.

Definition: Here the student makes use of a book of quotations and a good dictionary, looking for the definition of abortion that best supports her side of the debate.

Division: Here the student breaks abortion down into stages, choosing either favorable or unfavorable divisions.

Naming: Here the student seeks synonyms for "abortion," seeking to strike a positive or negative tone.

Conjugates: Here the student returns to a good dictionary, looking for root words and seeking powerful arguments for or against, using words like abortive.

Genus: Here the student attempts to place abortion into the category of other types of murder or other types of difficult decisions.

Species: Here the student differentiates between different types of abortion.

Similarity: Here the student creates as many powerful comparisons as possible, perhaps drawing upon metaphorical language.

Difference: Here the student draws upon comparisons where there is some similarity between abortion and something else, in order to point out the difference. In a debate, one team's similarities are the other team's differences.

Contraries: Here the student defines abortion, favorably or in condemnation, by pointing out all of the things it is not.

Adjuncts: Here the student lists those conditions and attitudes that allow or forbid abortion.

Consequents: Here the student lists the consequences of getting or denying an abortion.

Antecedents: Here the student seeks to illuminate the broadest possible causes and consequences of abortion.

Incompatibilities: Here the student seeks to put into words the immense significance of the elimination of abortion.

Causes: Here the student seeks to name the real reasons why abortions occur.

Effects: Here the student seeks to name the real result of an abortion.

Comparisons with things greater, less, or equal: Here the student places abortion into a system of relative good and evil.

Once each student has teased out some ideas on the topic, sparked by his assigned division, the team pools all of the images, comparisons, definitions, perceptions, attitudes, and vocabulary, and decides on a speaker. Unlike in formal debating, there are no rules about the introduction of new material or the time limit on each speaker. Rather, the first team leader simply gets up and begins to speak. Because the focus is the creation of *copia* as a direct result of invention, the challenge is to keep speaking as long as possible without being reduced to ineffectual redundancy. As soon as the speaker hesitates, the other team is allowed to speak. The rest of the team can supply the speaker with fresh ideas as she rests and awaits the first sign that the opposition is running out of material.

This game reveals the excitement of the racing, dense imagery and association invited by a schoolboy's *inventio*, an attitude toward language and ideas that can be brought to Shakespeare's characters. Formal debate is also useful for classical actors. It can be used to reinforce an intellectual understanding of the structuring of argument and an emotional experience of the patience required when one waits for rebuttal, the thrill of scoring effectively using the brilliance of the rival, and the breathless speed at which the words must be absorbed, confronted, and reshaped for the best possible response. Most importantly, however, it familiarizes the actor with the nature of an argument, the structuring of which is a skill that was also acquired by Elizabethan schoolboys.

⚘ 11 ⚘

Structuring Argument

What? the Sword, and the Word?
Do you study them both, Master Parson?

Shallow [Wives 3.1.44]

Public debate used to be a standard component of a liberal arts education. Sadly, insofar as classical actors are concerned, formal debate is disappearing from the general experience of young people, but actors can rectify this by setting up the essential conventions of debate, experiencing the challenges and the thrills firsthand, and then applying these discoveries to the rhetorical arguments found in the plays.

Rhetoric always exists to present an argument. The listener and the speaker might not be mighty opposites; the debate might be on the question of which of the two loves the other most profoundly. Another common rhetorical dialog takes the form of intellectual mountain climbing, with each subsequent speaker agreeing with the points already made and taking the argument forward along the same lines.

The first scene of *A Midsummer Night's Dream* provides us with several examples of different kinds of argument. The play opens with two speakers, each of whom provides a contrasting perspective of the same event.

Theseus: Now fair Hippolyta, our nuptial hour
Draws on apace: four happy days bring in
Another moon: but O, methinks, how slow
This old Moon wanes; She lingers my desires

Like to a Step-dame, or a Dowager,
Long withering out a young mans revenue.

Hippolyta: Four days will quickly steep themselves in night
Four nights will quickly dream away the time:
And then the Moon, like to a silver bow,
New-bent in heaven, shall behold the night
Of our solemnities. [1.1.1]

Although it is possible to play an antagonistic undercurrent between these two, the dialog demonstrates an argument in another key, that of comparisons between opposing points of view, allowing each its validity, acknowledging and enjoying difference.

Very soon, however, the stage is filled with characters who have radically different opinions on an issue, and who are determined to change the mind of the opponent or, failing that, affect the decision of Theseus who is asked to judge between them.

Theseus: Demetrius is a worthy Gentleman.

Hermia: So is Lysander.

Theseus: In himself he is.
But in this kind, wanting your fathers voice.
The other must be held the worthier.

Hermia: I would my father looked but with my eyes.

Theseus: Rather your eyes must with his judgment look. [1.1.52]

The swift give and take of debate sets the emotional temperature of this type of argument, where the dialog "ball" is passed from one speaker to the other at the speed of thought.

This, however, is just one rhythm for intense debate. The other allows each speaker as much time as it takes to develop her argument as fully as desired. Here is Lysander marshalling every argument he can think of, why Hermia should be allowed to marry the man of her choice–himself.

I am my Lord, as well derived as he,
As well possessed: my love is more than his:
My fortunes every way as fairly ranked
(If not with vantage) as Demetrius:
And (which is more than all these boasts can be)
I am beloved of beauteous Hermia.
Why should not I then prosecute my right?
Demetrius, I'll avouch it to his head,
Made love to Nedars daughter, Helena,
And won her soul: and she (sweet Lady) dotes,

Devoutly dotes, dotes in Idolatry,
Upon this spotted and inconstant man. [1.1.99]

Later in this same scene, when the young lovers are alone together, we have
an example of argument in the form of exchange of ideas, each new thought
building on the one before.

Lysander: Ay me, for aught that I could ever read,
  Could ever hear by tale or history,
  The course of true love never did run smooth,
  But, either it was different in blood.

Hermia: O cross! too high to be enthralled to low.

Lysander: Or else misgraffed, in respect of years.

Hermia: O spite! too old to be engaged to young.

Lysander: Or else it stood upon the choice of friends.

Hermia: O hell! to choose love by anothers eye.

Lysander: Or if there were a sympathy in choice,
  War, death, or sickness, did lay siege to it;
  Making it momentany, as a sound:
  Swift as a shadow, short as any dream,
  Brief as the lightning in the collied night,
  That (in a spleen) unfolds both heaven and earth;
  And ere a man hath power to say, behold,
  The jaws of darkness do devour it up:
  So quick bright things come to confusion.

Hermia: If then true Lovers have been ever crossed,
  It stands as an edict in destiny:
  Then let us teach our trial patience,
  Because it is a customary cross,
  As due to love, as thoughts, and dreams, and sighs,
  Wishes and tears, poor Fancies followers. [1.1.132]

The convention of this type of argument suggests that Hermia could never
have reached the insight of her final speech without the ladder of images she
and Lysander have built together. Of course this is also a sexy love scene
between two passionate young lovers, building toward their decision to run
away together, so the argument and the emotional journey work hand in glove
to shape the rising intensity of the scene.

Immediately after this, Hermia and her dear friend Helena have a more
familiar type of debate, one in which they disagree just about completely on
the issue of Demetrius.

Helena: O teach me how you look, and with what art
  You sway the motion of Demetrius heart.

Hermia: I frown upon him, yet he loves me still.

Helena: O that your frowns would teach my smiles such skill.

Hermia: I give him curses, yet he gives me love.

Helena: O that my prayers could such affection move.

Hermia: The more I hate, the more he follows me.

Helena: The more I love, the more he hateth me.

Hermia: His folly Helena is no fault of mine.

Helena: None but your beauty, would that fault were mine. [1.1.192]

Although it is possible to play the scene so that Helena irritates Hermia, this is not really an example of idea/rebuttal, but rather information/information, where the contrast is in the different ways Demetrius responds to the two women.

Spotting the argument is not always as easy as this. Soliloquies, for example, set a special challenge. While it might be tempting to conclude that a person talking to herself is trying to persuade herself of something, the overriding thrust of a soliloquy is seldom that simple. It is difficult to make the entire speech that follows an exercise in Helena convincing herself to betray Hermia and Lysander to Demetrius.

> How happy some, o'er other some can be?
> Through Athens I am thought as fair as she.
> But what of that? Demetrius thinks not so:
> He will not know, what all, but he do know,
> And as he errs, doting on Hermia's eyes;
> So I, admiring of his qualities:
> Things base and vile, holding no quantity,
> Love can transpose to form and dignity,
> Love looks not with the eyes, but with the mind,
> And therefore is winged Cupid painted blind.
> Nor hath loves mind of any judgement taste:
> Wings and no eyes, figure, unheedy haste.
> And therefore is Love said to be a child,
> Because in choice he is so oft beguiled,
> As waggish boys in game themselves forswear;
> So the boy Love is perjured every where.
> For ere Demetrius looked on Hermias eyne,
> He hailed down oaths that he was only mine.
> And when this Hail some heat from Hermia felt,
> So he dissolved, and showers of oaths did melt,
> I will go tell him of fair Hermia's flight:
> Then to the wood will he, to-morrow night
> Pursue her; and for this intelligence,
> If I have thanks, it is a dear expense:

> But herein mean I to enrich my pain,
> To have his sight thither, and back again. [1.1.226]

The decision to betray Hermia seems to come out of the air, rather than serving as the natural conclusion to the lengthy discussion of the nature of love that precedes it. However, if the entire speech is viewed as a lecture on love, then the betrayal of Hermia is just one more example of the crazy things that love makes you do, even to the point of such a dear expense, that is worthwhile to a lover if only she can be with the beloved as a result.

It is sometimes helpful to verbalize the "resolution" that might result in such a speech. For example, Helena's soliloquy might be the closing argument in a debate between five speakers, all claiming to know the real nature of love. The first to present his argument: Theseus. His thesis is that love is known by the impatience that it arouses in the lover. The second is Egeus, Hermia's father, whose argument takes the form of a negative statement: he sets out to offer an example of non-love.

> This man hath bewitched the bosom of my child:
> Thou, thou Lysander, thou hast given her rhymes,
> And interchanged love-tokens with my child:
> Thou hast by Moon-light at her window sung,
> With feigning voice, verses of feigning love,
> And stolen the impression of her fantasy,
> With bracelets of thy hair, rings, gawds, conceits,
> Knacks, trifles, Nosegays, sweet meats (messengers
> Of strong prevailment in unhardened youth)
> With cunning hast thou filched my daughter's heart. [1.1.27]

We have already looked at the joint presentation on the true nature of true love, as presented by Hermia and Lysander, followed by another negative statement, again a duet, from Hermia and Helena on all the indicators of non-love shown to and by Demetrius. It now rests with Helena to have the final word. What is this thing called love?

Her presentation begins obliquely. The theme has already been stated, the terms well established, and hers is a summation rather than the opening statement of the debate. Therefore, she can establish in her introduction the personal implications of the inequality of love: some are happy, others are not, when the daisy chain of loving someone who loves another is in place. This sets the emotional stakes for her first clear argument, demonstrating her understanding of the nature of love: its capacity to transform the beloved into an object of adoration. She heightens the power of this observation with reference to the cliché, "Love is blind," which allows her to introduce the figure of Cupid and then make a series of observations on the nature of love arising out of that personification: Love lacks judgement, indulges itself in unheeding haste, and is often tricked, just like a child. And, like boys at play, Love thinks little of making promises and not keeping them. A subtle shift of language allows Helena to move effortlessly from the metaphor to the actual: Love is perjured everywhere: Love lies, and Love's name is taken in vain. She then explains this with reference to her particular situation, which also takes us back to the opening argument: Demetrius used to say he loved her, now he loves Hermia. Eyes and oaths reoccur, uniting all of the images that have been presented so far.

And now Helena offers her ultimate proof, that she of all the speakers is most knowledgeable of the true nature of love. For not only has she observed it in Demetrius, she will now demonstrate it in herself. She will act with unheeding haste, showing no judgment. She will blind herself to the unworthiness of Demetrius as well as to the immorality of her own behavior. She will betray her best friend. She will do all this because she loves. Furthermore, she will demonstrate a capacity for enduring pain and humiliation that places her experience of love in the highest category of dear expense, willingly paid, simply to be able to see the beloved.

Every set speech can be analyzed as just such a unified rhetorical argument. The trick is to figure out what is being argued. Is it the presentation of an idea, or the rebuttal of something that has gone before? Is it contrasting perspective or summation and culmination? Is it the systematic destruction of the points made by someone else? Is it the systematic construction of a world view?

Let us have a look at a different character and see how an awareness of argument can help us to understand how his speeches are structured. Iago, we all agree, can be pretty persuasive, finding the capacity for gullibility in everyone from Roderigo to Barbantio, Cassio, and to Othello himself. When he cannot win by a combination of lies and persuasion, he stabs his opponents to death and then takes a vow of silence against all accusers. Having prepared the ground, here is how he persuades Othello to doubt the loving Desdemona. Othello declares that he will require proof before he will believe ill of his wife, and Iago obliges:

Iago: I know our Country disposition well:
           In Venice, they do let Heaven see the pranks
           They dare not show their Husbands.
           Their best Conscience,
           Is not to leave't undone, but kept unknown.

Othello: Dost thou say so?

Iago: She did deceive her Father, marrying you,
           And when she seemed to shake, and fear your looks,
           She loved them most.

Othello: And so she did.

Iago: Why go to then:
           She that so young could give out such a Seeming

> To seal her Fathers eyes up, close as Oak,
> He thought 'twas Witchcraft. [3.3.201]

Iago then returns to his favored strategy, pretending extreme reluctance to discuss the possibility of an affair between Cassio and Desdemona.

Now let us turn our attention to how this master-persuader shapes a soliloquy. Here is the one that brings to a close the first scene in Cyprus, when Desdemona and Othello are united in a passionate evocation of their powerful love, and Iago's plotting seems least likely to succeed.

> That Cassio loves her, I do well believe't:
> That she loves him, 'tis apt, and of great Credit.
> The Moor (how beit that I endure him not)
> Is of a constant, loving, Noble Nature,
> And I dare think, he'll prove to Desdemona
> A most dear husband. Now I do love her too,
> Not out of absolute Lust, (though peradventure
> I stand accountant for as great a sin)
> But partly led to diet my Revenge,
> For that I do suspect the lusty Moor
> Hath leaped into my Seat. The thought whereof,
> Doth (like a poisonous Mineral) gnaw my Inwards:
> And nothing can, or shall content my Soul
> Till I am evened with him, wife, for wife.
> Or failing so, yet that I put the Moor,
> At least into a Jealousy so strong
> That judgment cannot cure. Which thing to do,
> If this poor Trash of Venice, whom I trace
> For his quick hunting, stand the putting on,
> I'll have our Michael Cassio on the hip,
> Abuse him to the Moor, in the rank garb
> (For I fear Cassio with my Night-Cap too)
> Make the Moor thank me, love me, and reward me,
> For making him egregiously an ass,
> And practising upon his peace, and quiet,
> Even to madness. 'Tis here: but yet confused,
> Knaverys plain face is never seen, till used. [2.1.286]

While it is tempting to view this as a series of justifications of villainy, the accusation of adultery with Iago's wife Emilia, made against both Othello and Cassio, seem strangely emotionless, as does the abrupt declaration, "Now I do love her too."

So what is going on here? As is so often the case with a soliloquy, Shakespeare seems to be giving us a look inside the mind of this man, and it is not a very pleasant sight. There is a logic at work, of a sort, that takes us from Iago's observations about the scene which has just occurred, to Iago's own shifting feelings. Having observed the love all around, he decides that he feels the same emotion. Then, in seeking to explain that emotion, his mind turns to revenge, and then to the rather startling news that he too experiences the torments of jealousy. It is an easy step from that sensation to a desire to inflict Othello with more of the same. However, the causality seems backwards. Iago wants revenge, then finds a reason to justify revenge, and then decides that the revenge will suit the (probably imaginary) crime. The brilliance of the rhetorical argument is that we follow Iago through these linked ideas, when in truth the mind at work is, at best, confused and quite likely mad.

MODELS FOR STRUCTURED ARGUMENT

Through modelling on the experts, even the youngest Elizabethan school child could structure a persuasive argument. In addition, children could hear examples of structured argument in Sunday sermons and the last words of condemned criminals. Rhetorical strategies were so pervasive as to be "normal" and "natural" rather than artificial, and hence the natural medium for the expression of deep feeling.

As an introduction to the intensity of rhetorical presentation, here is an exercise for a group.

Star Chamber

In Shakespeare's England, which was a police state with censorship and secret police, individuals could be arrested for expressing treasonous opinions. Shakespeare's colleague, Ben Jonson, served time in prison for some of the political satire he dared to write, and two of Shakespeare's fellow shareholders were dragged off the streets immediately following Essex's doomed rebellion, because the company had been paid to play *Richard II* the day before. These two were brought before the Star Chamber, a collection of powerful men who met in secret to interrogate, judge, and sentence political prisoners. Shakespeare's friends were let go, because they successfully pleaded their ignorance of Essex's plans and their complete loyalty to the monarchy and their noble patrons.

Set up a Star Chamber, with five members of the group seated around the outside of the room. A sixth person is sent outside the room to wait and to prepare an imaginary situation of sudden arrest, no charges laid, and the absolute terror of the power of the five in the room. In preparation, these five can outline a general scenario of suspicion, but it need not follow any particular logic. Think of the sort of paranoia that plagues tyrants, and the strange lines of questioning they favor. Bring the sixth person back in to sit in the middle of the circle, perhaps unable to turn around so that some of the questioners are never seen. Ask about acquaintances, beliefs, and activities. Assume that the accused is lying and set traps. Ask the same question different ways.

Change the subject frequently and without explanation. Demand short answers and "yes or no" answers to complex questions. Cut off the victim mid-explanation. If the victim hesitates, one or more should start firing off all sorts of difficult additional questions.

After a two-minute interrogation, which should seem like hours to the accused, and on a prearranged signal, one of the interrogators should invite the accused to speak in self-defense, giving a two-minute time limit during which the accused must persuade the group to withdraw the charge of treason. As the accused speaks, listen to the structuring of the communication. Listen for repetition of words and phrases. Listen for words that join thoughts, that suggest connections between ideas (and, but, if, because, then, etc.). Even in this rattled state, and without any of an Elizabethan's training, the accused will grab hold of rhetorical devices. Take notes. The accused will think the notes are on content. They should be on structure. Reinforce the use of rhetoric by nodding your head as if in agreement whenever a word is repeated or one idea is linked to another. Keep a tally. Jot down descriptions of what you're hearing, not the content but the form. At the end of the two minutes, announce that the accused is free to leave. Then you can break out of the scenario and share what you heard. The accused will probably be unaware of the form because the content was all-important.

If others wish to explore rhetoric using the Star Chamber exercise, it is important that you do not duplicate any scenario. Once the group has explored rhetoric and discussed that exploration, the next "victim" is better served by a scenario that advances the story and integrates a growing consciousness of the importance of structuring argument. The second scenario could have the accused seated outside, knowing that the Star Chamber allows three minutes for a speech of self defense, and preparing. Once invited in, however, the accused would be interrupted by questions, allowed to give only a short answer, and then told, "continue with your argument." Those listening can pay special attention to exactly what words are used by the accused to get back to the preplanned speech.

The next volunteer could have a similar experience waiting and planning outside the chamber and expecting questions and interruptions. But this time, the first interrogator to interrupt could say, "Enough, we have no interest in that, but we will give you two minutes to persuade us that theatre should not be censored because it is not political but merely entertainment. If you succeed, then we will let you go free."

Each of the variations should set up some element of the unexpected, so that the accused is forced to structure thought within the rush of feeling.

After the Star Chamber exercise, students are willing to accept that there is at least an element of truth in the Greek's view that rhetorical strategies are natural, available to everyone to draw upon, even when speaking extempore under great stress.

Variations on the Formal Debate

Although debating can be an excellent preparation for an actor seeking to develop a personal facility with the building blocks of rhetoric, the adversarial form of such verbal sparring does not, in fact, match more than a small proportion of the human interactions dramatized in Shakespeare's plays. For that reason, it is important to practice some of the alternative formal interactions that can provide a variety of models for the rhetorical displays found in the plays.

As we have seen with the Star Chamber improvisation, speaking at length in self-defense, in contrast to enduring an intense cross-examination, places very specific demands on the individual to present one's perspective in a compelling manner. Simple variations on this theme are the credo and the motivational mosaic.

In the credo exercise, the actor is invited to speak for two minutes, extempore or using only a few notes, on those beliefs and values that she perceives as central to her definition of self. If an Elizabethan context sparks a more dramatic and charged performance, then consider the fate of the religious martyrs, who were allowed on their scaffolds to address the spectators in what was, for each of them, one last opportunity to confirm the beliefs for which they were willing to die.

In the motivational mosaic game, the group participates in an improvisation of a realistic situation in which individuals have strong desires and needs which they are not free to disclose. At various intervals in the improvisation, a time-out is called and one member of the group is invited to address the audience for no more than two minutes, during which she must describe, as vividly as possible, her motivations, her experiences in the improvisation to date, her plans for the future, and whatever else she might be feeling and thinking.

If these challenges are set after the actors have encountered the rhetorical "vessels," and if they have begun to enjoy the power of language, including metaphor, personification, allusion, and persuasive argument, then they will be ready to set aside modern language patterns in favor of overtly "artificial" language in the best sense of the word. However, if the actors "run dry" and find themselves unable to fill the allotted time, or resort to boring language usage, then it's time to deal out the rhetorical cards, which serve as prompts to rich language even as they demand an increased sophistication in delivery.

I also use the cards when introducing actors to the "yes, and" game. This is a variation on the adversarial debate, and involves each actor picking up on the comments of the prior speaker in order to build toward the greatest, most comprehensive understanding of the topic in question. There is a slight flavor of competition, in that you want to top the contribution of whomever you follow, but the end result is more like mountain climbing than mud wrestling. The point is for each speaker to lead the entire group further and higher, so that the actor who follows can start from that point and climb still further yet.

A slight variation on this rhetorical exchange, one that is slightly more competitive and a great preparation for games of wit and love scenes, is the game, "We are both the same, only I am more so." Here each speaker demonstrates that he is the one who most perfectly knows the essence of the shared attribute, whatever the group has elected to debate. We can find this rhetorical game at work in the most passionate of love scenes, as when Romeo and Juliet vie with each other to declare more perfectly their love:

Romeo: Lady, by yonder blessed Moon I vow,
     That tips with silver all these Fruit tree tops.

Juliet: O swear not by the Moon, th' inconstant Moon,
     That monthly changes in her circled Orb,
     Lest that thy Love prove likewise variable.

Romeo: What shall I swear by?

Juliet: Do not swear at all:
     Or if thou wilt, swear by thy gracious self,
     Which is the God of my Idolatry,
     And I'll believe thee.

Romeo: If my hearts dear love.

Juliet: Well do not swear, although I joy in thee:
     I have no joy of this contract to-night,
     It is too rash, too unadvised, too sudden,
     Too like the lightning which doth cease to be
     Ere one can say, it lightens, Sweet good night:
     This bud of Love by Summers ripening breath,
     May prove a beauteous Flower when next we meet:
     Goodnight, goodnight, as sweet repose and rest,
     Come to thy heart, as that within my breast.

Romeo: O wilt thou leave me so unsatisfied?

Juliet: What satisfaction canst thou have to-night?

Romeo: Th' exchange of thy Loves faithful vow for mine.

Juliet: I gave thee mine before thou didst request it:
     And yet I would it were to give again.

Romeo: Wouldst thou withdraw it;
     For what purpose Love?

Juliet: But to be frank and give it thee again,
     And yet I wish but for the thing I have,
     My bounty is as boundless as the Sea,
     My Love as deep, the more I give to thee
     The more I have, for both are Infinite. [2.2.107]

It does not serve such a scene to enquire after the structured argument, unless the definition of "argument" has been expanded to include the more pleasurable verbal competitions afforded by these alternatives to formal debate.

LISTENING WITH THE HEART, THE MIND, AND THE SOUL

> We cannot feel too little, hear too much.
>
> Henry [*HVIII* 1.2.128]

It is remarkable how quickly the basic building blocks of rhetoric become sufficiently familiar to reveal themselves to the modern actor's intellectual appreciation. When coupled with imitation, the mouth and tongue and breath quickly become acclimatized to the sensation of rhetorical speaking events. The danger, however, is that rhetoric remains an intellectual pleasure rather than a complete language system, equally suited to every sort of exchange. It is time to train the actors' ears as well as their minds and mouths.

One of the foundations of the theory of rhetoric as propagated by Greek and Roman classical authors, was the three-part foundation of *ethos, logos,* and *pathos.* It is almost impossible to separate these three elements within any language event, because they are interwoven and integral to the communication function of language. It is possible, however, to disentangle the concept of each of the three threads, and then *listen* for one of the threads as it blends into the unified whole of the speaker's desire to communicate.

Logos is fairly easily recognized as the intellectual function of rational thought. All language participates in such a function, and therefore is inherently logical, but some language patterns foreground *logos* in order to achieve the goal of the speech act. "If you get down from the table before you finish your broccoli, you will not get dessert," says the mother to the child in a doomed effort to demonstrate a logical proposition: if X occurs, then Y will follow.

Pathos, meaning any emotion, is a thread that actors are accustomed to foregrounding and, as we have seen, disengaging from language in contemporary conventions of communication. However, just as we could define all language as a function of rational thought, we too could define every speech communication as the action of giving shape to feeling. Therefore, every language strategy is connected to *pathos,* though some demonstrate that connection with unmistakable force. "Don't you dare get down from that chair, young man," screams the mother, successfully conveying the emotions at work at the dinner table.

Ethos, the Latin root of a word like "ethical," was a concept with which Shakespeare and his contemporaries would have been more familiar than we are today. Our contemporary definition is a more limited one, focused on ethical issues, personal morality, and that long list of concepts that includes justice, rights, honor, criminality, and so on. *Ethos*, however, has its rhetorical roots in a fairly simple oratorical strategy: the speaker presents some aspects of herself in order to clarify that her thoughts are worth listening to. This might be as simple as, "I'm a nutrition specialist, and I know that broccoli contains important vitamins that you will get nowhere else, so you should eat that broccoli." But the *ethos* of a speech event can also be established by a reference to the personal attributes, usually positive, in the listener, inclining him toward agreement with the speaker, as in, "I know you're a good little boy, and so you'll want to eat that broccoli before you get down from the table, won't you?"

Any word that contains or implies a reference to a moral system partakes of the thread of *ethos*. "It's not very nice of you to disobey me like that," says the mother, counting on her son having internalized the moral system that marks "nice" as a positive value and "disobey" as a negative one. Even something as subtle as, "Mother says, eat your broccoli, please," is powerfully encoded with *ethos*: "mother" and "please" having such positive moral weight at the family dinner table.

Ethos, then, is every aspect of language that conveys the shared value system that binds the speaker to the listener. We actually have very few words that are morally neutral, though the context in which value is ascribed can transform the word to its near opposite, an act of rebellion that every generation enjoys.

When I first started working in theatre, "cheap" was a positive-value word. This was due, in large part, to the budgets we enjoyed for any given production, and the words, "I can do it for cheap," were always greeted with applause during production meetings. However, when I began to work in a major festival, "cheap" became a negative-value word. This was only in part because budgets were bigger. So were expenses, and risks, and the intensity of scrutiny of cost versus benefit no less than in the poor little theatre company. "Don't be cheap," however, was used to convey opposition to a negative-value activity or opinion, more damning still when used in reference to an artistic choice: "That's so cheap!" Same word, same meaning, different value system, in every instance the thread of *ethos*.

If you try to deliver a speech, first focusing on *logos*, then on *pathos*, and finally on *ethos*, you will discover that it is almost impossible to separate the three threads in the act of speaking. However, it is remarkably easy to listen for the three threads, and knowing that the three threads are being listened for can sharpen your awareness of their interweaving in a speech. Sometimes you discover that you have been making insufficient use of the communication potential of all three threads, and therefore experiencing only a portion of the power of the language you have been given to speak.

Audience of Three

Four actors can work together to sharpen their ability to hear, and therefore to partake of, the three distinct threads that rhetoric was created to weave so brilliantly. One delivers the monologue and the other three listen for one of the three threads. After four speeches, everyone will have had a turn speaking and listening for each of the three.

The job of each listener is to signal that the assigned thread has been successfully foregrounded at that moment and therefore that the speaker has succeeded in reaching that listener. Each thread is acknowledged in a manner that reinforces the assigned thread. The *logos* listener keeps track of the score. Every time a logical point is made, the speaker gets a check. The *pathos* listener radiates back the feelings conveyed, magnified, and expressed with facial expression, gesture, and nonverbal vocalization (sighs, laughs, growls, moans). The *ethos* listener nods in approval with any positive-value word and shakes the head in disapproval of any negative-value word, this shake not representing, however, disagreement with the speaker but a shared moral reaction.

In listening, it is important that the potential, as well as the actual delivery, of the speech be noted with regard to each of the threads. The speaker regards every check, every emotive signal, and every nod or shake as success. After the first delivery of the speech, each of the listeners makes suggestions of how the speaker's delivery might heighten each listener's experience of the power of the speech.

Here is an example of a few short passages, in each one of which the foregrounding of one of the threads is obvious, and so the other two need to be clarified by the "Audience of Three" exercise. Portia, the heroine of *The Merchant of Venice*, delivers each of these at different times, demonstrating her command of the three pillars of rhetoric. Here is Portia's famous ethical argument on the concept of Mercy:

> The quality of mercy is not strained,
> It droppeth as the gentle rain from heaven
> Upon the place beneath. It is twice blest,
> It blesseth him that gives, and him that takes,
> 'Tis mightiest in the mightiest, it becomes
> The throned Monarch better than his Crown.
> His Sceptre shows the force of temporal power,
> The attribute to awe and Majesty,
> Wherein doth sit the dread and fear of Kings:
> But mercy is above this sceptred sway,
> It is enthroned in the hearts of Kings,
> It is an attribute to God himself;
> And earthly power doth then show likest Gods
> When mercy seasons Justice. Therefore Jew,
> Though Justice be thy plea, consider this,

That in the course of Justice, none of us
Should see salvation: we do pray for mercy,
And that same prayer, doth teach us all to render
The deeds of mercy. I have spoke thus much
To mitigate the justice of thy plea:
Which if thou follow, this strict court of Venice
Must needs give sentence 'gainst the Merchant there. [4.1.184]

Here is quite a different side of Portia, the emotional, irrational, love-struck
girl:

I pray you tarry: pause a day or two
Before you hazard, for, in choosing wrong
I lose your company, therefore forbear a while,
There's something tells me (but it is not love)
I would not lose you, and you know your self,
Hate counsels not in such a quality,
But lest you should not understand me well,
And yet a maiden hath no tongue, but thought,
I would detain you here some month or two
Before you venture for me. I could teach you
How to choose right, but I am then forsworn,
So will I never be, so may you miss me,
But if you do, you'll make me wish a sin,
That I had been forsworn: Beshrew your eyes,
They have o'er-looked me and divided me,
One half of me is yours, the other half yours,
Mine own, I would say: but if mine then yours,
And so all yours; O these naughty times
Put bars between the owners and their rights.
And so though yours, not yours (prove it so)
Let Fortune go to hell for it, not I.
I speak too long, but 'tis to peize the time,
To eke it, and to draw it out in length,
To stay you from election. [3.2.1]

Here is the logical Portia, cooly defusing excessive compliment and setting up
her plot to follow Bassanio to Venice:

I never did repent for doing good,
Nor shall not now: for in companions
That do converse and waste the time together,
Whose souls do bear an equal yoke of love,
There must be needs a like proportion
Of lineaments, of manners, and of spirit;
Which makes me think that this Antonio
Being the bosom lover of my Lord,

Must needs be like my Lord. If it be so,
How little is the cost I have bestowed
In purchasing the semblance of my soul;
From out the state of hellish cruelty,
This comes too near the praising of my self,
Therefore no more of it: hear other things:
Lorenzo I commit into your hands,
The husbandry and manage of my house,
Until my Lords return, for mine own part,
I have toward heaven breathed a secret vow,
To live in prayer and contemplation,
Only attended by Nerissa here,
Until her husband and my Lords return:
There is a monastery two miles off,
And there will we abide. I do desire you
Not to deny this imposition,
The which my love and some necessity
Now lays upon you. [3.4.10]

The dominant thread in each of these speeches is the one most likely to be present in first reading. It is the second and third thread that require special attention. This is where the audience of three can assist the actor in the experience of delivering a rhetorically powerful statement. It is almost impossible to express the emotional, the logical, and the ethical elements of a speech separately, because the language accomplishes such a tight weaving of the three. However, it is possible to deliver each of the speeches and observe the reactions of the trio of listeners, and shape the way that you convey *pathos*, *logos*, and *ethos*, so as to arouse the richest response from all three.

We can see at a glance that the first speech affords the *ethos* listener many opportunities to nod in agreement with the powerful ethical concepts of justice and mercy. The *pathos* listener will respond to the equally strong emotional thread, which otherwise might drop out of sight. Consider the emotional power of words like "gentle rain" or "dread and fear." The *pathos* listener will reflect back any feelings that words like "prayer" and "heaven" have for Portia, as well as whatever she might be feeling about the sentence under which Antonio stands to lose his life. The *logos* listener will chart the precision of Portia's logic. He will note the effectiveness of Portia's listing of evidence, the contrast she demonstrates between earthly and heavenly power, and the striking culmination of her argument, marked by "therefore."

The emotional connections often come most easily for a modern actor, and, knowing what Portia is going through at this point in the play, the second speech can quite easily be delivered as a highly charged expression of fear and longing. The *pathos* listener will have a great deal to reflect back at the speaker. It is therefore up to the *logos* and the *ethos* listeners to tease out the other two pillars, without which this speech could not function as effectively. The *ethos* listener will be able to nod affirmation on words like "forbear" and "quality," "right" and "rights," and shake the head with disapproval at "wrong," "forsworn," and "sin." This turns out to be a highly ethical speech, because Portia is torn between two rights, or two wrongs. The *logos* listener might assume that there will be less to respond to, because this speech, with its strong emotions, lacks an obvious logic; however, because all language systems participate in the essential elements of logic, that listener too will have something to which to respond. "For in losing wrong I lose your company" is a simple statement of logic. So is "So will I never be, so may you miss me." It will be the *logos* listener who will remind the speaker that this, too, is an argument, which culminates in the statement, "Prove it so,/Let fortune go to hell for it, not I."

Modern listeners find the *logos* listening the most difficult, because we are no longer trained in formal logic. It is far easier for the *ethos* person, who simply listens for any words that have moral value, positive or negative. I coach the *logos* listeners to respond to the obvious markers of logical construction, such as "if . . . then" or "therefore" as well as key conjunctions like "but" or "so." Most importantly, the *logos* listeners turn off their empathy and refuse to be swayed by moral content. They listen, instead, to how the argument is constructed, attempting to assess how successful the speaker is in persuading the listeners to a specific point of view.

For the speaker, the highly emotive facial expressions, reflecting back the feelings being evoked, and the positive nods or negative shakes in connection with moral concepts, are clear, effective markers of the feelings and the beliefs that the speech conveys moment by moment, word by word. It is the intense concentration of the *logos* listener, in contrast, that drives home the through-line of the argument, demonstrating how each shift in feeling, each powerful ethical word, connects to the need to persuade the listener of the character's point of view.

ஒ 12 ஓ
Tangled Webs

His speech was like a tangled chain: nothing impaired, but all disordered.
Theseus [*Dreams* 5.1.125]

The challenge that Shakespeare's language gives a modern actor and her audience is only partly the shift in meaning that has taken place in individual
words. True, it is disconcerting to encounter words that are no longer in our
vocabulary or, worse yet, words that mean something quite different today
than they did for Shakespeare. However, the actual meaning can usually be
intuited by context, assisted by the inflection and emphasis of the actor in
performance, who has had recourse to the definitions provided by scholars in
the footnotes of the edition he carried around in rehearsal. An actor may have
to do a bit of digging to figure out why those particular words turn out to
mean that particular thing, but once clear, it is usually a fairly straightforward
process to say the word with meaning, and hence have it mean what it should.

Actors can practice these tricks in gibberish exercises, in which an arbitrary
pattern of sound is manipulated by all of the strategies of nonverbal (facial
expression and gesture) and prelinguistic (sound qualities such as tone of voice,
volume, etc.) communication. Most professional voice training introduces an
actor to the immense flexibility of the natural speaking voice. Once a clarity
is achieved in rehearsal as to the action of a scene, the delivery of the text
crystallizes in whatever form best serves the telling of the story, the presentation of the event, the evocation of relationship and emotion.

Let us take a simple example. The word "presently" has come to mean "in
a moment or two," usually a wait that turns out to be significantly longer than
predicted. In Shakespeare's time, the word meant "in the present moment,"

and suggested an immediacy of action. "Go presently to the king," therefore would send the Elizabethan messenger racing as fast as humanly possible whereas a modern individual would have received a signal to visit the king in the near future, as soon as it might be convenient.

Saying the word "presently" with a fierceness, an urgency, a crispness, in combination with the *reaction* of the listener, who races off the stage, communicates immediately to the modern audience that the stakes are higher, the pressure of time greater, than might be expected simply from reading the word in a modern context. Here is a more difficult example, found in the declaration of love made by Olivia to the boy Cesario (who is Viola in disguise):

> Cesario, by the Roses of the Spring,
> By maid-hood, honor, truth, and every thing,
> I love thee so, that maugre all thy pride,
> Nor wit, nor reason, can my passion hide:
> Do not extort thy reasons from this clause,
> For that I woo, thou therefore hast no cause:
> But rather reason thus, with reason fetter;
> Love sought, is good: but given unsought, is better. [*12th Night* 3.1.149]

"Maugre" means here "in spite of" or "notwithstanding the power of," a word that was in use as late as the end of the nineteenth century but which doesn't even sound like what it means. However, the context is fairly clear and the line can be delivered with a strong emphasis on "pride," as a contrast to the passion that she cannot hide.

What, however, are we going to do with what follows? The meaning of these lines might be explained as follows:

Having explained that, even given the immense power of my pride, my own intelligence and rational self cannot do the correct thing and hide my love for you, let's talk about how you feel about me. Don't wrench out reasons for rejecting me from what I'm about to say, that because I'm chasing you, therefore you have no reason to love me. Instead, take your rational self and shackle it with a very good reason to love me: that love that you might seek is good, but love that you receive without expecting it is even better.

The general idea is probably clear at first or second reading, providing the actor with a very good idea of what she is trying to accomplish in saying these words. What is not so easily achieved, but which is necessary in order to own this speech, is why these words in this order mean that. An audience member or someone reading for general interest is free to be satisfied with a general understanding; and actor's comprehension must be specific and concrete.

A few of the words might need to be clarified. In preparing my informal translation, I looked up "extort" and "fetter" in the *Oxford English Dictionary*, which I had handy because I'd just looked up "maugre." This allowed me to confirm my intuition about the emotional weight of those words because of the associations of both with imprisonment, torture, legal process, abuse of power, loss of freedom, and honor.

But the real puzzle came in trying to figure out the interconnectedness of the phrases, given that so many of the grammatically required linking words have been dropped to create the pithy, striking rhetoric of the last four lines. Here is how they might appear if all of the connecting words were in place.

Do not extort thy reasons from this clause, [which follows, thusly,]
For that I woo [thee], thou therefore hast no cause [to woo me in return/
    love me?]:
But rather [than extorting reasons], [take your] reason [and] thus, [in the
    following manner] with [the following] reason fetter [your reason];
Love sought, is good, but [Love] given unsought [is] better.

Many of the links and repeated words, though they clarify things, are not really necessary and they do nothing to increase the impact of the communication Olivia is trying to accomplish. One of the missing phrases accomplishes an even more important task, and that is allowing Olivia to avoid clarifying what she means. Is she saying that because she, the girl, is declaring her love, therefore the boy isn't going to have to come up with romantic things to whisper in her ear, or plan elaborate strategies to win her love, because he already has it? Or is she addressing a greater danger, that because she had broken a gender taboo and initiated the wooing, he will be repulsed by her, finding her forwardness sufficient reason to judge her unsuitable as an object of his affection? The careful structuring of the idea within the rhetorical strategy allows her listener, Cesario/Viola, and the audience, to fill in the missing phrase.

These four lines demonstrate two of the rhetorical strategies that cause modern actors and audiences a great deal of difficulty. The first is the density of the language, achieved by the elimination of as many words as possible, so that great complexity of thought and feeling can be conveyed by language that can be spoken at something approximating the speed of thought. The absence of words that serve a grammatical function allows the speech to leap from noun to verb, from image to action, from concept to emotion, and the striking juxtapositions suggest the many varied and conflicting impressions, feelings, and ideas at work in the moment.

The second rhetorical strategy is the manipulation of the familiar sequence of words in a grammatically correct sentence, so that the words of greatest significance are positioned for greatest effect. "But rather reason thus with reason fetter" is a sequence of words rearranged from the expected order, which would be, "But rather, you should fetter your reason thusly, with the following reason," or, in condensed form, "But rather fetter reason thus with reason." Of course then we would have neither the rhyme, nor the end-of-line positioning of the powerful image of the fetters of a prison cell.

The combination of density and inversion with purposeful ambiguity can result in passages that are very difficult to clarify intellectually. A sensitive delivery of the sequence of sounds as shaped by the rhythm of the poetry puts an actor in touch with the emotional heart of the moment, which can then be conveyed powerfully to an audience, but until the actor knows why those words, in that precise order, mean what she intuits they must mean, the performance of those lines runs the risk of being filled with sound and fury, but signifying nothing.

Sometimes editors, in an attempt to assist the careful reader, provide an explanation for a troublesome passage. Except when the translation is as convoluted and incomprehensible as the original, these clarify the meaning and confirm the actor's intuition, but they still do not allow for true ownership of this particular sequence of words. For that, the actor must add in all of the missing words, sort out what options are allowed for in the ambiguous absences, and reorder the words and phrases into a familiar sentence structure.

Here is an example of just such a convoluted passage, and the process of acquiring ownership of thought and feeling. Celia and Rosalind have just asked Orlando to withdraw from the wrestling match in which he would be risking his life.

I beseech you, punish me not with your hard thoughts, wherein I confess me much guilty to deny so fair and excellent Ladies any thing. But let your fair eyes, and gentle wishes go with me to my trial, wherein if I be foiled, there is but one shamed that was never gracious: if killed, but one dead that was willing to be so: I shall do my friends no wrong, for I have none to lament me: the world no injury, for in it I have nothing: only in the world I fill up a place, which may be better supplied, when I have made it empty. [*AYLI* 1.2.183]

Much has been made of Orlando's lack of formal education; one of the purposes of this speech is to convey to the audience that this is a young man of natural wit with a strong command of the art of speaking. Although the sentences are complex in structure, the flow of thought suggests a clear and noble personality with nothing to hide. Orlando is presented as a young man already sensitive to the ironies of the adult world. The careful use of repeated words helps the listeners on stage (the two princesses) and off (the audience) follow his delicate comparisons:

wherein	*if* I be foiled, there is but one shamed that was never gracious:		
	if killed, but one dead that was willing to be so:		
I shall do my friends	*no* wrong,	*for* I have none to lament me:	
the world	*no* injury,	*for* in it I have nothing:	

At the end of the speech, Orlando gives voice to something very like despair, which in a less comic world might bring about a very unhappy ending: "only in the world I fill up a place, which may be better supplied when I have made it empty." To make the transition from the regular parallel structures, the word "only" marks a contrasting perspective, and the second "world" echoes the first, as "empty" echoes "nothing." The simple power of the speech comes in large part from the juxtaposition of words, sometimes in antithesis, as in "one shamed that was never gracious," where the concept of grace, that is, nobility, and shame are contrasted, or in parallel comparison: foiled and killed, friends and the world, fair eyes and gentle wishes.

When we encounter a passage like this, it is important that we remember that Shakespeare could have, if he wished, created clear, flowing, always comprehensible passages. Let us assume that form matches content in some profoundly significant way. Although logic is a part of rhetoric, and can be brought into service at any time, it can also be jettisoned for the sake of powerful spoken communication. So too is grammar, though it often serves the needs of rhetoric, regularly put aside to make a point. Clarity and simplicity are suitable for certain types of effective communication, but we simply cannot view convolution and density as failed rhetoric. Rather, they are examples of rhetoric applied for a specific communication challenge, chosen because they are the perfect means by which the communication can occur.

When writing dramatic poetry, Shakespeare blends the requirements and capacities of the Iambic Code with the flexibility allowed by the art of rhetoric. In prose passages, the rhetorical structures alone give shape to the language, although Shakespeare's sensitivity to sound and rhythm remains striking and inspiring.

RHETORICAL PUNCTUATION

Give me some breath, some little pause.

Buckingham [*RIII* 4.2.24]

If you have an opportunity to compare the punctuation used in the folio or quarto edition of a play and that used by a modern editor, you will be struck by how freely the commas, colons, semicolons, and even periods have been changed. What this marks, in essence, is the shift from using punctuation as a marker of the Elizabethan rhetorical system to using punctuation in the accepted modern grammatical practices of formal writing supplemented, when required, by contemporary patterns of using punctuation to suggest dramatic interpretation.

The closest we will ever get to what Shakespeare actually wrote is one of the available editions of a published play, with who knows how many changes made intentionally or in error. But even if we do not ascribe the punctuation of the quartos and folios to Shakespeare's hand, we can assume that the publisher was attempting to make the play readable, and used punctuation to assist the silent reader in this task. Modern editors do the same thing. The difference is that modern editors are trying to make Shakespeare clear to modern readers schooled in modern grammar. Shakespeare's first editors were creating books for readers educated in the same rhetorical system so familiar to Shakespeare and his actors.

For that reason alone, I think it is important to return to the punctuation of Shakespeare's first editions. The commas, colons, semicolons, periods, question marks, and exclamation marks were added by someone who had in his inner ear the speech rhythms of Shakespeare's theatre. Let me give you an example of what happens when a modern editor's punctuation shapes your exploration of a piece of text.

Here is a modern version of Mowbray's speech, which we looked at for clues arising from the Iambic Code. I have copied the format from the *Riverside Shakespeare*:

> A heavy sentence, my most sovereign liege,
> And all unlook'd for from your Highness' mouth.
> A dearer merit, not so deep a maim
> As to be cast forth in the common air,
> Have I deserved at your Highness' hands.
> The language I have learnt these forty years,
> My native English, now I must forego,
> And now my tongue's use is to me no more
> Than an unstringed viol or a harp,
> Or like a cunning instrument cas'd up,
> Or being open, put into his hands
> That knows no touch to tune the harmony.
> Within my mouth you have enjail'd my tongue,
> Doubly portcullis'd with my teeth and lips,
> And dull unfeeling barren ignorance
> Is made my jailer to attend on me.
> I am too old to fawn upon a nurse,
> Too far in years to be a pupil now.
> What is thy sentence [then] but speechless death,
> Which robs my tongue from breathing native breath?

Here is the same text in the folio and then the quarto:

> A heauy sentence, my most Soueraigne Liege,
> And all vnlook'd for from your Highnesse mouth:
> A deerer merit, not so deepe a maime,
> As to be cast forth in the common ayre
> Haue I deserued at your Highnesse hands.
> The Language I haue learn'd these forty yeares

(My natiue English) now I must forgo,
And now my tongues vse is to me no more,
Then an vnstringed Vyall, or a Harpe,
Or like a cunning Instrument cas'd vp,
Or being open, put into his hands
That knowes no touch to tune the harmony.
Within my mouth you haue engaol'd my tongue,
Doubly percullist with my teeth and lippes,
And dull, vnfeeling, barren ignorance,
Is made my Gaoler to attend on me:
I am too old to fawne vpon a Nurse,
Too farre in yeeres to be a pupill now:
What is thy sentence then, but speechlesse death,
Which robs my tongue from breathing natiue breath?

A heauy sentence, my most soueraigne Liege,
And all vnlookt for from your Highnesse mouth,
A deerer merit not so deepe a maime,
As to be cast forth in the common ayre
Haue I deserued at your Highnesse hands:
The language I haue learnt these forty yeeres,
My natiue English now I must forgo,
And now my tongues vse is to me, no more
Than an vnstringed violl or a harpe,
Or like a cunning instrument casde vp,
Or being open, put into his hands
That knowes no touch to tune the harmonie:
Within my mouth you haue engaold my tongue,
Doubly portculist with my teeth and lippes,
And dull vnfeeling barren ignorance
Is made my Gaoler to attend on me:
I am too olde to fawne vpon a nurse,
Too far in yeeres to be a pupill now,
What is thy sentence but speechlesse death?
Which robbes my tongue from breathing natiue breath.

Generally, modern punctuation is too "correct" relative to the flowing energies of a scene. Modern editors like to put in periods whenever a thought has been completed, even if the forward-moving energy of the speech is better represented by a colon or semicolon. Editors like to use commas entirely grammatically, whereas in the first texts they are sprinkled to much greater effect as markers for quick breath resulting in an evocative syncopated rhythm. Modern editors must work quite a bit harder than the first editors simply to clarify what is being read. The shifts in familiar patterns in structuring sentences means that modern readers need careful guidance to follow a thought; the first readers were better able to recognize the rhetorical strategy at work and so didn't need the same sort of overt markers. Generally, modern punctuation slows and intellectualizes as it clarifies; rhetorical punctuation from the first texts results in surging rip-tides of oratory.

In exploring rhetorical punctuation, we must realize that we are in the area of speculation. We have no direct evidence of Shakespeare's punctuation practices, and the use of punctuation, the use of rhetorical structures, and the printing industry were undergoing radical change in Shakespeare's life. We simply cannot assume a pre-set, comprehensive, and enduring connection between punctuation and anything else.

Even so, there is clearly a pattern in the use of commas, colons, semicolons, and other punctuation marks. Not every instance supports the observable pattern, which could mean that the existing punctuation mark is an error, or the pattern is loosely structured and open to a wide variety of alternatives. Sufficient examples of punctuation in keeping with the general patterns do suggest that the marks were a reliable means of communication, from first editor to first readers, of the way that the words should be imagined as spoken.

Historians have suggested that the earliest punctuation marks were inserted so that those reading aloud might pause appropriately, to assist the listener in understanding the progression of the argument or the flow of the narrative. There was need for some sort of mark to suggest the end of a thought, the equivalent of our period. There was also a need for something at the other end of the scale, the barest possible pause to shape the speaker's flow, drawing the listener's attention to what had just been said, and what was about to be said. We are equally familiar with the comma, and if we are given a passage to read aloud on sight, we make use of the period and comma today very much as these pointers were used in their earliest published form.

Something inbetween the two markers is also needed; the thrust of the argument or story can be ongoing, even when one thought has finished and a new one is about to begin. We are familiar with the semicolon and colon, although many of us interchange these marks with commas or with periods because the correct grammatical use is not as clearcut. We also do not have as ready a verbal cadence to match these median pointers.

The other use of punctuation is to assist in the comprehension of the grammatical structure of a sentence. The tension between punctuation for sense and punctuation to mark cadence remains to plague writers and their teachers and editors today. Rather than getting caught up in any sort of debate about what is or is not grammatically correct punctuation, we place our entire focus on how punctuation suggests cadence, how these pointers instruct the speaker.

The comma and the period each signal a speaking strategy that is the same for Shakespeare's first publishers as for us today. The comma signals the slightest of pauses. Perhaps the speaker breathes in, perhaps just a very short silence. The end sound of the word before the comma holds steady or rises slightly, to suggest clearly that the thought is not completed, but this can be a very slight modulation because everything else is in accordance with the incomplete nature of the thought. There is little chance that the listener will mistake a comma for a period.

On a period, however, the speaker makes a clear cadence of the voice. The drop in pitch, corresponding to the clear completion of a thought, and any other indication of conclusion enacted by the speaker with facial expression or gesture, work together to give the listener a clear marker. Because these signals are so clear and so significant, it is extremely difficult for an actor who has learned a text with modern punctuation to challenge the preliminary reading engendered by those markings. Once you've memorized a period, you have to make a conscious effort to link that idea with another to bypass the power of the period marker, even more so because you were not particularly conscious of memorizing the punctuation along with the words. The subtle shapings of commas present even more pervasive and irritating shapings. The editor has, in effect, instructed you to link this noun with this, and separate those two from the three that follow, by putting in that comma, when it might just as easily have been a different linking that you memorized.

Here is the best example of the havoc an editor can play with groupings of nouns and verbs, through alterations in the location of commas. Here, I have reproduced the punctuation that appears in a popular internet site, operated by the Massachusetts Institute for Technology, or MIT:

What a piece of work is a man! how noble in reason! how infinite in faculty! in form and moving how express and admirable! in action how like an angel! in apprehension how like a god! the beauty of the world! the paragon of animals! And yet, to me, what is this quintessence of dust? man delights not me: no, nor woman neither, though by your smiling you seem to say so. [*Hamlet* 2.2.303]

Here now is the Riverside version:

What [a] piece of work is a man, how noble in reason, how infinite in faculties, in form and moving, how express and admirable in action, how like an angel in apprehension, how like a god! The beauty of the world; the paragon of animals; and yet to me what is this quintessence of dust? Man delights not me—nor women neither, though by your smiling you seem to say so.

This is the same speech as it appears in the second quarto:

What peece of worke is a man, how noble in reason, how infinit in faculties, in forme and moouing, how expresse and admirable in action, how like an Angell in apprehension, how like a God: the beautie of the world; the paragon of Annimales; and yet to me, what is this Quintessence of dust: man delights not me, nor women neither, though by your smilling, you seeme to say so.

And the folio:

What a piece of worke is a man! how Noble in Reason? how infinite in faculty? in
forme and mouing how expresse and admirable? in Action, how like an Angel? in
apprehension, how like a God? the beauty of the world, the Parragon of Animals; and
yet to me, what is this Quintessence of Dust? Man delights not me; no, nor Woman
neither; though by your smiling you seeme to say so.

Now let us compare the Riverside to the folio and quarto.

What [a] piece of work is a man, [exclamation mark in the folio, followed by a small
letter]
    how noble in reason, [question mark in the folio, followed by a small letter]
    how infinite in faculties, [in folio the word is faculty, followed by a question mark,
then a small letter]
    in form and moving, [no comma in the folio]
    how express and admirable [folio has question mark followed by small letter here]
in action,
    how like an angel [folio has question mark followed by small letter here] in appre-
hension,
    how like a god! [folio has question mark followed by small letter here; 2nd quarto
has
    a colon; in both, the following word is *not* capitalized]
    The beauty of the world; [folio has comma]
    the paragon of animals;
    and yet to me [both folio and 2nd quarto have comma]
    what is this quintessence of dust? [2nd quarto has colon followed by small letter]
    Man delights not me—[neither folio nor 2nd quarto uses a dash. Folio has semicolon
followed by "no,"; 2nd quarto has just a comma]
    nor women neither,
    though by your smiling [2nd quarto has comma here]
    you seem to say so.

We can see by this comparison that there are only three punctuation marks
that are the same in the three versions we are comparing. The folio makes
much more use of exclamation marks and question marks, indicators of rhetorical emphasis. And these markers divide up the verbs and nouns in quite a
different way. Is the connection, as the Riverside suggests, "how noble in
reason, how infinite in faculties, in form and moving, how express and admirable in action, how like an angel in apprehension, how like a god!" or is
Hamlet's point, "how noble in reason, how infinite in faculties, in form and
moving how express and admirable, in action how like an angel, in apprehension how like a god!" This is the way the speech appears in Signet edition.
Quite a different thought. Quite a different flow.

Also note, in neither the folio nor the quarto is there any indication of the
end of a thought at this point in Hamlet's speech, yet the Riverside editor feels
obliged to capitalize the next word, making just such a division in flow and
thought between the first part and the second.

Punctuation for Sense

In assessing the relative theatrical success of the contrasting modern versions of Hamlet's speech, we, like the modern editors, judge on the basis of modern conventions. What conventions were available to the first publishers? From the few manuscripts that have survived the four hundred years since these plays were first performed, we know that Shakespeare and his contemporaries punctuated very lightly, while the typesetters of his day felt free to add punctuation to suit their own tastes and to serve the needs of a reading public. They also would have heard these plays spoken aloud, and might well select markings to suggest the customary oratorical strategies available to actors. Before we can decide whether that style of speaking will serve us in the modern theatre, we need to understand the conventions for punctuation that were in use at the time.

Modern punctuation sets a significant difference for the usage of the colon and the semicolon. In Shakespeare's time, punctuation, like spelling, was less strictly regulated. But a far more important difference is that punctuation was used to suggest the length of pause for breath to be taken by the speaker, and the intonation required to link the phrase ending to the one following. The period, then as now, marks the fullest intake of breath and the cadencing of the voice to signal the end of a thought. We find far fewer periods in the first publications of the plays than in modern ones, and this is the single most important adaptation that the modern actor must make: do not assume that the end of a grammatical thought is the end of a rhetorical structure. Cadence far less than you do in modern plays, and do everything in your power to clarify—with tone of voice and emotional coloring and energy flow—the connection between the ideas in the speech.

The comma, then as now, suggests the shortest of pauses, a quick intake of breath, and generally Shakespeare's first editors threw them into the texts far more often than grammatically necessary. They appear often to mark patterns of emphasis that were common in oration. For example, a modern editor would have Puck say:

> Sometime for a three-foot stool mistaketh me;
> Then slip I from her bum, down topples she,
> And "tailor" cries, and falls into a cough;
> And then the whole quire hold their hips and loff,
> And waxen in their mirth, and neeze, and swear
> A merrier hour was never wasted there. [*Dream* 2.1.52]

In the folio there is an extra comma after hips. The intonation suggests a meaning of "not only did they hold their hips, they also laughed," rather than the less charged "they both held their hips and laughed." There is also an extra comma after stool, as if the speaker marks a slight pause before the end of the speech, to draw out the joke most effectively.

It is in the use of colons and semicolons that the modern editors follow the most significantly different set of conventions. Today, we use the semicolon to join two complete sentences that have some meaningful connection which is suggested by the punctuation rather than conveyed by the use of a specific linking word such as "because" or "on the other hand."

> My dog has fleas; my cat has a flea collar.
> Although my dog has fleas, my cat has a flea collar.
> My dog has fleas because my cat has a flea collar.
> My dog has fleas. On the other hand, my cat has a flea collar.

In written form, the semicolon efficiently sets up the juxtaposition but allows for a variety of speculations as to the exact nature of the connection. In spoken form, the semicolon invites the voice to rise on the first "fleas," suggesting an unfinished thought, followed by a pause greater than a comma, and then the second part of the sentence cadencing on the final word. Less formal writing might suggest this with

My dog has fleas. . . . My cat has a flea collar.

Colons, on the other hand, are used to introduce extra information. We most often use it to set up things like lists.

The car was filled to the roof rack: boxes, blankets, baby carriage, baby seat, baby.

As we can see from the folio version of Hamlet's speech, colons are used where today we would use commas or semicolons. Sometimes they link phrases, sometimes grammatically complete sentences. Clearly, they suggest a rhetorical strategy that is not grammatical.

A further test of the validity of what I call rhetorical punctuation, as found in the first publications of these plays, can be made upon those speeches that we looked at first without any punctuation. I reproduce them here complete with long spellings, so that you can spot all possible correlations between the discoveries made with and without the clues from the folio.

> Had'st thou but shooke thy head, or made a pause
> When I spake darkely, what I purposed:
> Or turn'd an eye of doubt upon my face;
> As bid me tell my tale in expresse words:
> Deepe shame had struck me dumbe, made me break off,
> And those thy feares, might have wrought feares in me.
> But, thou didst understand me by my signes,
> And didst in signes againe parley with sinne,

Yea, without stop, didst let thy heart consent,
And consequently, thy rude hand to acte
The deed, which both our tongues held vilde to name.
Out of my sight, and never see me more:
My Nobles leave me, and my State is braved,
Even at my gates, with rankes of forraigne powres;
Nay, in the body of this fleshly Land,
This kingdome, this Confine of blood, and breathe
Hostilitie, and civil tumult reignes
Betweene my conscience, and my Cosins death. [*John* 4.2.231]

Greefe fils the roome up of my absent childe:
Lies in his bed, walkes up and downe with me,
Puts on his pretty lookes, repeats his words,
Remembers me of all his gracious parts,
Stuffes out his vacant garments with his forme;
Then, have I reason to be fond of griefe?
Fare you well: had you such a losse as I,
I could give better comfort then you doe.
I will not keepe this forme upon my head,
When there is such disorder in my witte:
O Lord, my boy, my Arthur, my faire sonne,
My life, my joy, my food, my all the world:
My widow-comfort, and my sorrowes cure. [*John* 3.4.93]

We can venture through these two speeches line by line, just as we did when we sought clues from the Iambic Code. We will use the punctuation to guide our patterns of breathing, so that a comma will draw a quick breath, a period demand a full stop, and the colon and semicolon a breath somewhere in between. More importantly, we will use the colons as suggestions of the building of a rhetorical argument, so that they mark a transition that might be verbalized as, "Having said what I have just said, I am now able to continue with my next point, which is as follows." We will note how capitalizations and long spellings might suggest words of heightened significance. At the same time, we will remember that this is poetry, and continue to make use of the rising energy of each verse line as well as the forward driving force of the rhetorical argument. And so we begin with John and Hubert.

Had'st thou but shooke thy head, or made a pause

The action verb leaps out, in its simplicity and clarity. Because I know where this is all going, I am all the more likely to let a vivid picture pop into my head, of Hubert standing silently, not moving, when I first proposed the elimination of young Arthur.

When I spake darkely, what I purposed:

As earlier, when there was no special marking, the image of dark speaking leaps out. I also notice the colon after "proposed" and realize that I've just made the opening manoeuver in my rhetorical argument. Having caught Hubert's attention, I'm ready to proceed.

> Or turn'd an eye of doubt upon my face;

The semicolon suggests that I've reached a more significant juncture in the argument, something akin to changing directions. As soon as I move on to the next line, my strategy is confirmed.

> As bid me tell my tale in expresse words:

This was a qualifier, placing the blame of my guilt on his complicity. What actually occurred is an example of masterful manipulation of his loyal servant by a king:

John: If this same were a Church-yard where we stand,
And thou possessed with a thousand wrongs:
Or if that surly spirit melancholy
Had baked thy blood, and made it heavy, thick,
Which else runs tickling up and down the veins,
Making that idiot laughter keep mens eyes,
And strain their cheeks to idle merriment,
A passion hateful to my purposes:
Or if that thou couldst see me without eyes,
Hear me without thine ears, and make reply
Without a tongue, using conceit alone,
Without eyes, ears, and harmful sound of words:
Then, in despite of brooded watchful day,
I would into thy bosom pour my thoughts:
But (ah) I will not, yet I love thee well,
And by my troth I think thou lov'st me well.

Hubert: So well, that what you bid me undertake,
Though that my death were adjunct to my Act,
By heaven I would do it.

John: Do not I know thou wouldst?
Good Hubert, Hubert, Hubert throw thine eye
On yon young boy: I'll tell thee what my friend,
He is a very serpent in my way,
And wheresoere this foot of mine doth tread,
He lies before me: dost thou understand me?
Thou art his keeper.

Hubert: And I'll keep him so,
That he shall not offend your Majesty.

John: Death.
Hubert: My Lord.
John: A Grave.
Hubert: He shall not live.
John: Enough.
          I could be merry now, Hubert, I love thee.
          Well, I'll not say what I intend for thee. [3.3.40]

The memory of that conversation must be with us both as I continue:

Deepe shame had struck me dumbe, made me break off,

Suddenly, the alliteration coupled with the long spelling draws my eye and
ear to the connection between deep shame and silence. The commas make me
want to rush on to the next line:

And those thy feares, might have wrought feares in me.

The comma marks the midline inversion, and I'm very glad to find a period,
a place to stop and regroup, to change the key in which I am composing this
verbal music. I'm fascinated to note the correspondence between this punctuation and my earlier thoughts on the transition marked by the first word of
the next line:

But, thou didst understand me by my signes,

The extra, ungrammatical comma reinforces the significance of that little word
"but." I still don't completely understand what I mean when I refer to signs,
except that the long spelling indicates that there might be something more
going on here. Another quick look at the scene in act three suggests some
subtle signs or signals in my words, and his, as my next line suggests:

And didst in signes againe parley with sinne,

It is impossible to miss the long spelling on that terrible word at the end of
this line, and I'm glad that the comma signals the shortest intake of breath so
I can move on to:

Yea, without stop, didst let thy heart consent,

I can feel the speed picking up here, as I work my way through the section
that follows the period and the transitional "but."

And consequently, thy rude hand to acte

There is no punctuation at all at the end of this line, and the long spelling of the final word invites me to punch it out and move on to the next line:

> The deed, which both our tongues held vilde to name.

Another period. I feel like I have raced through that terrible section, and now I'm ready to change key yet again, and seek an entirely new strategy for my argument.

> Out of my sight, and never see me more:

Well, that was a change. But I note the colon at the end of the line. I only say that in order to move on to what follows:

> My Nobles leave me, and my State is braved,

Here the capital letters suggest that significance of the nobles and the state for my status as king, and in fact for the safekeeping of England herself.

> Even at my gates, with rankes of forraigne powres;

The strange spelling of the words at the end of the line slow me down, in a way that lends gravity to what I am saying. There is something particularly terrible about invasion by foreign troops and, having said that, I have reached a semicolon, and must prepare to make some sort of contrasting statement.

> Nay, in the body of this fleshly Land,

This time, the semicolon seems to signal an intensification of the original statement, as the imagery becomes almost sensual in its physicality. The capitalization of "land" reinforces the significance I noticed earlier, and the comma suggests a quick breath before moving on to the next line:

> This kingdome, this Confine of blood, and breathe

A combination of two long spellings and a capital letter draw my energy away from blood, saving me from selecting for special consideration the least interesting of the words in this line.

> Hostilitie, and civil tumult reignes

The ungrammatical comma before the "and" draws attention to the word it follows, a word that I'd spotted as significant with the help of the Iambic Code, and the long spellings draw attention away from tumult, again toward the less obviously significant words.

> Betweene my conscience, and my Cosins death.

I'm surprised that the first word of this line is more significant than either "conscience" or "death," but I suspect that I am being lured away from a modern pattern of emphasis toward something more subtle, wherein the obvious words take care of themselves and the special attention is given elsewhere in the line, as a means of saving this speech from the trap of melodrama.

Now let us turn to Constance and her grief:

> Greefe fils the roome up of my absent childe:

Here we find quite a different effect, as the first and last words, so clearly charged with feeling, also receive the long spelling, as does the middle noun. The colon reminds me that I am not just expressing my feelings, but attempting to persuade, to demonstrate, to change the way my listeners look at the situation. Having stated this essential premise, I can move on to the next stage of my presentation:

> Lies in his bed, walkes up and downe with me,

Again, it is interesting to find such simple, telling words given the added weight of the long spelling. The comma at the end of the line gives me the shortest possible time to pause before moving on.

> Puts on his pretty lookes, repeats his words,

The pattern continues. I open my imagination to just how Arthur might look, but keep the flow moving as suggested by the commas.

> Remembers me of all his gracious parts,

There is no time to do more than say these words, let these memories wash over me, and move forward to my next line:

> Stuffes out his vacant garments with his forme;

The semicolon invites some sort of transition. I'm struck by the words at the beginning and the end of the line, which arouse images that work against the dominant feelings of grief. I can't help but imagine stuffing oneself at a banquet or stuffing old clothing to make a scarecrow. And just what is the form of grief?

Then, have I reason to be fond of griefe?

The semicolon clearly signalled the shift with the word "then" that I'd noted earlier, but now I drive toward a question mark. Is this rhetorical, or am I expecting an answer? And isn't it interesting that grief is spelled differently here than in the first line?

Fare you well: had you such a losse as I,

The colon after the farewell phrase seems absolutely perfect. Those words are not an ending, but rather a springboard to the words that follow. The long spelling of loss simply drives home the absolute simplicity of her painful situation. Arthur is not dead, though he might as well be, because he is lost to her.

I could give better comfort then you doe.

If we discount the question mark, this period marks the first shift in key. What else can I say?

I will not keepe this forme upon my head,

Because I now know what is happening in the scene, that she is taking off her formal headgear with these words, much to the dismay of the king of France who is trying to comfort her, I find greater significance in the word form than I did before. I also suddenly realize that it is the same word, and same spelling, as when used to describe the shape of grief.

When there is such disorder in my witte:

The long spelling of wit, followed by the semicolon, forces me to consider very carefully just where I am going with this confession of confused thinking. But of course it need not reflect a rational, premeditated strategy; the rhythm is absolutely right for what follows:

O Lord, my boy, my Arthur, my faire sonne,

The commas force me to slow down and sit for a moment with each image, and the long spellings of the last two words draw out a lingering pain.

My life, my joy, my food, my all the world:

This line feels like four stabs of pain, and the commas separate them clearly in my mind, giving me the opportunity of hearing, for the first time, the internal rhyme of boy with joy, a crystalization of all that I have lost. The colon invites me to view all that has preceded this moment as preparation for my final communication, in fact my last lines in the play:

My widow-comfort, and my sorrowes cure.

How painful the hyphen makes the image of his comfort to me, and how deeply the long spelling of sorrow moves me, into empathy for this woman's plight.

ANALYZING SENTENCES

In addition to our familiar grammatical strategies that allow for the creation of compound complex sentences, Shakespeare was free to make use of a few additional devices in service of the rhetorical power or poetic intensity required by the situation. These strategies fall into two general categories: inversions and compressions.

Although we do not often vary from the simple sentence structure of subject/verb/predicate, we can recognize the meaning of a sentence or phrase in which the inversion has occurred, and appreciate the special impact of such an inversion. Think, for example, of an advertising slogan such as "Squirbles: Drink Them for Fun!" The "correct" word order would be "Drink squirbles for fun," but "squirbles" draws our eye and ear much more powerfully to the intended focus of the slogan. This sort of inversion is possible because individual words that mark subordinate clauses or verb phrases, or that identify a noun phrase as a subject or object of a verb, are such clear markers of how those words function in the construction of the sentence that we do not need to encounter the sentence in the correct order to understand the correct relationship between the parts of the sentence.

However, we still expect to see the more familiar sentence order when we read, and we count on getting important information from the organization of the parts of any sentence. We expect the active subject to come very early in the sentence, if not first, and we expect words that relate to each other to be close together, if not side by side.

Compression is another familiar linguistic trick that emerges when patterns of words are so familiar as to be predictable, allowing us to leave out words, confident in the assumption that the listener or reader will "fill in the blanks" as needed. So we know that "Your mother would," as a response to "I can't think of a single person who would want to own a painting on black velvet," actually means, "Your mother is, in fact, the one single person you do know who would want very much to own a painting on black velvet." Compression is the proof of the adage, "Less is more." The short, compressed response has just the impact the speaker wishes, and the meaning is perfectly clear.

Shakespeare's theatre allowed for some spectacular inversions and compressions. We can only assume that the audience was attuned to hear sentences of such complexity, rearranged so very completely, and compressed recklessly; the intonation and emphasis of the actor speaking would of course point the way. The modern actor is in a much trickier position. The modern audience is not so tuned, and the modern actor faces the daunting task of getting these complex sentences up off the page, into the mouth and mind, and then find a strategy for emphasis and intonation to "sell" the sentence, which often involves leading the audience through the maze step by step.

Let us take it as a given that the shape of the sentence reflects the content in some important way. A simple sentence might present a profound emotion: "The king is dead; long live the king." But only a complex sentence can reflect the glorious leaps of the mind, the tortured uncertainties of the spirit, the blind longings of the soul. And so, in order to perform Shakespeare's complex sentences, an actor needs to be able to think some complex thoughts. Then, because of the compression, everything speeds up and the mind must move like lightning through the pattern of phrases and connections.

There are no shortcuts through these syntactical nightmares. It can be overwhelmingly intimidating or depressingly frustrating to encounter one of these monsters in your assigned lines. And, unlike the Iambic Code, the encounter of your intuitions and Shakespeare's language never seems to get any easier; there is no hope of having the entire intellectual process of analysis and conscious exploration become subliminal, familiar, natural. Let us assume, therefore, that if a character is driven to build a lengthy and highly complex sentence, filled with inversions and compressions, the character's mental state can only be comprehended by the actor undertaking the laborous journey into the heart of the puzzle.

Let us have a go at some of the sentence patterns in major speeches, ranging from early to late, and from formal argument to flights of fancy and passion, including male and female speakers, well-known and obscure speeches, prose and poetry.

Here is the widowed Duchess of Gloucester, trying to persuade John of Gaunt to take action to avenge the murder of his brother, her husband.

> Finds brotherhood in thee no sharper spur?
> Hath love in thy old blood no living fire?
> Edwards seven sons (whereof thyself art one)
> Were as seven vials of his Sacred blood,
> Or seven fair branches springing from one root:
> Some of those seven are dried by nature's course,
> Some of those branches by the Destinies cut;
> But Thomas, my dear Lord, my life, my Gloucester,
> One Vial full of Edward's Sacred blood,
> One flourishing branch of his most Royal root
> Is cracked, and all the precious liquor spilt;
> Is hacked down, and his summer leaves all faded

By Envys hand and Murders bloody Axe.
Ah Gaunt! His blood was thine, that bed, that womb,
That metal, that self-mould, that fashioned thee,
Made him a man: and though thou liv'st and breath'st,
Yet art thou slain in him: thou dost consent
In some large measure to thy Fathers death,
In that thou seest thy wretched brother die,
Who was the model of thy Fathers life.
Call it not patience (Gaunt) it is despair,
In suffering thus thy brother to be slaughtered,
Thou show'st the naked pathway to thy life,
Teaching stern murder how to butcher thee:
That which in mean men we intitle patience
Is pale cold cowardice in noble breasts:
What shall I say, to safeguard thine own life,
The best way is to venge my Gloucesters death. [*RII* 1.2.9]

The first two lines, a pair of questions, demonstrate Shakespeare's favorite tricks of reordering and condensing in order to sharpen the effectiveness of the Duchess's argument.

Finds brotherhood in thee no sharper spur?
Hath love in thy old blood no living fire?

Rewritten into a more straightforward order, and with the missing words inserted, these two lines might read:

Can brotherhood find no sharper spur in thee?
Does love have no living fire in thy old blood?

By slipping the prepositional phrase (marked by "in") into the middle of the line, each question can end with the more powerful image: sharp spurs and living fire. By inverting both questions the same way, the parallel structure draws our ear and mind to the connection between the two questions. The fact that Gaunt is so reluctant to avenge his brother's death suggests that his age is having an effect on his ability to feel passion about anything.

The next eleven lines form one sentence that presents the argument that, as a son of a great king, Gloucester's death has great spiritual, as well as political, significance.

Edwards seven sons (whereof thyself art one)
Were as seven vials of his Sacred blood,
Or seven fair branches springing from one root:
Some of those seven are dried by nature's course,
Some of those branches by the Destinies cut;
But Thomas, my dear Lord, my life, my Gloucester,

One Vial full of Edward's Sacred blood,
One flourishing branch of his most Royal root
Is cracked, and all the precious liquor spilt;
Is hacked down, and his summer leaves all faded
By Envys hand and Murders bloody Axe.

The first three lines take us to an important colon. They establish the proposition, with one parenthetical thought and two alternative comparisons. The nominal group is the seven sons of King Edward III. The verb is "were" which places all of the significance of the second half of the sentence on what follows, the two options: seven vials or seven branches. The repetition of the word seven, plus the clear indicators "as . . . or . . ." make it easy to follow the branching of the sentence into the two alternatives. After the branching, the sentences take slightly different directions. "Vials" is modified by the phrase "of his sacred blood," while "branches" is modified by "springing from one root." This contrasting language pattern allows each image to be self-sufficient and striking, but still linked at the important juncture. These are divergent, not parallel, images.

The next three lines of poetry each begin with an important linking word that takes us forward from the colon. "Some" is used twice, again to signal similar responses to the first part of the sentence. The parallel nature of the construction is reinforced by the next two words; the phrase "Some of those" creates an almost ritualized quality to this section of the sentence. But then the two phrases are quite differently constructed. The first, "Some of those seven are dried by nature's course," follows a regular syntactical strategy, using the passive voice of the verb "to dry," and then identifying the force that has done the drying. The second, "Some of those branches by the Destinies cut," uses the same verb structure, but inserts the force that has done the action before the verb itself. This allows for an echo of the hard "c" from "course" to "cut" and also, as with the pair of phrases that immediately precedes this, suggests the similarities and the differences at the same time. Vials are dried up and branches are cut. Nature and Destiny are at work. Similar, but not exactly the same, because the drying up of the blood is a function of aging, and the cutting of branches a more abrupt, though accidental, death.

At this point we have in the folio a semicolon, and then the third word which could well have followed the colon, which marked the setup to this section of the Duchess's argument. "But" evokes here the same sudden change in direction as it would in a modern speech. At this point, the layering on of modifying phrases grow dense, and we must clarify the essential components of the sentence: "But Thomas . . . is cracked . . . is hacked." This is the same two-option construction as began the sentence, with the verb "to be" now in the present tense. Everything else tells us more about Thomas and more about the two verbs. The repetition of the possessive pronoun makes it easy to understand that "dear lord" and "life" and "Gloucester" are all equal modifiers of "Thomas" and that the Duchess is making an important connection between his noble title, her formal relationship with him, and the depth of her love for him. Similarly, the repetition of "one" helps us to follow the two modifying phrases that follow. The double-duty images of a vial of blood and a branch of a root return for the third time, with significant new words. Thomas is a "full" vial and a "flourishing" branch, and the root is now "most royal." Remember that this speech started with the Duchess suggesting that John of Gaunt's blood is old; Thomas, in contrast, was young, vigorous, a far better demonstration of the genetic inheritance of Edward III's royal lineage. At this point, the structure of the sentence reaches its greatest complexity. We have one vial that is cracked, and one branch that is hacked down. But the two nouns and the two verbs are paired with each other rather than with the corresponding sentence component. However, it is not too difficult to follow the interwoven threads, because of the natural link between noun and verb, and by the additional information which is linked directly to each of the verbs with the word "and." So we learn that the cracked vial resulted in all the precious liquid being spilled, and the hacked branch resulted in the fading of all of the summer leaves. We've seen verbs in the passive voice before in this sentence: Nature and Destiny were responsible for the drying and cutting. Here, at last, as the sentence builds toward its climactic conclusion, the agents of the cracking and hacking are finally mentioned: envy's hand and murder's bloody axe. This is where we feel the impact of the complex sentence structure. Earlier, the drying was linked to Nature only, and the cutting to Destiny. Here, the paired nouns and paired verbs are separated by the paired agents, so that envy's hand and murder's bloody axe merge into a single entity, a single action, a murder prompted by envy, and the two alternative images for Edward's sons become one moment of death. And she is only halfway there. The Duchess must build on this powerful evocation of the murder of Gaunt's brother by driving home the three-way connection between the two brothers and each brother to the shared parents.

> Ah Gaunt! His blood was thine, that bed, that womb,
> That metal, that self-mould, that fashioned thee,
> Made him a man: and though thou liv'st and breath'st,
> Yet art thou slain in him: thou dost consent
> In some large measure to thy Fathers death,
> In that thou seest thy wretched brother die,
> Who was the model of thy Fathers life.

"His blood was thine" is the simplest statement in the sentence. What follows is a list of four nouns, each introduced by "that" to draw our ear to their exact parallel nature: bed, womb, metal, and self-mould. This list forms a precise picture of the passing of genetic material, through the sexual act that brings a man's seed to a woman's womb, that creates sons who bear a physical and emotional similarity to their father, and who pass on that similarity, in turn, to their sons. Remember that this interaction is taking place within the context of the upcoming trial by combat that threatens the life of Gaunt's son, the Duchess's nephew, grandson of Edward III. The four nouns form two pairs: bed is to womb as metal is to self-mould. We can hear this if we mark the connection between the womb and the mould into which the metal is poured.

The sentence then pulls one of those tricks that is possible because the simple word "that" is suddenly used to form a different grammatical function. It shifts from an indicator for emphasis and clarity, as in "that bed over there" to a replacement for the original noun, meaning "the one that did it." So once we have finished with the two sets of paired nouns, we move on to the significance of all of this: the same activity that created you, created him. "Fashioned" and "made" can be used as verbs to describe the activity of procreation and metal-working; the first suggests the careful artistry of the craft while the second is much more functional a verb, but it required a direct object. What was made? Answer: a man. Again, the Duchess draws a comparison between Gaunt's lack of masculine passion and her dead husband's undeniable masculinity.

We have now reached another colon, so whatever the Duchess has been setting up in this sentence, it is now time to drive the point home. "And though ... yet ..." sets up the point she must make. The first half uses active verbs: living and breathing; the second reverts to the passive voice. She cannot say "you are dead," but she can say, "thou art slain." Then, there is no agent suggested, no "by whom," but instead the clarifying phrase that explains how a living, breathing man can be slain—"in him." In other words, the part of you that is in him is dead.

But that is also not the point of the sentence. That concept—that by sharing the same parents they are so positioned that the death of one creates a paradox whereby the living brother can still be said to have been slain—is presented so as to drive home the greatest accusation: that Gaunt has been a passive witness to the murder of his own father. The syntax is relatively straightforward and the careful antithesis created by "thy father's death ... thy father's life" allows her to present this difficult concept. The placing of "in some large measure" between "consent" and "to thy father's death" does not create a problem; nor does the location of the modifying phrase "who was the model" separated from "wretched brother" by the word "die" because of the clear identifying function of the pronoun "who." Now we reach the last sentence of her argument.

> Call it not patience (Gaunt) it is despair,
> In suffering thus thy brother to be slaughtered,
> Thou show'st the naked pathway to thy life,
> Teaching stern murder how to butcher thee:
> That which in mean men we intile patience
> Is pale cold cowardice in noble breasts:

What shall I say, to safeguard thine own life,
The best way is to venge my Gloucesters death.

Here, the rhetorical punctuation of the folio gives us a clear pathway to follow for delivering the rhetorical argument, but the grammatical construction of the sentence is entirely confusing. The Riverside editors have put a period at the end of the first line, preferring the clarity of the simple contrast between patience and despair to the more complex function of the concept of despair in the rhetorical argument. With a comma in place of a period, the phrase, "it is despair" is the lead-in to the next phrase: the Duchess must describe the despair, explain how Gaunt's actions demonstrate despair. If we insert an imagined "because" following this comma, we can see how the rising intensity of the endgame of her argument is working here. What is so fascinating about these constructions is that, by having grammar bow to rhetoric, Shakespeare captures the rhythms of a speaker who knows the point she wants to make but not exactly how it is going to come out. The power of language is not clean and tidy, but racing, raging, unravelling in the split second she thinks of what to say next.

After the imagined "because" following "despair," the thought would be much clearer if the next two lines were reversed. It is despair because you show the murderers an unimpeded path toward the next murder—yours—by allowing your brother to be slaughtered, in fact you teach the murderers how to butcher you. This is truly a type of despair. By reordering the three phrases, we can still follow the connection and benefit from the juxtaposition of the two images: showing the naked pathway, which is more obscure, followed by teaching the butchers, which is clear. In addition, by starting this explanation with "in suffering thus" and leaving out the "because" there is a brief moment, before the thrust of the argument is clarified, when it appears as if the explanation will end with that phrase. It is despair to suffer the death of a brother. This is the despair she is feeling. The rhetorical construction allows both meanings to coexist. Strict grammar would force the Duchess to choose between one of the meanings, and to convey the second with additional words. The elision of "because" and the inversion of the sentence allows for the emotional density of the rhetorical argument. It is simultaneously logical (if you do this, then that will occur) and emotional (I know what despair feels like. You are acting out of despair.). The Riverside editors clean up the end of the speech, by putting a period after "breasts" and a question mark followed by a capital so that "What can I say?" becomes an almost comically familiar phrase. The punctuation of the folio captures, I think, the breathless energy that must link the question and the summation of the argument, though the actor must inflect "What can I say," so that the rhetorical question is clear. And the colon is far preferable than the period. The actress must link the final argument with the closing summation as powerfully as possible.

Let us look at another speech from this remarkable play, one which we have already used as an example of the Iambic Code at work, and then explore the difference in modern and Elizabethan punctuation. Mowbray's farewell to England will also serve as an excellent example of the construction of an argument. His first sentence is built upon a contrast:

> A heavy sentence, my most Sovereign Liege,
> And all unlooked for from your Highness mouth:
> A dearer merit, not so deep a maim,
> As to be cast forth in the common air
> Have I deserved at your Highness hands.

"Dearer merit" and "deep maim" benefit from the alliteration and the asymmetrical construction: dearer but not deeper. There is a second unspoken contrast, between the heavy sentence and what Mowbray feels he deserves. The positioning of "mouth" and "hands" reinforces this antithesis: the king might speak a sentence but what might he also give in the way of reward for past services rendered? With the colon, we know that the word "mouth" is the leaping off point for what follows; it is then most effective if the contrasting word "hands" sits right before the period that marks the culmination of this stage of the argument. The inversion of the sentence, resulting in the disconnection of "have I deserved" from the two nouns that the phrase modifies, "merit" and "maim," is justified by the rhetorical power it creates. The small words "as" and "in" help us to follow the function of the phrase, which tells us exactly what the maim is, "to be cast forth in[to] the common air," and this is the theme of the rest of the speech. Mowbray could have said many things in response to Richard's betrayal. He could have brought up the fact that he has done murder for Richard (he is responsible for the death of Thomas of Gloucester, whose widow we met in the previous scene) or he could have questioned the King's intervention in what was otherwise a legitimate trial by combat. Instead, he expands on the precise nature of the "deep maim." The construction of this opening sentence sets up the rest of the speech by what might otherwise appear as simply an awkward placement of the modifying phrase, "As to be cast forth in the common air." Awkwardness is seldom just that. Shakespeare could be clear when that was what was required. Convolution, inversion, ungrammatical separations, and unexpected juxtapositions are all rhetorical strategies of great power. They also suggest the working of the human mind: Mowbray's thoughts lingered too long on the deep maim, he had to say just what it was, even though the phrase gets in the way of the logical flow of the sentence, and that lingering then takes hold and his tongue gives shape to what he is feeling.

> The Language I have learned these forty years
> (My native English) now I must forego,
> And now my tongues use is to me no more,

Than an unstringed Viol, or a Harp,
Or like a cunning Instrument cased up,
Or being open, put into his hands
That knows no touch to tune the harmony.

The little word "or" appears three times as Mowbray searches for the perfect metaphor for what it feels like to be cut off from one's native language. First, he thinks of an instrument unstringed, perhaps a viol or a harp. Then he thinks of any wonderful musical instrument locked up in its case. Then, as an alternative, he offers the image of someone opening up the case and putting the instrument into the hands of someone who does not know how to play it. We have no trouble following the train of thought, although it is not smooth and the phrases created by the use of "or" are not pleasantly balanced. Even more awkward is "now my tongue's use is to me no more, than. . . ." Modern editors take out the comma so that "no more than" makes grammatical sense on the page; it is more effective however in the theatre to take a slight pause for breath and for emphasis before launching into the imagery. But what are we to make of "my tongue's use is to me no more?" Why not just say, "is no more use to me"? These are all single-syllable words, and the meter is equally well served by "and NOW my TONGUE is NO more USE to ME" as it is by "and NOW my TONGUE's use IS to ME no MORE." However, if you try to say these two versions aloud, you will discover that they have quite different tonal qualities and Shakespeare's version twists the tongue and requires a slower delivery. The sequence of three "s" sounds simply doesn't roll off the tongue the way "no more use to me" does.

We have no evidence that Shakespeare deliberated consciously over various possible wordings, and made choices to guide his actors, thinking to himself, "I'll put it this way so that the actor has to slow down and really feel this, that will get the effect I want here." In fact, from everything we know, Shakespeare wrote quickly and edited very little before bringing the works to the theatre. So if the tonal quality of the line contains any theatrical messages, they are probably intuitive. That ordering of words just seemed right, somehow, for Mowbray and for the presentation of Mowbray's situation by the working mouth and lips and tongue and breath of the actor for whom Shakespeare wrote the role. Shakespeare was, after all, an actor and a shareholder in a theatre company. He cared much more for the success of the plays in front of an audience than for how the words would appear to literary scholars. Even if he had consciously considered his language, he would analyze this speech for its rhetorical strategies, not for its grammar. We need to speak the words, feel the impact of the sounds as we do this, and accept that the flexibility of language is being used to serve the theatrical moment, not simply to create archaic and/or poetical structures.

Back to Mowbray. He proceeds to talk about very much what we have been discussing: the sensation of a speaker of language:

Within my mouth you have engaoled my tongue,
Doubly portcullised with my teeth and lips,
And dull, unfeeling, barren ignorance,
Is made my Gaoler to attend on me:
I am too old to fawn upon a Nurse,
Too far in years to be a pupil now:
What is thy sentence then, but speechless death,
Which robs my tongue from breathing native breath?

When I was a child, a British airline had a television commercial advertising tours to England in which some deep-voiced English actor intoned part of the following speech in a way that gave me goosebumps. I realize now that it was, in part, the glorious rhetorical strategy of using the same first word in every phrase that ensured the sonorous effect. Who could have believed that anyone could pull it off to this extent? This entire speech is one grammatically sentence; despite the folio's period after "Mary's Son," you must wait for the verb until the second to last line.

This royal Throne of Kings, this sceptered Isle,
This earth of Majesty, this seat of Mars,
This other Eden, demi-paradise,
This Fortress built by Nature for her self,
Against infection, and the hand of war:
This happy breed of men, this little world,
This precious stone, set in the silver sea,
Which serves it in the office of a wall,
Or as a Moat defensive to a house,
Against the envy of less happier Lands,
This blessed plot, this earth, this Realm, this England,
This nurse, this teeming womb of Royal Kings,
Feared by their breed, and famous by their birth,
Renowned for their deeds, as far from home,
For Christian service, and true Chivalry,
As is the sepulchre in stubborn Jewry
Of the Worlds ransom, blessed Mary's Son.
This land of such dear souls, this dear dear Land,
Dear for her reputation through the world,
Is now Leased out (I die pronouncing it)
Like to a Tenement or pelting Farm.

The speaker, John of Gaunt, is dying and short of breath, but in the way of so many other death scenes, his final words are endowed with the glory that comes from having one foot in this world and one in the next. Earlier in the scene, Gaunt had explained, "Where words are scarce, they are seldom spent in vain, / For they breathe truth, that breathe their words in pain" [2.1.7]. With that sort of a setup, we can imagine everyone in the audience listening very carefully, and savoring the paean to national pride. Thank goodness, because look what Gaunt springs on his audience—one of the most convoluted sentences in the cannon:

> This Nurse, this teeming womb of Royal Kings,
> Feared by their breed, and famous by their birth,
> Renowned for their deeds, as far from home,
> For Christian service, and true Chivalry,
> As is the sepulchre in stubborn Jewry
> Of the worlds ransom, blessed Mary's Son.

The first phrase, "this nurse," and the phrases after, "this land of such dear souls, this dear dear land," are wonderfully simple and suggest through imagery and repetition the love Gaunt feels, like what he feels toward his nanny, this home of everyone he holds dear. But between the phrases is an idea that has to do with the great sweep of history, every last one of the great kings of England, and the nature of their fame in the entire world. The stakes have to be as high as possible, and the phrases pile on, each one filled with the most powerful images, but grammar has gone out the window. How do these phrases connect? When reading this aloud for the first time, it's difficult to tell what modifies what. But if we can examine the words on the page, working purely in the literary mode, we realize that "Feared by their breed, and famous by their birth," modifies "Kings," and so does "Renowned . . . as far from home." Next, it's easy to see that "As is the sepulchre in stubborn Jewry," tells us just how far away from home the kings are known. "The world's ransom, blessed Mary's Son," says the same thing twice, in two different ways; both these phrases mean Jesus Christ. His tomb or sepulchre is in Jerusalem, and the winning back of this city from the non-Christian Ottoman Empire was the goal of the Crusades which dominated the political agenda of so many medieval kings. Jerusalem is also the home of the Jewish faith, those people who stubbornly, at least from a Christian point of view, refused to accept Jesus as the messiah promised by the Old Testament prophets. The last piece can now be placed into the speech. "For Christian service, and true chivalry" is parallel to another phrase that begins with the same word, "for their deeds," so the kings are renowned for their deeds *and* for their service and chivalry. But there is a second possibility, that the deeds are for the purpose of Christian service and true chivalry, which would be an apt description of the crusades from John of Gaunt's point of view.

So even now we cannot say that we have come to the end of what this tangled web might mean. But we have gone far enough for now, because only by saying the words, and giving ourselves over to the rhythms of the rhetoric, without trying to know in advance what it all means, can we discover its rhetorical power and its human truth. Allow your character, poor John of Gaunt, not to know what he's going to say next, not to know why he must layer the phrases, but knowing that this layering captures the truest sense of the greatness of these kings. I'll try to capture the flow of the rising tide of feeling and include some bracketed questions that suggest the leap that the transition conveys.

> [what sort of kings?]
>
> [*firmly*] Feared by their breed, and famous by their birth,
>
> > [famous? why do you say that? how famous?]
>
> [*slightly more intense*] Renowned for their deeds, as far from home,
>
> > [yeah, right, like when they invaded France?]
>
> [*making an important additional point*] For Christian service, and true Chivalry,
>
> > [OK, that sort of deed, I remember that]
>
> [*returning to the main argument, with a growing intensity to emphasize the extreme distance of fame*] As is the sepulchre in stubborn Jewry,
>
> > [what sepulchre? I'm lost again]
>
> [*clarifying the great significance, the emotional point of the entire section, marking the huge spiritual values of Jesus Christ himself*] Of the Worlds ransom, blessed Mary's Son
>
> > [I agree, the most important grave site in the Western world]

Suddenly, the passage comes clear, and we see that the craft of rhetoric uses grammar because the long list of nouns and noun phrases introduced by the word "this" do, in fact, lead to a verb and predicate, and also abuses grammar for rhetorical effect. The five-line passage we've been working on would require the addition of several more linking words to transform it into a grammatically clear and correct sentence. But those linking words have been elided out, excised to create a striking rhythm and an emotional leaping from image to image that captures the way we think and communicate with intensity. If you included it in an essay as your own writing, recorded as prose, the teacher would mark all over it with a red pencil. But once we've spotted the simple trick of the rhetorical structure, we can say these words and be understood.

Since Shakespeare was capable of writing so clearly, are we to take these complexly tangled webs as bad writing? When I'm correcting essays, I often find myself scrawling "AWK" in the margin, meaning that the sentence is awkwardly constructed and could do with a rewrite. Is it possible that we have been left with some disasters which Shakespeare left uncorrected in his speed to get his manuscripts to the actors in the company? Or is the problem the four-hundred-year shift and the supremacy of grammar over rhetoric in our school systems?

Here is another tangled web that horrifies every actor taking on the role of

Ariel in *The Tempest*. In the guise of a harpy, Ariel makes vanish the banquet brought to the castaways by the dancing spirits under his command. When some draw swords to attack him, he responds:

> You fools, I and my fellows
> Are ministers of Fate, the Elements,
> Of whom your swords are tempered, may as well
> Wound the loud winds, or with bemocked-at-Stabs
> Kill the still-closing waters, as diminish
> One dowle that's in my plume: My fellow ministers
> Are like-invulnerable: if you could hurt,
> Your swords are now too massy for your strengths,
> And will not be uplifted: But remember
> (For that's my business to you) that you three
> From Milan did supplant good Prospero,
> Exposed unto the Sea (which hath requit it)
> Him, and his innocent child: for which foul deed,
> The Powers, delaying (not forgetting) have
> Incensed the Seas, and Shores; yea, all the Creatures
> Against your peace: Thee of thy Son, Alonso
> They have bereft; [3.3.60]

Up until this point, all seems to be flowing smoothly. But what happens next? Here is how Ariel tops this great beginning, and to deny you any assistance, I reproduce it in "free fall," without punctuation:

> and do pronounce by me
> Lingering perdition worse than any death
> Can be at once shall step by step attend
> You and your ways whose wraths to guard you from
> Which here in this most desolate isle else falls
> Upon your heads is nothing but heart-sorrow
> And a clear life ensuing.

Whose wraths? What exactly will fall on their heads? What are they being guarded from? What or who will do the guarding? Before you answer those questions intellectually, let's see how the lines might come at the castaways listening so intently to this strange creature. We'll borrow a technique we have used before and take it line by line. Not sentence by sentence. Let's back up a bit.

> Him and his innocent child for which foul deed

The contrast between innocent victim and foul deed is powerful, and the causality clear. If Ariel paused here, the listeners would say, "OK, punishment, probably, but what?"

The powers delaying not forgetting have

It's clear, even without punctuation, when the words are said aloud, that "delaying, not forgetting" tells us about the powers, and leaves us still in suspense about the punishment these powers will inflict for the foul deed. We think, "What, what, have what??"

Incensed the seas and shores yea all the creatures

This we understand. We've lived through a shipwreck. The strange shapes offered us a banquet and then took it away. We can feel how incensed they all are against us. But if Ariel made us wait, we'd want to know exactly what they've been incensed to do. Anything worse than we've already had?

Against your peace thee of thy son Alonso

The midline inversion helps us to hear what punctuation informs the reader's eye: Ariel turns midway through this line and addresses just one of the group, the king Alonso, who turned a blind eye to the deposition of Prospero, and so is an accessory. He is also, at this moment, in mourning for his son, drowned in the storm. If he raises his head, surely he is saying, "What punishment for me?"

They have bereft and do pronounce by me

The first part of the line answers the question of Alonso's punishment. There is a direct link between his culpability so many years ago and his loss today. But then, what is going to be pronounced? More punishment? Will Alonso lose his kingdom? His life? And what about the others, more guilty of the crime?

Lingering perdition worse than any death

Well, that answers the question about death. There is a punishment much worse. How long will they be stuck on this island? Until they all die? Is this a type of purgatory, and will they never be allowed to forget their griefs and sins? Imagine that you're listening to this, and you begin to rebel a little against this pronouncement. Ariel responds by increasing the intensity on the single-syllable words that come marching out in the next line:

Can be at once shall step by step attend

There's no denying the pounding power of these words, like a curse, and the soul responds even as the mind grapples to achieve the exact meaning. Is the punishment coming at once? Or do those words simply describe a sudden death, contrasted with lingering perdition? Or is it both of those?

> You and your ways whose wraths to guard you from

Now the imagery comes clear. Perdition is like a courtier, the sort that always hangs around, never leaves you alone, and goes with you everywhere, attending you and walking right beside you, matching his step to yours. And suddenly, there are more characters in this little drama, called wraths. Whose are they? Perditions? Or the Powers who delayed but didn't forget. Does it matter? What a terrible word, summoning up nightmares of the furies from ancient Greek legends or the evil fairies of childhood tales. And yet, the line ends with something of a promise. They can be guarded from. Something, someone, can somehow stand between you and the wraths, whoever they are. How? Who?

> Which here in this most desolate isle else falls

We don't get the answer to our question, but instead a heightening of the images of terror. Wraths will fall from above, in an attacking motion, in this terrible, terrifying place. But again, that lovely word, second to the last, "else." We're burning to know how we can avoid the punishment.

> Upon your heads is nothing but heart's sorrow

When we first hear this line, we feel as if the wraths falling on our heads are the embodiment of the sorrow. And yet, that can't be right, can it? In the middle of the line is that strange construction, that takes a moment to unravel, so that we are aware of the negative even as Ariel moves on to the closing image:

> And a clear life ensuing.

The hope is now before us. Heart's sorrow is not the wrath, but the very thing that guarantees avoiding the wraths, because of what follows, a clear life. The convoluted structure of the thought was purposeful, it led us through the maze to torment us, to deny us easy answers, and to suggest the complexity and paradox of the pain that heals, and the sorrow that saves. Now that we have worked our way through it, here is how it appears with folio punctuation:

> and do pronounce by me
> Lingering perdition (worse than any death
> Can be at once) shall step, by step attend
> You, and your ways, whose wraths to guard you from,
> Which here, in this most desolate isle, else falls

Upon your heads, is nothing but heart-sorrow,
And a clear life ensuing.

Persuasion

Here is another example, that demonstrates the structuring of an argument
to persuade. A close analysis of its power clarifies how rhetorical structures
function in the shaping of thought and feeling.

Hold thy desperate hand:
Art thou a man? thy form cries out thou art:
Thy tears are womanish, thy wild acts denote
The unreasonable Fury of a beast.
Unseemly woman, in a seeming man,
And ill beseeming beast in seeming both,
Thou hast amazed me. By my holy order,
I thought thy disposition better tempered,
Hast thou slain Tybalt? wilt thou slay thy self?
And slay thy Lady, that in thy life lies,
By doing damned hate upon thy self?
Why rail'st thou on thy birth? the heaven and earth?
Since birth, and heaven, and earth, all three do meet
In thee at once, which thou at once wouldst lose.
Fie, fie, thou sham'st thy shape, thy love, thy wit,
Which like a Usurer abound'st in all:
And usest none in that true use indeed,
Which should bedeck thy shape, thy love thy wit:
Thy Noble shape, is but a form of wax,
Digressing from the Valour of a man,
Thy dear Love sworn but hollow perjury,
Killing that Love which thou hast vowed to cherish.
Thy wit, that Ornament to shape and Love,
Misshapen in the conduct of them both:
Like powder in a skilless Soldiers flask,
Is set afire by thine own ignorance,
And thou dismembered with thine own defence.
What, rouse thee, man, thy Juliet is alive,
For whose dear sake thou wast but lately dead.
There art thou happy. Tybalt would kill thee,
But thou slew'st Tybalt, there are thou happy.
The law that threatened death becomes thy Friend,
And turned it to exile, there art thou happy.
A pack of blessing light upon thy back,
Happiness Courts thee in her best array,
But like a misshaped and sullen wench,
Thou puttest up thy Fortune and thy Love:
Take heed, take heed, for such die miserable.

Go get thee to thy Love as was decreed,
Ascend her Chamber, hence and comfort her:
But look thou stay not till the watch be set,
For then thou canst not pass to Mantua,
Where thou shalt live till we can find a time
To blaze your marriage, reconcile your Friends,
Beg pardon of thy Prince, and call thee back,
With twenty hundred thousand times more joy
Than thou went'st forth in lamentation.
Go before Nurse, commend me to thy Lady,
And bid her hasten all the house to bed,
Which heavy sorrow makes them apt unto.
Romeo is coming. [3.3.108]

The roots of the rhetorical strategies in Shakespeare's plays stretch back to the art of oratory as developed in the great city-state of Athens, where every citizen participated in management of the city. Arguing persuasively for going to war or making a peace-treaty was the right and responsibility of every free man (slaves and women were not citizens of Athens). At this moment in *Romeo and Juliet*, the Friar must persuade Romeo not to kill himself in despair, but in fact to move forward from the terrible mischance that threatens to destroy the young man who has just unwittingly caused the death of his best friend, murdered his new cousin-by-marriage, and learned that he has been banished forever from Verona and hence from his bride Juliet.

If ever there were need for rhetorical power, this is it. The Friar, as a man of god, might be expected to find this relatively easy. But as we have learned from earlier scenes, and also from his actions earlier in this scene, the Friar is not exactly a sermonizing machine. He likes flowers. He loves Romeo deeply, as his spiritual son. He is flustered and terrified by the knocking at the door, as he will be later when he mismanages the scene in the crypt. But language comes to his aid. His love and spirituality empower him to say just what Romeo needs to hear at this moment.

Let's use this speech to explore the strategies of rhetoric that exist at the level of individual words. These are the figures of speech, ways of patterning words to draw attention to the pattern because of the connection between patterns in language and patterns in thought. One example will help clarify what this means. The Friar asks Romeo,

Hast thou slain Tybalt? wilt thou slay thyself?
And slay thy Lady, too that lives in thee,
By doing damned hate upon thyself? [3.3.116]

Three times in two lines he uses the word "slay" in order to point out an unfortunate pattern. Having killed Tybalt, Romeo now prepares to kill himself. He has forgotten that a third person will be killed by this action, emotionally if not physically. While there might be a reason to counter one slaying with another, suicide as an expression of a murderer's remorse and guilt, the third slaying makes no sense, and this repeated use of the word brings this to Romeo's attention, accomplishing the Friar's goal, which is to persuade him to a completely different view of the past, present, and future.

Slay is a powerful word and the repetition reinforces the importance of the concept of murder. But patterns in thought can be conveyed by the repetition of simple linking words. Let's look at the words that the Friar uses next in his argument:

> Why rail'st thou on thy birth, the heaven, and earth?
> Since birth, and heaven, and earth, all three do meet
> In thee at once; which thou at once wouldst lose. [3.3.119]

The eye quickly spots the repetition of the trio of important words, "birth," "heaven," and "earth," but equally important to the success of the pattern is the simple word "and."

Bite off the next section and see what rhetorical figures come to the Friar's aid.

> Fie, fie, thou shamest thy shape, thy love, thy wit;
> Which, like a usurer, abound'st in all,
> And usest none in that true use indeed
> Which should bedeck thy shape, thy love, thy wit:
> Thy noble shape is but a form of wax,
> Digressing from the valour of a man;
> Thy dear love sworn but hollow perjury,
> Killing that love which thou hast vowed to cherish;
> Thy wit, that ornament to shape and love,
> Misshapen in the conduct of them both,
> Like powder in a skitless soldier's flask,
> Is set afire by thine own ignorance,
> And thou dismembered with thine own defence. [3.3.122]

We have the same pattern of repeating three key words, "shape," "love," and "wit," here separated by a few lines, and highlighted by the repeated use of the simple word "thy." Then the same three words return, each used to set up a longer thought. The first two of these are contained in two lines of verse each, but the third requires fully five lines in which the Friar drives home the importance of wit to both shape and love, which are repeated once more to clarify the connection. Look at how this section ends. The repetition of "thine own" helps to set up the horrible images of "set afire with thine own ignorance," and "dismembered with thine own defence."

In the next section, the Friar repeats subtle variations of the phrase, "there art thou happy" almost like a ritualized chant, in keeping with the rocking, hugging comfort a parent gives a distraught child.

> What, rouse thee, man! thy Juliet is alive,
> For whose dear sake thou wast but lately dead;
> There art thou happy: Tybalt would kill thee,
> But thou slew'st Tybalt; there are thou happy too:
> The law that threatened death becomes thy friend
> And turns it to exile; there art thou happy:
> A pack of blessings lights up upon thy back;
> Happiness courts thee in her best array;
> But, like a misbehaved and sullen wench,
> Thou pout'st upon thy fortune and thy love:
> Take heed, take heed, for such die miserable. [3.3.135]

"Take heed, take heed" is the Friar's last use of striking repetition which has provided so much of the emotional power of the speech. These are a type of hammering, and when they disappear, it is as if the Friar has become gentler, calmer. Romeo's need for a large dose of tough love is suggested by how long it has taken the Friar to reach the less overtly patterned instructions:

> Go, get thee to thy love, as was decreed,
> Ascend her chamber, hence and comfort her:
> But look thou stay not till the watch be set,
> For then thou canst not pass to Mantua;
> Where thou shalt live, till we can find a time
> To blaze your marriage, reconcile your friends,
> Beg pardon of the prince, and call thee back
> With twenty hundred thousand times more joy
> Than thou went'st forth in lamentation.
> Go before, nurse: commend me to thy lady;
> And bid her hasten all the house to bed,
> Which heavy sorrow makes them apt unto:
> Romeo is coming. [3.3.146]

The speech is still beautifully patterned, but with phrases of equal length rather than repeated words. Compare "to blaze your marriage," "reconcile your friends," and "beg pardon of the prince" with "and call thee back with twenty hundred thousand times more joy than thou went'st forth in lamentation." The first three, similar phrases of verb/linking word(s)/noun set up a pattern that is boldly broken by the joyous final promise which requires two and a half lines to express.

Romeo and Juliet represents Shakespeare mid-career, sure of his craft and using the Iambic Code and the strategies of rhetoric to great dramatic effect almost perfectly in keeping with character and situation. It is useful to have a look at earlier plays, to seek out examples of rhetoric that are less subtly employed than in the Friar's brilliant emotional rescue of the suicidal Romeo.

Richard III contains one of my favorite examples of overt rhetoric. Queen Margaret has been wandering around the palace like a revengeful ghost, most appropriately because the historical record shows that she was back in France during these events and could not possibly have been present. She has watched the wife of the man who assumed the throne after the death of Margaret's husband and son, spewing hatred of this newest Queen for usurping Margaret's title. Now the tide has turned. The usurper, Elizabeth, has seen her husband die and her own two sons murdered in the tower by their evil uncle, Richard. While Elizabeth is bewailing her fate, Margaret gives her a philosophical lesson on that very subject. To reinforce the image of teaching, Margaret uses the sort of obvious rhetoric that one might hear in a schoolhouse, when one of the students is asked to "decline," or recite in order, on the topic of "the course of justice."

> I called thee then, vain flourish of my fortune:
> I called thee then, poor Shadow, painted Queen,
> The presentation of but what I was;
> The flattering Index of a direful Pageant;
> One heaved a high, to be hurled down below:
> A Mother only mocked with two fair Babes;
> A dream of what thou wast, a garish Flag
> To be the aim of every dangerous Shot;
> A sign of Dignity, a Breath, a Bubble;
> A Queen in jest, only to fill the Scene.
> Where is thy Husband now? Where be thy Brothers?
> Where are thy two Sons? Wherein dost thou Joy?
> Who sues, and kneels, and says, God save the Queen?
> Where be the bending Peers that flattered thee?
> Where be the thronging Troops that followed thee?
> Decline all this, and see what now thou art.
> For happy Wife, a most distressed Widow:
> For joyful Mother, one that wails the name:
> For one being sued to, one that humbly sues:
> For Queen, a very Caitiff, crowned with care:
> For she that scorned at me, now scorned of me:
> For she being feared of all, now fearing one:
> For she commanding all, obeyed of none.
> Thus hath the course of Justice wheeled about,
> And left thee but a very prey to time,
> Having no more but Thought of what thou wast,
> To Torture thee the more, being what thou art,
> Thou didst usurp my place, and dost thou not
> Usurp the just proportion of my Sorrow?
> Now thy proud Neck, bears half my burthened yoke,

From which, even here I slip my wearied head,
And leave the burthen of it all, on thee.
Farewell, Yorks wife, and Queen of sad mischance,
These English woes, shall make me smile in France. [4.4.82]

Let's start with the obvious rhetorical figures. Look at the repetition of words at the beginning of phrases in the section that follows "Decline all this":

For happy Wife, a most distressed Widow:
For joyful Mother, *one* that wails the name:
For one being sued to, *one* that humbly sues:
For Queen, a very Caitiff, crowned with care:
For she that scorned at me, *now* scorned of me:
For she being feared of all, *now* fearing one:
For she commanding all, obeyed of none.

That is balanced by the repeating of words that conclude phrases, "me" and "all." The repetitions set up the contrasting words that demonstrate how far Elizabeth has fallen. Wife has become widow, queen has become caitiff, meaning slave, scorned at becomes scorned of. Verbs shift from active to passive or vice versa: "being sued to" becomes "humbly sues," "feared of all" becomes "fearing one." The final comparison combines opposite words and shift in verb: "commanding all" becomes "obeyed of none."

Another familiar rhetorical device is a series of questions. The repeating of the interrogators, with that "wh" sound that has a misleading softness, is used by Margaret to hypnotize and torment her victim:

Where is thy Husband now? *Where* be thy Brothers?
Where are thy two Sons? *Wherein* dost thou Joy?
Who sues, and kneels, and says, God save the Queen?
Where be the bending Peers that flattered thee?
Where be the thronging Troops that followed thee?

There's just enough variety to keep this from becoming mechanical. Three uses of "where" is followed by "wherein" and "who" before we conclude with two more uses of "where." Four half-line questions are followed by three full-line questions, the last two shaped into exactly parallel structures, both beginning with "where be the," ending with "thee," and using "that" as an anchor, so that "bending peers" contrasts "thronging troops," and "flattered" contrasts "followed."

When rhetorical figures are used to compress complex thought, sentences can get quite difficult to follow unless the subtle inflections of the voice are called into play. Margaret's speech contains a sequence that is difficult for the mind when read silently but comes clear when spoken:

Thus hath the course of Justice whirled about,
And left thee but a very prey to time,
Having no more but Thought of what thou wast,
To Torture thee the more, being what thou art.

The first two lines are clear, and wonderfully evocative if you think of justice as a powerful rider on a great stallion, following a fox on a course through the countryside, suddenly wheeling his horse so that it rears up over the discovered victim, and then switch the image to think of time as a bird of prey like a hawk, circling before it plunges down onto the terrified field mouse. But what about the last two lines? Say the lines aloud, using the Iambic Code:

HAVing no MORE but THOUGHT of WHAT thou WERT
to TORture THEE the MORE being WHAT thou ART.

We know from our work on the code that "having" and "being" need to be highlighted because the first is used for the attacking energy of the inverted first foot while the second is a two-syllable word compressed into a single-syllable slot. Knowing that, we can see the contrast between having something and being something, and hold those in the back of our minds as we see just what is being contrasted. At the end of the two lines, the final words toward which the lines build, are "wert" and "art," past and present. The rhetorical figure heightens our awareness of the contrast: "what thou" is repeated. The other repetition, which is not combined with a parallel structuring of words, is "more" which is used in two quite different ways. Margaret says that Elizabeth has nothing but ("no MORE but") thought . . . to increase the pain ("torture thee the MORE"). What she does not say outright, but what the figure implies, is that because she can remember what it was like, and because that is all she has left, the pain of what she currently has to endure is not only increased, but the perfect example of how justice works, by torturing you with the perfectly crafted punishment.

Now look closely at how the two lines work together. Margaret is saying that Elizabeth, the prey of time, has nothing left but thoughts of what she used to be. The palaces and fancy clothes are all gone. All she has are memories. Fine, that's a complete thought. She is also saying that it needs nothing more than the thoughts of what Elizabeth used to be to torture her all the more when compared to what she is right now. That's another complete thought, and we've seen how Margaret can play the torturer by using just words and images, never touching her rival, yet causing immense pain.

In other words, the phrase "having no more but thought of what thou were" is a hinge, modifying the phrase before and the phrase following, but *not* linking the three phrases into a single simple observation. There are, in fact, three observations: the two I have paraphrased above, and a third, that all of this is a very special type of justice.

If you're thinking that there is no way you could convey all of this, with emphasis and intonation, then I'd have to agree. The point of rhetoric is that the communication takes place between someone who uses rhetorical devices and someone who *hears* them. The real secret for exploring this four-line sequence is that the responsibility rests with the actress playing Elizabeth to work through what it means, so that when she hears it in its compressed form, she can understand it, and react as Elizabeth would react, because Elizabeth would understand what Margaret is saying, and Margaret would know that Elizabeth understands. Modern actresses can pretend to understand, or act out a generalized, "this is a good hit here," and "ouch, she got me there," without knowing why these exact words, in this precise order, are the climax of the speech.

As something of an aside, look at the first ten lines, the setup to the rhetorical tour-de-force. The metaphor at work here is a theatrical presentation or pageant of the sort prepared by a town to honor a monarch like Elizabeth as she travelled around her kingdom. Shakespeare, his actors, and his audience would be familiar with such pageants, and were, at the moment these words were spoken, sitting watching a "scene." In these first ten lines, Margaret is presenting a comparison between herself and Elizabeth through the metaphor of an actor playing the role of a queen on the stage. Two things emerge from this. Margaret is able to speak so powerfully about Elizabeth's fall from power in the rest of the speech not only because she hates the woman and has a powerful drive to hurt her deeply, but also because she herself has been there, done that. Elizabeth is still just acting the role that Margaret herself has already played, the scorned caitiff, the wailing widow who has lost her only child, the victim of time and justice. In other words, don't assume that vicious revenge is the only thing going on here. Consider also pity, empathy, sympathy, recognition of one's own guilt, and the appropriateness of one's own downfall.

If that comment helps the actress to get more deeply into the reality of the moment, despite the rhetorical flourishes, the next comment might take us in the opposite direction. Remember that the role was originally played by a man, wearing a good deal of makeup (paint) in a dress donated to the company by some noblewoman, who would leave the theatre and walk the streets as a member of a new and barely tolerated profession (aligned with the devil, according to the puritans) even though during the play he'd been treated like a queen. So the actor, too, knew what it was like to be powerful and then to be despised. He also knew he was not a queen, and that everything he was about to say was part of the pageant, a jest, a type of dream, the presentation of the idea of "dignity" by a poor shadow.

The heightened language of rhetoric is simultaneously intensely real, reflecting authentic human interactions, and intensely artificial. A modern actor who accesses one without the other is more likely to drown in tears than to soar on the wings of breath and thought made possible by the mastery of the art of language.

So far, our examples of rhetoric have been taken from dramatic verse. One of the most useful discoveries that can come to a modern actor through a familiarity with rhetoric is the structuring of prose speeches. Without the line breaks and caesuras, we are thrown back onto punctuation to chart the rhythms of prose. But we simply cannot trust the punctuation, because we cannot know its source and because it is a literary device, of great help to a reader but little help to a listener. However, the familiar repetitions that mark rhetorical figures of speech prove the source of prose structures in a most delightful way. Here are two examples from *As You Like It*. The first is Jaques's self-analysis, and the second is Rosalind's analysis of the events near the end of the play.

I have neither the Scholars melancholy, which is emulation: nor the Musicians, which is fantastical; nor the Courtiers, which is proud: nor the Soldiers, which is ambitious: nor the Lawyers, which is politic: nor the Ladys, which is nice: nor the Lovers, which is all these: but it is a melancholy of mine own, compounded of many simples, extracted from many objects, and indeed the sundry contemplation of my travels, in which by often rumination wraps me in a most humorous sadness. [4.1.10]

O, I know where you are: nay, 'tis true: there was never any thing so sudden, but the fight of two Rams, and Caesars Thrasonical brag of I came, saw, and overcame. For your brother, and my sister, no sooner met, but they looked: no sooner looked, but they loved; no sooner loved, but they sighed: no sooner sighed but they asked one another the reason: no sooner knew the reason, but they sought the remedy: and in these degrees, have they made a pair of stairs to marriage, which they will climb incontinent, or else be incontinent before marriage; they are in the very wrath of Love, and they will together. Clubs cannot part them. [5.2.29]

Neither of these speeches is particularly difficult to hear and understand. Jaques's long list of different types of melancholy is anchored by the repetitions, and Rosalind builds a stair of words to match the stairs the lovers climb toward marriage. By writing out these speeches so that the repeated words line up, we can see the pattern instantly.

I have neither	the Scholars	melancholy	which is	emulation
nor	the Musicians		which is	fantastical
nor	the Courtiers		which is	proud
nor	the Soldiers		which is	ambitious
nor	the Lawyers		which is	politic
nor	the Ladys		which is	nice
nor	the Lovers		which is	all these
but it is a		melancholy		of mine own

```
For               your      brother and

                  my        sister
no sooner                              met
         but      they      looked
no sooner                   looked
         but      they      loved
no sooner                   loved
         but      they      sighed
no sooner                   sighed
         but      they      asked one another          the reason
no sooner                   knew                        the reason
         but      they      sought        the remedy
```

An example of a considerably more complex rhetorical passage in prose is found in *Henry V* when King Henry is wooing the French princess Katherine. Not surprisingly, given his victory at Agincourt where so many of the French nobility have just perished, the young lover must put to good use all of the arts of persuasion to order to win her love. While still a prince, Henry studied the fine art of rambling prose under that charismatic old tutor, Falstaff, while at the same time learning from his father the linguistic devices necessary to inspire his people with flights of great poetry, all of which he puts to good use when he becomes king. Earlier in *Henry V*, his skill with language was put to the test of inspiring weary and desperate men facing a far greater enemy; he responded to a general's wish to have ten thousand more men to fight at Agincourt with the words, "No, my faire Cousin: / If we are marked to die, we are enow / To do our Country loss: and if to live, / The fewer men, the greater share of honour" [4.3.19]. He then launched into a speech that contains the famous line, "We few, we happy few, we band of brothers" [4.3.60]. And now, here he is, using all of his skill with language to create a "rhapsody of words" [*Hamlet* 3.4.48] with which to win a gentle battle for the heart of France. Let us look at this passage as it appears in the folio.

Marry, if you would put me to Verses, or to Dance for your sake, Kate, why you undid me: for the one I have neither words nor measure; and for the other, I have no strength in measure, yet a reasonable measure in strength. If I could winne a Lady at Leape-frogge, or by vauting into my Saddle, with my Armour on my backe; under the correction of bragging be it spoken. I should quickly leape into a Wife: Or if I might buffet for my Love, or bound my Horse for her favours, I could lay on like a Butcher, and sit like a Jack an Apes, never off. But before God Kate, I cannot looke greenely, nor gaspe out my eloquence, nor I have no cunning in protestation; onely downe-right Oathes, which I never use till urg'd, nor never breake for urging. If thou canst love a fellow of this temper, Kate, whose face is not worth Sunne-burning? that never lookes in his Glasse, for love of any thing he sees there? let thine Eye be thy Cooke. I speake to thee plaine Souldier: If thou canst love me for this, take me? if not? to say to thee that I shall dye, is true; but for thy love, by the L. No: yet I love thee too. And while thou liv'st, deare Kate, take a fellow of plaine and uncoyned Constancie, for he perforce must do thee right, because he hath not the gift to wooe in other places: for these fellowes of infinit tongue, that can rhyme themselves into Ladyes favours, they doe always reason themselves out againe. What? a speaker is but a prater, a Ryme is but a Ballad; a good Legge will fall, a strait Backe will stoope, a blacke Beard will turne white, a curl'd Pate will grow bald, a faire Face will wither, a full Eye will wax hollow: but a good Heart, Kate, is the Sunne and the Moone, or rather the Sunne, and not the Moone; for it shines bright, and never changes, but keepes his course truly. If thou would have such a one, take me? and take me; take a Souldier: take a Souldier; take a King. And what say'st thou then to my Loue? speake my faire, and fairely, I pray thee. [*HV* 5.2.132]

Next, let us break the speech down into its component sentence units, as indicated by the folio punctuation, and rearrange each sentence on the page so as to draw attention to the parallel construction of phrases. In addition, we can italicize key words that are repeated in order to link sentence to sentence.

Marry, if you would put me   to   Verses,
                 or   to Dance for your sake, *Kate*, why you undid me:
        for the one   I have neither words   nor measure;
and   for the other, I have no strength   in measure,
                 yet a *reasonable* measure
                 in strength.

If I could winne a *Lady* at   Leape-frogge, or by vauting into
                 my Saddle,
        with my Armour on my backe; under the correction of bragging
        be it *spoken*.
        I should quickly   leape into a Wife;
Or if I might buffet for my *Love*,
        or   bound my Horse for her favours,
I could   lay on like a Butcher,
        and   sit like a Jack an Apes, never off.

But before God *Kate*, I cannot   *looke* greenely,
        nor   gaspe out my eloquence,
        nor I have no cunning in protestation; onely downe-right Oathes,
             which I never use till urg'd.
             nor never breake for urging.

If thou canst love a *fellow* of this temper, *Kate*, whose face is not worth
    Sunne-burning?

that never *lookes* in his Glasse, for *love* of any thing he sees there? let
thine *Eye* be thy Cooke.

I *speake* to thee *plaine Souldier:*
If thou canst *love* me for this,
take me? if not? to say to thee that I shall dye, is true;
but for thy   *love*, by the L. No:
yet I   *love* thee too.

And while thou liv'st, deare *Kate*,
take a *fellow* of *plaine* and uncoyned Constance.
for   he perforce must do thee right,
because he hath not the gift to wooe in other places:
for these *fellowes* or infinit tongue,

	that can	*rhyme* themselves into *Ladyes* favours,
they doe alwayes		*reason* themselves out againe.

What?   a *speaker* is but   a prater,
          a *Ryme* is but   a Ballad,
          a good Legge   will fall,
          a strait Backe   will stoope,
          a blacke Beard   will turne white,
          a curl'd Pate   will grow bald,
          a *faire* Face   will wither,
          a full *Eye*   will wax hallow:
but   a good Heart, *Kate*, is the *Sunne*   and the Moone,
or rather   the *Sunne*, and not the Moone;
for it shines bright,
and never changes,
but keepes his course truly.

If thou would have such a one,   *take* me?
            and   *take* me;
                           take a *Souldier:*
                           take a *Souldier;*
                           take a King.

And what   say'st thou then to my *Loue?*
            speake my   *faire*, and
                   fairely, I pray thee.

Katherine's only answer to this wooing is, "Is it possible that I should love the
enemy of France?" This resistance to his eloquence will provide a modern
Henry with the motivation to make so many and so diverse attempts at persuasion, each shift in strategy marked by a period. Within each sentence, we
can see the skillful repetition of key words to shape the thought, including the
long list of physical attributes that change as a man ages and the simple yet
effective ladder, "take me? and take me; take a Souldier: take a Souldier; take

a King." What is also fascinating, in rhetorical terms, is the sentence at the midway mark: "If thou canst love a fellow of this temper, Kate, whose face is not worth Sunne-burning? that never lookes in his Glasse, for love of any thing he sees there? let thine Eye be thy Cooke" which contains no patterning within the sentence but echoes or prefigures word usage in the rest of the speech with "fellow," "Kate," "sun," "look," "love," and "eye." Henry also makes use of associated words, so that when he asks Katherine to let her eye by her cook, he is building upon his earlier reference to a butcher, and when he refers to prating, rhymes, and ballads he is taking us back to his first thought about being asked to create love poetry for his lady. There is also a more serious thread linking "oath," "true," "right," and "plain" with "Constancy," the one gift he offers her in lieu of eloquent, cunning protestations and a gracious, courtly dance partner.

Puns

How every fool can play upon the word.

Lorenzo [*Merchant* 3.5.43]

One of the most amusing discoveries I made when I first began to study classical rhetorical devices, is that the various categories of puns all make an appearance in the lists of tropes, each with its own fancy Greek label. I had always thought that puns were a form of comic wordplay that some people can generate to amuse others, amusement signalled by a loud groan of appreciation. I knew that Shakespeare was very fond of puns, an attribute of his writing that seemed to embarrass most scholars, along with his fondness for a *double entendre*.

Puns, along with all of the other examples of amusing wordplay that his witty characters seem to so enjoy (in fact, a skill at wordplay seems to be the single identifying mark of wit in the world of the plays), set a significant challenge to the modern actor. Some of the puns quite simply do not work any more, because pronunciation has changed in four hundred years and the words no longer sound alike. Falstaff, a greater player with words and therefore, we can assume, a very witty fellow, has this to say when he has been caught out in one more outrageous falsehood:

Give you a reason on compulsion? If Reasons were as plentiful as Blackberries, I would give no man a Reason upon compulsion, I. [*1HIV* 2.4.238]

You can't miss what you never knew existed, and so a modern audience doesn't miss the pun, though they might wonder for a microsecond why reasons are being compared to blackberries. The modern actor might have learned from the notes that "reason" was pronounced "raison" in Shakespeare's day, and be very glad he doesn't have to play the groaner, though his appreciation for the speed with which Falstaff's brain works might be increased.

When the pun is necessary for there to be any humor in the situation, the actor can only hope that the director will cut the line or allow the development of some funny business to provide the comic fuel for the scene that the pun can no longer provide. This holds true for all sorts of comic moments, as all of the players of clowns and fools will confirm. There is nothing so deadly as spouting off what you know would have had them laughing until they wept four hundred years ago, but which today is greeted with yawns and empathetic embarrassment.

By returning to our rhetorical devices, we are reminded that puns and other wordplay were a strategy to further the argument of the orator. We can see this more clearly in the serious puns; for example, when Angelo, in contemplating the heinous bargain he struck with Isabella, her virginity in exchange for her brother's life, says,

> This deed unshapes me quite, makes me unpregnant
> And dull to all proceedings. A deflowered maid,
> And by an eminent body, that enforced
> The Law against it? But that her tender shame
> Will not proclaim against her maiden loss,
> How might she tongue me? yet reason dares her no,
> For my Authority bears of a credent bulk,
> That no particular scandal once can touch
> But it confounds the breather. [*Measure* 4.4.20]

Angelo's argument at this moment might be stated as, "Let me demonstrate the depths of sin to which I have descended," and part of the burden of proof is carried by the irony he points out, that he, who was responsible for enforcing the law against premarital sex, broke that law, and that he encountered Isabella and was able to strike his terrible bargain, because her brother had been caught at the same crime. And how was the brother found out? Because his fiancée was pregnant! Three interconnected strings of wordplay advance Angelo's argument. The first involves the word "enforce," which brings together the image of enforcing the law, and also forcing himself on her in a form of sexual coercion. The second involves images of pregnancy, as Angelo describes how the pressure of his sinful secret transforms his customary sense of self. He is used to participating in his legal duties in a most "pregnant" manner, in the other sense of the word, defined in the *Oxford English Dictionary* as "Of an argument, proof, evidence, reason, etc.: Pressing, urgent, weighty; compelling, cogent, forcible, convincing; hence, clear, obvious." Shakespeare uses the word "unpregnant" elsewhere in a similar sense, as when Hamlet berates himself for not taking his revenge for his father's murder:

> Yet I,
> A dull and muddy-mettled Rascal, peak
> Like John a-dreams, unpregnant of my cause,
> And can say nothing. [2.2.566]

When Angelo talks about the "bulk" of his authority, there is another echo of a woman's pregnancy in his choice of word to describe the status of his public persona.

The third cluster of words that form a type of pun or wordplay to advance the argument can be heard in Angelo's choice of "body," "tongue," and "breather," all perfectly clear alternatives to "holder of public office," "proclaim," and "proclaimer." But this grouping of synonyms, all unexpected and unusual, heard or spoken alongside direct references to the sexual act: "a deflowered maid," "her tender shame," "her maiden loss," cannot avoid arousing a sexual association, reinforced by the use of the verb "touch."

It is the tendency of modern actors to avoid pointing out the wordplay in serious moments, in the mistaken impression that such bitter irony and dark laughter would not enhance the dramatic power of the scene. Worse yet, they might not ascribe the deliberate inclusion of such wordplay to Angelo, but rather write it off as a typical bit of generic Shakespearean poetry. Far better to use it as a clue to the man's state of mind and mental agility. How horrifying, to be capable of that level of intellectual acuity, to see and make sense of the implications of his actions, to communicate exactly what is at stake for himself and the audience, and still be unable to stop himself. No wonder, when caught out, he takes the opposite approach to Falstaff and, rather than attempting to talk his way out of his mess, he responds, simply:

> I am sorry, that such sorrow I procure,
> And so deep sticks it in my penitent heart,
> That I crave death more willingly than mercy,
> 'Tis my deserving, and I do entreat it. [5.1.474]

and remains silent for the rest of the play.

There are times that modern actors find it difficult to accept Shakespeare's love of puns. It's bad enough in comic situations, but when the dying John of Gaunt spouts this extended riff on his name, who could blame us for wondering just what is going on in this man's mind? King Richard has just arrived at the bedside of his dying uncle, and says, "What comfort man? How is't with aged Gaunt?" Gaunt replies:

> Oh how that name befits my composition:
> Old Gaunt indeed, and gaunt in being old:
> Within me grief hath kept a tedious fast,
> And who abstains from meat, that is not gaunt?
> For sleeping England long time have I watched;

Watching breeds leanness, leanness is all gaunt.
The pleasure that some Fathers feed upon,
Is my strict fast, I mean my Childrens looks,
And therein fasting, hast thou made me gaunt:
Gaunt am I for the grave, gaunt as a grave,
Whose hollow womb inherits nought but bones. [2.1.73]

That even Shakespeare intended this to be over the top is signalled by Richard's response, "Can sick men play so nicely with their names?" The following exchange then takes place:

Gaunt: No, misery makes sport to mock it self:
         Since thou dost seek to kill my name in me,
         I mock my name (great King) to flatter thee.

Richard: Should dying men flatter with those that live?

Gaunt: No, no, men living flatter those that die.

Richard: Thou now a dying, say'st thou flatterest me.

Gaunt: Oh no, thou diest, though I the sicker be.

Richard: I am in health, I breathe, I see thee ill.

Gaunt: Now he that made me, knows I see thee ill:
         Ill in my self to see, and in thee, seeing ill [2.1.85]

Clearly, Gaunt has not lost one ounce of his linguistic skill, and with his last breath he is fighting for the survival of England. His punning about his name, in this context, makes perfect sense, as he drives home the argument, forcing Richard to acknowledge the damage he is doing England.

Wit

It seems a natural progression to move from the word games that arise from *topoi* directly to that quality of dialog that is best described as witty. The word has come to mean not only the agility with which the individual plays with language, but the caliber of intellect that is suggested by such verbal gymnastics.

As You Like It and other comedies contain countless examples of wit: beautifully structured statements that capture gems of perception about character and humanity. Rosalind is given some of the best of these witty sayings which are so precise that they fall into the category of *sententiae*, which means "sentences," as the term was used to describe what we today would call "quotable quotes." Here are a few examples, built around rhetorical figures. Look for repetitions and parallel structuring of phrases, the familiar features of rhetorical figures.

. . . I drove my Suitor from his mad humour of love, to a living humour of madness . . . [3.2.417]

. . . men have died from time to time, and worms have eaten them, but not for love. [4.1.106]

. . . men are April when they woo, December when they wed: Maids are May when they are maids, but the sky changes when they are wives. [4.1.147]

In *Much Ado About Nothing* we find another wonderfully witty woman, Beatrice, puncturing the pretensions of others with a few well chosen words: "He that hath a beard, is more than a youth: and he that hath no beard, is less than a man: and he that is more than a youth, is not for me: and he that is less than a man, I am not for him" [2.1.36]. She's well matched in Benedict, who offers his own witty observations: "That a woman conceived me, I thank her: that she brought me up, I likewise give her most humble thanks: . . . Because I will not do them the wrong to mistrust any, I will do myself the right to trust none: and the fine is, (for the which I may go the finer) I will live a Bachelor" [1.1.238,242]. Is it any wonder that their friends conspire to bring these two quipsters together?

There is no denying that many of these rhetorical games are sexually charged. Let us have a look at the famous duet from *The Taming of the Shrew*:

Petruchio: My self am moved to woo thee for my wife.

Kate: Moved, in good time, let him that moved you hither
Remove you hence: I knew you at the first
You were a moveable.

Petruchio: Why, what's a moveable?

Kate: A joined stool.

Petruchio: Thou hast hit it: come sit on me.

Kate: Asses are made to bear, and so are you.

Petruchio: Women are made to bear, and so are you.

Kate: No such jade as you, if me you mean.

Petruchio: Alas good Kate, I will not burden thee,
For knowing thee to be but young and light.

Kate: Too light for such a swain as you to catch,
And yet as heavy as my weight should be.

Petruchio: Should be, should: buzz.

Kate: Well ta'en, and like a buzzard.

Petruchio: O slow-winged Turtle, shall a buzzard take thee?

Kate: Ay for a Turtle, as he takes a buzzard.

Petruchio: Come, come you Wasp, i' faith you are too angry.

Kate: If I be waspish, best beware my sting.

Petruchio: My remedy is then to pluck it out.

Kate: Ay, if the fool could find it where it lies.

Petruchio: Who knows not where a Wasp does wear his sting? In his tail.

Kate: In his tongue?

Petruchio: Whose tongue.

Kate: Yours if you talk of tails, and so farewell.

Petruchio: What with my tongue in your tail.
             Nay, come again, good Kate, I am a Gentleman.

Kate: That I'll try. [2.1.202]

And with that, Kate strikes him, with good reason after such a filthy joke. This is a scene that works entirely on the level of sexually charged verbal warfare, even if the actors don't really understand what they're actually saying. If they do consult the editor's notes, they will discover the essential rhetorical strategy that both players are using.

It is possible to set up the language game of this scene, and in fact all witty exchanges, as a series of linguistic dominos. Just how this works is most easily seen in a simpler exchange between a master-manipulator and a bright young child. This is Richard, duke of Gloucester, engaging with his young nephew the duke of York. The fact that Richard will soon have this boy murdered adds a touch of dramatic irony to what otherwise appears, on the surface, to be an entirely friendly game of word-dominoes.

York: I pray you, Uncle, give me this Dagger.

Richard: My Dagger, little Cousin? with all my heart.

Prince Edward: A Beggar, Brother?

York: Of my kind Uncle, that I know will give,
               And being but a Toy, which is no grief to give.

Richard: A greater gift than that, I'll give my Cousin.

York: A greater gift? O, that's the Sword to it.

Richard: Ay, gentle Cousin, were it light enough.

York: O then I see, you will part but with light gifts,
               In weightier things you'll say a Beggar nay.

Richard: It is too weighty for your Grace to wear.

York: I weigh it lightly, were it heavier.

Richard: What, would you have my Weapon, little Lord?

York: I would that I might thank you, as, as, you call me.

Richard: How?

York: Little. [*RIII* 3.1.110]

The first domino is the word "greater," which has two meanings, more important, and larger in size. York seizes upon this to place his next domino, linking the sword, which is larger than the dagger, to the word "greater." Gloucester then responds by pointing out that the sword is too heavy for a young boy, at which point York makes use of the double meaning of the word "light," as in not weighty and also not valuable. He makes a double play by drawing upon the double meaning of the word "weighty," as in heavy as well as important. Gloucester then plays the straight man to set up York's rhetorical coup, "I weigh it lightly, were it heavier." On the surface, this is nonsense, or so convoluted and condensed a sentence to be almost incomprehensible, though it means, simply, even if it were heavier, he would value it but as an insignificant gift. But the shape of the sentence is the clue to its rhetorical power and the success of the boy's wit. It is as if he has crafted a domino piece that fits perfectly in the middle of a square of other dominoes. By condensing the thought into a few words, and those taken from the exchange just completed, York is able to answer his uncle's question and score on multiple levels. York is able to cap his achievement in the next exchange, by picking up on his uncle's "little lord," to say he would thank him but little for such a gift.

Richard is rather an expert at this sort of sparring, as has been demonstrated in a much more sexually charged scene earlier in the play. Richard describes his wooing of Lady Anne as a "keen encounter of our wits" [1.2.115], but one that is played over the body of a dead king, with the highest possible stakes personally and politically:

Gloucester: Fairer than tongue can name thee, let me have
Some patient leisure to excuse my self.

Lady Anne: Fouler than heart can think thee,
Thou canst make no excuse current,
But to hang thy self.

Gloucester: By such despair, I should accuse my self.

Lady Anne: And by despairing shalt thou stand excused,
For doing worthy Vengeance on thy self,
That didst unworthy slaughter upon others.

Lady Anne: Didst thou not kill this King?

Gloucester: I grant ye.

Lady Anne: Dost grant me Hedg-hog,
Then God grant me too
Thou mayst be damned for that wicked deed,
O he was gentle, mild, and virtuous.

Gloucester: The better for the King of heaven that hath him.

Lady Anne: He is in heaven, where thou shalt never come.

Gloucester: Let him thank me, that holp to send him thither:
For he was fitter for that place than earth.

Lady Anne: And thou unfit for any place, but hell.

Gloucester: Yes one place else, if you will hear me name it.

Lady Anne: Some dungeon.

Gloucester: Your Bed-chamber. [1.2.81,101]

These two brief excerpts illustrate the shape of the battle of wits. They match each other idea for idea, with parallel phrases and using direct antithesis or reusing each other's words to different or increased effect. Modern actors might find the rigidity of the exchange antinaturalistic, but it is the precise mirroring of shape as well as content that makes the give and take such a demonstration of intellectual facility. Lest we think this is just a game, we must remember that the greater the rhetorical effect, the stronger the emotion underlying it, driving it, demanding shape for the expression of the feeling and the accomplishment of the argument. We can see this in the following exchange between Richard and Queen Elizabeth. Richard has decided to woo Elizabeth's daughter, sister to the charming duke of York and his older brother Edward, both murdered in the tower. Elizabeth asks how she could possibly persuade her daughter to receive Richard as a suitor:

Richard: Infer fair Englands peace by this Alliance.

Elizabeth: Which she shall purchase with still lasting war.

Richard: Tell her, the King that may command, entreats.

Elizabeth: That at her hands, which the kings King forbids.

Richard: Say she shall be a High and Mighty Queen.

Elizabeth: To wail the Title, as her Mother doth.

Richard: Say I will love her everlastingly.

Elizabeth: But how long shall that title ever last?

Richard: Sweetly in force, unto her fair lifes end.

Elizabeth: But how long fairly shall her sweet lie last?

Richard: So long as Heaven and Nature lengthens it.

Elizabeth: So long as Hell and Richard likes of it.

Richard: Say, I her Sovereign, am her Subject low.

Elizabeth: But she your Subject, loathes such Sovereignty.

Richard: Be eloquent in my behalf to her.

Elizabeth: An honest tale speeds best, being plainly told.

Richard: Then plainly to her, tell her my loving tale.

Elizabeth: Plain and not honest, is too harsh a style.

Richard: Your Reasons are too shallow, and too quick.

Elizabeth: O no, my Reasons are too deep and dead,
Too deep and dead (poor Infants) in their grave.

Richard: Harp not on that string Madam, that is past.

Elizabeth: Harp on it still shall I till heart-strings break.

Richard: Now by my George, my Garter, and my Crown.

Elizabeth: Profaned, dishonoured, and the third usurped. [4.4.343]

To the modern actor, the precise balance of this exchange might signal a ritualized formality that excludes any possibility of deep feeling and spontaneous interaction. The potency of rhetoric allows the coexistence of both the ritual and the emotion, the one summoning and supporting the other.

Comic Duets

Comic exchanges of wit differ only in mood from the deadly serious sparring of a villain such as Richard. In order to recapture our comic spirit, let us return to the forest of Arden, to an exchange between two masters of the comic put-down, Orlando and Jaques, both of whom, we have seen, can make good use of rhetorical devices:

Jaques: I thank you for your company, but good faith I had as lief have been my self alone.

Orlando: And so had I: but yet, for fashion sake I thank you too, for your society.

Jaques: God buy you, let's meet as little as we can.

Orlando: I do desire we may be better strangers.

Jaques: I pray you mar no more trees with Writing Love-songs in their barks.

Orlando: I pray you mar no more of my verses with reading them ill-favouredly.

Jaques: Rosalind is your loves name?

Orlando: Yes, just.

Jaques: I do not like her name.

Orlando: There was no thought of pleasing you when she was christened.

Jaques: What stature is she of?

Orlando: Just as high as my heart.

Jaques: You are full of pretty answers: have you not been acquainted with goldsmiths wives, and conned them out of rings?

Orlando: Not so: but I answer you right painted cloth, from whence you have studied your questions.

Jaques: You have a nimble wit; I think 'twas made of Atalanta's heels. Will you sit down with me, and we two, will rail against our Mistress the world, and all our misery.

Orlando: I will chide no breather in the world but my self against whom I know most faults.

Jaques: The worst fault you have, is to be in love.

Orlando: 'Tis a fault I will not change, for your best virtue: I am weary of you.

Jaques: By my troth, I was seeking for a Fool, when I found you.

Orlando: He is drowned in the brook, look but in, and you shall see him.

Jaques: There I shall see mine own figure.

Orlando: Which I take to be either a fool, or a Cipher.

Jaques: I'll tarry no longer with you, farewell good signior Love.

Orlando: I am glad of your departure: Adieu good Monsieur Melancholy. [*AYLI* 3.2.253]

The fun of some of the put-downs are lost to us today, but it is still a great sparring match between well-matched opponents.

Shakespeare on occasion provides us with a striking mismatch of rhetorical skill. Here is Touchstone, a court fool, interacting with the simple shepherd Corin:

Corin: And how like you this shepherd life Master Touchstone?

Touchstone: Truly shepherd, in respect of itself, it is a good life; but in respect that it is a shepherds life, it is naught. In respect that it is solitary, I like it very well: but in respect that it is private, it is a very vile life. Now in respect it is in the fields, it pleaseth me well: but in respect it is not in the court, it is tedious. As is it a spare life (look you) it fits my humour well: but as there is no more plenty in it, it goes much against my stomach. Has't any Philosophy in thee shepherd?

Corin: No more, but that I know the more one sickens, the worse at ease he is: and that he that wants money, means, and content, is without three good friends. That the property of rain is to wet, and fire to burn: That good pasture makes fat sheep: and that a great cause of the night, is lack of the Sun: That he that hath learned no wit by Nature, nor Art, may complain of good breeding, or comes of a very dull kindred.

Touchstone: Such a one is a natural Philosopher. [*AYLI* 3.2.11]

Here we see contrasting rhetorical strategies set upon a comic collision. The verbal meanderings and games of Touchstone are sure to leave Corin confused and at a loss for a witty response, save for the fact that the old shepherd has his own way with words, and can spin, even with his simple phrasing and images from daily life, a compelling response that wins the grudging respect of his better-educated companion.

And so, finally, back where we began, with the great battle of wits between perfectly matched lovers. Returning to Kate and Petruchio's sexy exchange, we can see the domino trick as they play with multiple meanings of light (not heavy, but also sexually wanton), of be/bee, of buzz (the sound of the bee) into buzzard (the bird of prey), and of turtle (not only the snapping turtle that can kill a buzzard, Kate's meaning, but also the turtle dove, symbol of love). We can also see the parallel shape of lines and the repetition of key words as they are tossed back and forth between the two players.

Falstaff and the Comic Manipulation of Rhetoric

Sir John Falstaff is a master of the English language. True, he uses it for mockery and self-indulgence, but in his parodies of formal rhetoric he demonstrates the easy fluidity of someone who can turn a phrase with the best of them. His rapid-fire competitions with Prince Hal, in which each attempts to insult the other more vividly and unexpectedly, demonstrate the topics of invention as strikingly as any school-boy could wish, and his manipulation of argument is a textbook on persuasion. Here is Falstaff's parody of Hal's father, and that man's formal logic, during another riotous evening at the Boar's Head tavern:

Harry, I do not only marvel where thou spendest thy time; but also, how thou art accompanied: For though the Camomile, the more it is trodden, the faster it grows; yet Youth, the more it is wasted, the sooner it wears. Thou art my Son: I have partly thy Mothers Word, partly my Opinion; but chiefly, a villainous trick of thine Eye, and a foolish hanging of thy nether Lip, that doth warrant me. If then thou be Son to me, here lieth the point: why, being Son to me, art thou so pointed at? Shall the blessed Son of Heaven prove a Micher, and eat Black-berries? a question not to be asked. Shall the Son of England prove a Thief, and take Purses? a question to be asked. There is a thing, Harry, which thou hast often heard of, and it is known to many in our Land, by the Name of Pitch: this Pitch (as ancient Writers do report) doth defile; so doth the company thou keepest: for Harry, now I do not speak to thee in Drink, but in Tears; not in Pleasure, but in Passion; not in Words only, but in Woes also. [2.4.398]

Here, in contrast, is the King's speech on the same topic:

I know not whether God will have it so,
For some displeasing service I have done;
That in his secret Doom, out of my Blood,
He'll breed Revengement, and a Scourge for me:
But thou dost in thy passages of Life,
Make me believe, that thou art only marked
For the hot vengeance, and the Rod of heaven
To punish my Mistreadings. Tell me else,
Could such inordinate and low desires,
Such poor, such bare, such lewd, such mean attempts,
Such barren pleasures, rude society,
As thou art matched withal, and grafted too,
Accompany the greatness of thy blood,
And hold their level with thy Princely heart? [3.2.5]

From these two examples we see Shakespeare's capacity to use all of the strategies of rhetoric in service of a powerful expression of a man's thoughts, feelings, and morality, and also his ability to misuse the tools of rhetoric in service of comic characterization and parody. What is most startling is that, for us and for Prince Hal, the King's speech is entirely effective, even though we have already heard, in advance, Falstaff's mockery of its form and content.

ACHIEVABLE COMPLEXITIES

The Gentleman is Learned, and a most rare Speaker,
To Nature none more bound; his training such,
That he may furnish and instruct great Teachers,
And never seek for aid out of himself.

Henry [*HVIII* 1.2.111]

This book has taken us through some of the most complex and subtle aspects of Shakespeare's language, and a modern actor could well be forgiven for despairing at any point along the way. What with the language being four hundred years old, and the Iambic Code being so unfamiliar and complicated—to say nothing of the nuances of that immense system of language known as rhetoric which was second-nature to Elizabethan schoolboys but requires an immense intellectual effort on the part of a graduate of a modern school system who struggles with the basic parts of speech—is it any wonder that an actor would much rather embrace an approach that values intuition and communicating with a modern audience over the intellectual contortions of codes and schemes?

I can offer two observations in support of my belief that the complexities of Shakespeare's language can and should be mastered by modern actors. The first is that the workings of the Iambic Code and the systems of rhetoric exist because they reflect the most theatrical and effective uses of the English language, and that Shakespeare and his fellow dramatists would never have used such systems if they did not support the essential function of dramatic dialog: the striking presentation of characters and situations in a manner best suited to showcasing that thing that actors do best.

The second observation is that every speaker of the English language already possesses, subconsciously and intuitively, a rich and comprehensive understanding of the rhythmic patterns that make up the code and the shapings of thought and feeling that form the basis of all rhetoric. We know these things, and can use these attributes of the language, because we are surrounded by speakers who use the language to communicate. We communicate regularly using complex patterns of sound and sense, though seldom with conscious awareness of the connection between the content of our speaking and the form it takes. Our language is rhythmic. Our language is structured. We master the tricks of manipulating sound and shape along with our facility as adult speakers.

There are, however, several very important conditions that preclude an actor's reliance on the intuitive understanding of language when working on Shakespeare's plays. The first is our modern distrust of the ornate, the artificial (in the Elizabethan sense of the word), the lengthy and awesome celebrations of the potency of our language. An actor must work very hard to overcome her habitual reliance on expletives, redundancies, hesitations, and the blandest of vocabularies, not only to recapture an Elizabethan love of the language, but also to discipline the mind and the voice to a higher standard of excellence than is currently considered normal in our culture.

Even more important than this shift in attitude is the increased capacity for comprehension that comes with a conscious awareness of the Iambic Code and rhetoric. There is much in Shakespeare's plays that is incomprehensible to a modern audience because of the shifts in the English language. There is much more that is lost to a modern audience because modern actors have assumed that the complex patterns they read on the page cannot possibly be "actable." However, once they learn to feel the rhythm in their emotional gut, they are far better prepared to render the poetry vividly and theatrically. And once they can spot the "orcas" and convey the human impulse to communicate that has shaped the language into those specific patterns, they are far better placed to deliver the powerful speeches of the characters in all of their theatrical power.

Recommended Reading

Abbott, E.A. *A Shakespearian Grammar: An Attempt to Illustrate Some of the Differences Between Elizabethan and Modern English.* London: Macmillan, 1886.

Baldwin, T.W. *William Shakespere's Small Latine & Lesse Greeke.* Urbana: University of Illinois Press, 1956.

Barber, Charles. *Early Modern English.* London: Andre Deutsch, 1976.

Barton, John. *Playing Shakespeare.* London: Methuen, 1984.

Berry, Cicely. *The Actor and His Text.* London: Harrap, 1987.

Blake, N.F. *Shakespeare's Language: An Introduction.* London: Macmillan, 1983.

Bolton, W.F. *Shakespeare's English: Language in the History Plays.* Oxford: Basil Blackwell, 1992.

Brine, Adrian, and Michael York. *A Shakespearean Actor Prepares.* Lyme, NH: Smith & Kraus, 2000.

Brook, G.L. *The Language of Shakespeare.* London: Andre Deutsch, 1976.

Brubaker, Edward S. *Shakespeare Aloud: A Guide to his Verse on Stage.* Lancaster, PA: E.S. Brubaker, 1976.

Cohen, Robert. *Acting in Shakespeare.* Mountain View, CA: Mayfield, 1991.

Daw, Kurt. *Acting Shakespeare and His Contemporaries.* Portsmouth, NH: Heinemann, 1998.

Dent, R.W. *Shakespeare's Proverbial Language: An Index.* Berkeley: University of California Press, 1981.

Doyle, John, and Ray Lischner. *Shakespeare for Dummies.* Foster City, CA: IDG Books Worldwide, 1999.

Gilbert, Anthony J. *Shakespeare's Dramatic Speech.* Lewiston, NY: Edwin Mellen Press, 1997.

Görlach, Manfred. *Introduction to Early Modern English.* Cambridge: Cambridge University Press, 1978.

Gurr, Andrew. *The Shakespearian Playing Companies.* Oxford: Clarendon Press, 1996.

Hedges, David, and Mita Scott Hedges. *Speaking Shakespeare: A Handbook for the Student Actor and Oral Interpreter.* New York: American Press, 1967.

Hulme, Hilda M. *Explorations in Shakespeare's Language: Some Problems of Lexical Meaning in the Dramatic Text.* London: Longmans, 1962.

Joseph, Sister Miriam. *Rhetoric in Shakespeare's Time: Literary Theory of Renaissance Europe.* New York: Harcourt, Brace & World, 1962.

———. *Shakespeare's Use of the Arts of Language.* New York: Hafner, 1966.

Kastan, David Scott, ed. *A Companion to Shakespeare.* Oxford: Blackwell Publishers, 1999.

Linklater, Kristin. *Freeing Shakespeare's Voice: The Actor's Guide to Talking the Text.* New York: Theatre Communications Group, 1992.

Morrison, Malcolm. *Classical Acting.* Portsmouth, NH: Heinemann, 1996.

Onions, C.T. *A Shakespeare Glossary.* Revised by Robert D. Eagleson. Oxford: Clarendon Press, 1986.

Partridge, Eric. *Shakespeare's Bawdy: A Literary and Psychological Essay and a Comprehensive Glossary.* London: Routledge & Kegan Paul, 1968.

Rodenburg, Patsy. *The Actor Speaks: Voice and the Performer.* London: Methuen, 1997.

———. *The Need for Words: Voice and the Text.* New York: Routledge, 1993.

———. *The Right to Speak: Working with the Voice.* New York: Routledge, 1992.

Ronberg, Gert. *A Way with Words: The Language of English Renaissance Literature.* London: E. Arnold, 1992.

Roston, Murray. *Renaissance Perspectives in Literature and the Visual Arts.* Princeton, NJ: Princeton University Press, 1987.

Rubinstein, Frankie. *A Dictionary of Shakespeare's Sexual Puns and Their Significance.* London: Macmillan, 1984.

Salmon, Vivian, and Edwina Burness, eds. *A Reader in the Language of Shakespearian Drama.* Amsterdam: J. Benjamins, 1987.

Schmidt, Alexander. *Shakespeare-Lexicon: A Complete Dictionary of All the English Words, Phrases, and Constructions in the Works of the Poet.* Berlin: G. Reimer, 1886.

Shewmaker, Eugene F. *Shakespeare's Language: A Glossary of Unfamiliar Words in Shakespeare's Plays and Poems.* New York: Facts on File, 1996.

Smith, Bruce R. *The Acoustic World of Early Modern England: Attending to the O-factor.* Chicago: University of Chicago Press, 1999.

Spurgeon, Caroline. *Shakespeare's Imagery and What It Tells Us.* Cambridge: Cambridge University Press, 1935.

Suzman, Janet. *Acting with Shakespeare: Three Comedies.* New York: Applause Theatre Book Publishers, 1996.

Van Tassel, Wesley. *Clues to Acting Shakespeare.* New York: Allworth Press, 2000.

Vickers, Brian. *The Artistry of Shakespeare's Prose.* London: Methuen, 1968.

———. *Classical Rhetoric in English Poetry.* London: Macmillan, 1970.

Williams, Gordon. *A Glossary of Shakespeare's Sexual Language.* London: Athlone Press, 1997.

Wilson, Thomas. *The Art of Rhetoric* (1560). Edited by Peter E. Medine. University Park: Pennsylvania State University Press, 1994.

Wright, George T. *Shakespeare's Metrical Art.* Berkeley: University of California Press, 1988.

Bibliography

Ashley, Leonard R.N. *Elizabethan Popular Culture*. Bowling Green, OH: Bowling Green State University Popular Press, 1988.

Aydelotte, Frank. *Elizabethan Rogues and Vagabonds*. New York: Barnes & Noble, 1967.

Barton, John. *Playing Shakespeare*. London: Methuen, 1984.

Berry, Cicely. *The Actor and His Text*. London: Harrap, 1987.

Berry, Ralph. *Shakespeare and Social Class*. Atlantic Highlands, NJ: Humanities Press International, 1988.

Billington, Sandra. *A Social History of the Fool*. Brighton, Sussex: Harvester Press, 1984.

Biswas, D.C. *Shakespeare in His Own Time*. Delhi: Macmillan, 1979.

Blake, N.F. *Shakespeare's Language: An Introduction*. London: Macmillan, 1983.

Booty, John E., ed. *The Book of Common Prayer, 1559: The Elizabethan Prayer Book*. Charlottesville: University Press of Virginia, 1976.

Bradbrook, M.C. *Themes and Conventions of Elizabethan Tragedy*. Cambridge: Cambridge University Press, 1935.

Brine, Adrian, and Michael York. *A Shakespearean Actor Prepares*. Lyme, NH: Smith & Kraus, 2000.

Bryson, Anna. *From Courtesy to Civility: Changing Codes of Conduct in Early Modern England*. Oxford: Clarendon Press, 1998.

Burgess, Anthony. *Shakespeare*. Harmondsworth: Penguin Books, 1970.

Carroll, William C. *Fat King, Lean Beggar: Representations of Poverty in the Age of Shakespeare*. Ithaca, NY: Cornell University Press, 1996.

Cohen, Robert. *Acting in Shakespeare*. Mountain View, CA: Mayfield, 1991.

Collmann, Herbert Leonard. *Ballads & Broadsides: Chiefly of the Elizabethan Period*. New York: B. Franklin, 1971.

Cook, Ann Jennalie. *Making a Match: Courtship in Shakespeare and His Society*. Princeton, NJ: Princeton University Press, 1991.

Cressy, David. *Birth, Marriage, and Death: Ritual, Religion, and the Life-Cycle in Tudor and Stuart England*. Oxford: Oxford University Press, 1997.

Davis, Michael Justin. *The Landscape of William Shakespeare*. Exeter, Devon: Webb & Bower, 1987.

Daw, Kurt. *Acting Shakespeare and His Contemporaries*. Portsmouth, NH: Heinemann, 1998.

Evans, G. Blakemore, ed. *The Riverside Shakespeare*. Boston: Houghton Mifflin, 1974.

Fido, Martin. *Shakespeare*. Maplewood, NJ: Hammond, 1978.

Frye, Roland Mushat. *The Renaissance Hamlet: Issues and Responses in 1600*. Princeton, NJ: Princeton University Press, 1984.

Garber, Marjorie. *Coming of Age in Shakespeare*. London: Methuen, 1981.

Gurr, Andrew. *The Shakespearian Playing Companies*. Oxford: Clarendon Press, 1996.

Hall, Peter. *Making an Exhibition of Myself*. London: Sinclair-Stevenson, 1993.

Hankins, John Erskine. *Backgrounds of Shakespeare's Thought*. Hamden, CT: Archon Books, 1978.

Hawley, William M. *Shakespearean Tragedy and the Common Law: The Art of Punishment*. New York: Peter Lang, 1998.

Haynes, Alan. *Sex in Elizabethan England*. Stroud, Gloucestershire: Sutton, 1997.

Hibbert, Christopher. *The Court at Windsor: A Domestic History*. London: Allen Lane, 1977.

Hoeniger, F. David. *Medicine and Shakespeare in the English Renaissance*. Newark: University of Delaware Press, 1992.

Horizon Magazine, with Louis B. Wright, eds. *Shakespeare's England: A Horizon Caravel Book*. New York: American Heritage Pub. Co., 1964.

Hurstfield, Joel, and Alan G.R. Smith. *Elizabethan People: State and Society*. New York: St. Martin's Press, 1972.

Hussey, Maurice. *The World of Shakespeare and His Contemporaries: A Visual Approach*. London: Heinemann, 1971.

Hyland, Peter. *An Introduction to Shakespeare: The Dramatist in His Context*. New York: St. Martin's Press, 1996.

James, Max H. *Our House Is Hell: Shakespeare's Troubled Families*. Westport, CT: Greenwood Press, 1989.

James I, King of England. *The English Bible, Translated out of the Original Tongues by the Commandment of King James the First, Anno 1611*. New York: AMS Press, 1967.

Jonson, Ben. *Timber: or, Discoveries Made Upon Men and Matter*. 1641. Edited by Felix E. Schelling. Boston: Ginn & Co., 1892.

Joseph, Sister Miriam. *Shakespeare's Use of the Arts of Language*. New York: Hafner, 1966.

Kastan, David Scott, ed. *A Companion to Shakespeare*. Oxford: Blackwell Publishers, 1999.

Kinney, Arthur F. *Elizabethan Backgrounds: Historical Documents of the Age of Elizabeth I*. Hamden, CT: Archon Books, 1975.

Komroff, Manuel, ed. *The Apocrypha; or, Non-canonical Books of the Bible: The King James Version*. New York: Tudor Publishing Company, 1936.

Laroque, François. *The Age of Shakespeare*. Translated by Alexandra Campbell. New York: Harry N. Abrams, 1993.

Laslett, Peter. *The World We Have Lost: Further Explored*. London: Methuen, 1983.

Laurence, Anne. *Women in England, 1500–1760: A Social History*. New York: St. Martin's Press, 1994.

Linklater, Kristin. *Freeing Shakespeare's Voice: The Actor's Guide to Talking the Text*. New York: Theatre Communications Group, 1992.

MacDonald, Michael. *Mystical Bedlam: Madness, Anxiety, and Healing in Seventeenth-Century England*. Cambridge: Cambridge University Press, 1981.

McMurtry, Jo. *Understanding Shakespeare's England: A Companion for the American Reader.* Hamden, CT: Archon Books, 1989.

The Merriam-Webster Dictionary. Springfield, MA: Merriam-Webster, 1997.

Miller, Allan. *A Passion for Acting: Exploring the Actor's Creative Processes.* New York: Back Stage Books, 1992.

Miriam Joseph, Sister. *Shakespeare's Use of the Arts of Language.* New York: Hafner Pub. Co., 1966.

Morrison, Malcolm. *Classical Acting.* Portsmouth, NH: Heinemann, 1996.

Moston, Doug. *The First Folio of Shakespeare* (1623). New York: Applause Books, 1995.

Norwich, John Julius. *Shakespeare's Kings.* London: Viking, 1999.

Orlin, Lena Cowen. *Elizabethan Households: An Anthology.* Washington, DC: Folger Shakespeare Library, 1995.

Papp, Joseph, and Elizabeth Kirkland. *Shakespeare Alive!* New York: Bantam, 1988.

Patterson, Annabel M. *Shakespeare and the Popular Voice.* Oxford: Basil Blackwell, 1989.

Perry, Maria. *The Word of a Prince: A Life of Elizabeth I from Contemporary Documents.* Woodbridge, England: Boydell Press, 1990.

Pinciss, Gerald M., and Roger Lockyer, eds. *Shakespeare's World.* New York: Continuum, 1989.

Prichard, R.E., ed. *Shakespeare's England: Life in Elizabethan and Jacobean Times.* Stroud, Cloucestershire: Sutton, 1999.

Rickey, Mary Ellen, and Thomas B. Stroup, eds. *Certaine Sermons or Homilies, Appointed to Be Read in Churches, in the Time of Queen Elizabeth I, 1547–1571* (1623). Gainesville, FL: Scholars' Facsimiles & Reprints, 1968.

Ronberg, Gert. *A Way with Words: The Language of English Renaissance Literature.* London: E. Arnold, 1992.

Saccio, Peter. *Shakespeare's English Kings: History, Chronicle, and Drama.* Oxford: Oxford University Press, 1977.

Salgādo, Gāmini. *The Elizabethan Underworld.* London: J.M. Dent & Sons, 1977.

Schell, Edgar T., and J. D. Shuchter, eds. *English Morality Plays and Moral Interludes.* New York: Holt, Rinehart and Winston, 1969.

Schoenbaum, Samuel. *Shakespeare, the Globe, and the World.* New York: Oxford University Press, 1979.

Shahar, Shulamith. *Childhood in the Middle Ages.* London: Routledge, 1990.

Shaheen, Naseeb. *Biblical References in Shakespeare's Plays.* Newark: University of Delaware Press, 1999.

Sim, Alison. *Pleasures and Pastimes in Tudor England.* Stroud, Gloucestershire: Sutton, 1999.

——. *The Tudor Housewife.* Montreal:McGill-Queen's University Press, 1996.

Simpson, J.A., and E.S.C. Weiner, eds. *The Oxford English Dictionary.* 20 vols. Oxford: Clarendon Press, 1989.

Slater, Ann Pasternak. *Shakespeare, the Director.* Brighton, Sussex: Harvester, 1982.

Slavitt, David R. *The Metamorphoses of Ovid.* Baltimore: Johns Hopkins University Press, 1994.

Smith, Lacey Baldwin. *The Horizon Book of the Elizabethan World.* New York: American Heritage Pub. Co., 1967.

Smith, Bruce R. *Homosexual Desire in Shakespeare's England: A Cultural Poetics.* Chicago: University of Chicago Press, 1991.

Spurgeon, Caroline. *Shakespeare's Imagery and What It Tells Us.* Cambridge: Cambridge University Press, 1935.

Stern, Tiffany. *Rehearsal from Shakespeare to Sheridan.* Oxford: Clarendon Press, 2000.

Stone, Lawrence. *The Family, Sex, and Marriage in England, 1500–1800.* New York: Harper & Row, 1977.

Suzman, Janet. *Acting with Shakespeare: Three Comedies.* New York: Applause Theatre Book Publishers, 1996.

Thomas, Keith. *Religion and the Decline of Magic: Studies in Popular Beliefs in Sixteenth and Seventeenth Century England.* London: Weidenfeld and Nicolson, 1971.

Thomson, Peter. *Shakespeare's Professional Career.* Cambridge: Cambridge University Press, 1992.

Thurley, Simon. *The Royal Palaces of Tudor England: Architecture and Court Life, 1460–1547.* New Haven, CT: Yale University Press, 1993.

Trussler, Simon. *Shakespearean Concepts: A Dictionary of Terms and Conventions, Influences and Institutions, Themes, Ideas, and Genres in the Elizabethan and Jacobean Drama.* London: Methuen Drama, 1989.

Van Tassel, Wesley. *Clues to Acting Shakespeare.* New York: Allworth Press, 2000.

Vickers, Brian. *The Artistry of Shakespeare's Prose.* London: Methuen, 1968.

———. *Classical Rhetoric in English Poetry.* London: Macmillan, 1970.

Wildeblood, Joan, and Peter Brinson. *The Polite World: A Guide to English Manners and Deportment from the Thirteenth to the Nineteenth Century.* London: Oxford University Press, 1965.

Williams, Gordon. *A Glossary of Shakespeare's Sexual Language.* London: Athlone Press, 1997.

Williams, Neville. *All the Queen's Men: Elizabeth I and her Courtiers.* London: Weidenfeld and Nicolson, 1972.

Wilson, John Dover, ed. *Life in Shakespeare's England: A Book of Elizabethan Prose.* New York: Barnes & Noble, 1969.

Wither, George. *A Collection of Emblemes, ancient and moderne* (1635). Columbia: University of South Carolina Press, 1975.

Wittkower, Rudolf. *Allegory and the Migration of Symbols.* London: Thames and London, 1987.

Wright, George T. *Shakespeare's Metrical Art.* Berkeley: University of California Press, 1988.

General Index

Index of Plays
and Characters

About the Author

LESLIE O'DELL is Associate Professor of Theatre and English at Wilfrid Laurier University and Text Consultant for the Stratford Festival in Ontario.